THE GRACE OF DIFFERENCE

American Academy of Religion
Academy Series

edited by
Susan Thistlethwaite

Number 80
THE GRACE OF DIFFERENCE

by
Marilyn J. Legge

Marilyn J. Legge

THE GRACE OF DIFFERENCE
A Canadian Feminist
Theological Ethic

Scholars Press
Atlanta, Georgia

THE GRACE OF DIFFERENCE
A Canadian Feminist Theological Ethic

by
Marilyn J. Legge

Library of Congress Cataloging in Publication Data

Legge, Marilyn J.
 The grace of difference : A Canadian feminist theological ethic / Marilyn
J. Legge.
 p. cm. — (American Academy of Religion academy series ; no.
80)
 Includes bibliographical references.
 ISBN 1-55540-736-6 (hard). — ISBN 1-55540-737-4 (pbk.)
 1. Christianity—Canada. 2. Christian ethics—Canada. 3. Women—
Canada. 4. Feminism—Religious aspects—Christianity. I. Title.
II. Series.
BR570.L44 1992
277.1'082'082—dc20
               92-16229
               CIP

Printed in the United States of America
on acid-free paper

Dedicated to

Garth and Joyce Legge, devoted parents,
Beverly Harrison, cherished mentor and friend,
and Michael Bourgeois, beloved covenant companion--

their yearning for justice and love is blessing indeed.

TABLE OF CONTENTS

ACKNOWLEDGMENTS

Having been raised in manses in ecumenical and cross-cultural environments in northern Ontario, Quebec, and Central Africa, I have been enriched by lifelong global connections as a Canadian student of politics, culture, and theology. Work in such diverse settings as an Ontario logging camp among Ojibway, French, Finnish, and English Canadians; a rural development movement in Sri Lanka; a Toronto shelter for women in crisis; and window glazing in New York City has kept my learning as a white, western, middle-class woman engaged with issues of everyday life, especially those of class, race, and gender. Because of these roots and my abiding commitment to women's well-being, I share with many liberation theologians the fervent concern to honour the particularity of specific contexts and voices, thereby minimizing the domination of moral theology by abstraction and false universalism. This study represents one project which undertakes the task of providing methodological access to women's excluded voices and to their integration in Canadian theological ethics.

This dissertation could never have been written without the support, friendship, and encouragement of many people. My study at Union Theological Seminary was initiated by the Emmanuel College Traveling Fellowship and a United Church of Canada grant. I extend my deep appreciation to Douglas C. Jay, Principal of Emmanuel College, Raymond Whitehead, Elizabeth Anderson, and Ann Naylor who have offered wise counsel and sustenance over the course of this project; and to Audrey Anderson, Ruth Evans, Shelley Finson, Gwyneth Griffith, Jane Henson, Wendy Hunt, Glenys Huws, Debra Martens, Janet Silman, Mary Hembrow Snyder, Cheryl Wagner, Rhea Whitehead, and Richard Witham for their solidarity, laughter, and love.

I am profoundly indebted to Beverly Wildung Harrison, advisor, mentor, and friend, whose work and faith have shaped not only this project but also my life's pilgrimage. I celebrate her guidance and wisdom, as well as her belief in me. I have also been honoured to have on my dissertation committee Elizabeth Bettenhausen, Tom F. Driver, and Larry L. Rasmussen. I am indebted to their work and insightful suggestions. My vocation in theological education has also been nourished by tutoring with Beverly Harrison, James Cone, and Dorothee Sölle; their vision will always inspire me. While at Union I lived, struggled, and learned with colleagues I honour here: Elizabeth Bounds, Eric Brandt, Pamela Brubaker, Chung Hyun Kyung, Marie Giblin, Lois Kirkwood, Dwight Hopkins, Ada-María Isasi-Díaz, Sally MacNichol, Margaret Mayman, Mark Taylor, and Howard Wiley.

After moving to Saskatoon to teach theology at St. Andrew's College, my writing was made possible by the College's Board of Regents, which authorized a minimum teaching load so that I could complete this dissertation, and by President William Adamson, my faculty colleagues, staff, and students who protected my time and energies. The College also provided a Garner Trust grant toward preparation of the dissertation manuscript for publication. I also thank those friends in Saskatchewan who empowered me through the final stages: Laura Balas, Catherine Barnsley, Cheryl Black, Joanne Brown, Charlotte Caron, Richard Donald, Barbara Elliott, Susan Gingell, Margaret McKechney, Frederick Seller, Carol Stevenson Seller, Jennifer Watts, and Kay Willson. Sections of earlier drafts of the dissertation were read by Elizabeth Bounds, Susan Gingell, Debra Martens, and Kay Willson, all of whom offered helpful criticisms and suggestions. The task of editing a later version of the entire manuscript was generously and skillfully undertaken by Jane Doull.

My parents, Garth and Joyce Legge, provided emotional, spiritual, and material resources throughout my graduate studies. I am also immeasurably grateful to my brother, Murray, and sister-in-law, Peggy Millson; my sister, Valerie, and brother-in-law, Marcel Saint-Cyr; and the Bourgeois family, Lois, Gary and Deborah, Philip, and Ann: all have supported me with love, understanding, and compassion. Finally, I acknowledge the blessing of Michael Bourgeois, my partner, colleague, and friend for life. His steadfast companionship, insight, skill, and humour have enabled this dissertation to see the light of day.

CHAPTER ONE

INTRODUCTION TO THE STUDY:
ASSUMPTIONS, METHOD, AND SOURCES

Thesis Direction

Despite ardent claims to the contrary, women, as the subjects or as the creators of theological ethics, are all but invisible in Canadian theological practice. Even in the radical Christian tradition women have not been adequately included. Justice requires us to change this situation. This project, therefore, will search for the voices of women, especially marginalized women, in order to do theological ethics accountable to women's experiences in Canada.[1]

In this thesis I aim to recover salient features of Christian and cultural practices in Canada that will place women's well-being and

---

[1]Helpful essays on feminist sources, norms, and methods include the excellent collection by Barbara H. Andolsen, Christine E. Gudorf, and Mary D. Pellauer, eds., *Women's Consciousness, Women's Conscience: A Reader in Feminist Ethics* (Minneapolis: Winston Press, 1985); Beverly Wildung Harrison, *Making the Connections: Essays in Feminist Social Ethics*, ed. Carol S. Robb (Boston: Beacon Press, 1983); Anne Llewellyn Barstow, Karen McCarthy Brown, Cheryl Townsend Gilkes, Mary E. Hunt, and Elisabeth Schüssler Fiorenza, "Roundtable Discussion: On Feminist Methodology," *Journal of Feminist Studies in Religion* 1, no. 2 (Fall 1985), 73-88; Patricia Schechter, Beverly W. Harrison, Kwok Pui Lan, Margaret R. Miles, Renita J. Weems, and Marjorie Suchocki, "Roundtable Discussion: A Vision of Feminist Religious Scholarship," *Journal of Feminist Studies in Religion*, 3 (Spring 1987), 91-111; and Carter Heyward, "Heterosexist Theology: Being Above It All," ibid., 29-38.

struggles for right relationship at the centre of the work of Canadian theological ethics. This task must combine a variety of sources for its critique and reconstruction: sharing our experiences, naming injustices in our lives, and imagining a different future, one where women's worth and well-being will be respected and enhanced. Full consideration of all aspects of this topic lies beyond the scope of this thesis; nor can I hope to deal fully with the diverse discourses necessary to engage the realities of women's lives. Instead, my aim is to investigate a method for Christian ethics that will transform theological norms of the Canadian Radical Christian tradition, such as justice and mutuality, into new formulations which are accountable to women's experience.

This thesis argues that genuine contextual theologies capable of concretely naming sin and hope, and of moving us to fuller participation in claiming responsibility for our lives-in-relation, will emerge from both the struggles for cultural sovereignty and for economic justice in national and global spheres. No theology can be adequate to the task of enabling people to name God/dess as the "power of relation" among us without giving due attention to the life-experience of people in their concrete situation, especially those on the margins.[1]

If theology is a living response to a liberation that has been experienced and lived,[2] what are the sources for doing theology in Canada? Exploring the discourses of Christian theology and ethics, political economy, and cultural-literary theory, I will bring together three resources for doing Christian feminist ethics in a Canadian context: the radical faith-and-justice tradition, feminist social analysis, and cultural

---

[1]Use of the term "power of relation" for the realm of God comes from Carter Heyward, *The Redemption of God: A Theology of Mutual Relation* (Washington, D.C.: University Press of America, 1982), 6 ff., and Beverly W. Harrison, "Restoring the Tapestry of Life: The Vocation of Feminist Theology," the Nelle Morton Lecture, March 8, 1984, *The Drew Gateway* 54, no. 1 (1984), 45; see also Harrison, "Sexism and the Language of Christian Ethics," in *Making the Connections*, 39-41. The term God/dess, according to Rosemary Radford Ruether, is "a written symbol intended to combine both the masculine and feminine forms of the word for the divine while preserving the Judeo-Christian affirmation that divinity is one." *Sexism and God Talk: Toward a Feminist Theology* (Boston: Beacon Press, 1983), 46.

[2]Sheila Collins, *A Different Heaven and Earth* (Valley Forge: Judson Press, 1974), 34; see also Dorothee Sölle, "Theology and Liberation," in Benjamin Smillie, ed., *Political Theology in Canada* (Waterloo, Ontario: Wilfred Laurier University Press, 1982), 130.

analysis, including literary criticism. In relation to these resources I will draw especially on feminist perspectives in theological ethics that will open up the distinctive contribution of my method.

A groundwork of insights from sociological and political economic evaluations is indispensable for understanding the fabric of Canadian life. I will examine women's experiences within a critical social analysis of the political economy of women in Canada; this analysis is the initial methodological step for confronting rather than reproducing situations of gender, class, and racial/ ethnic oppression. This data, however, can only sketch the outline of the mosaic; the colours must be gleaned from the metaphors and images of artists and writers, from the everyday cultural dimension that offers insights and conveys meaning and purpose for our common life.

This study grants special importance to those in Canada who suffer most from the contradictions of gender, race, and class. They suffer from marginalization because they are socially excluded from power, wealth, and honour. They experience victimization because of the principal evil in society: injustice.[1] Most of them are women, of whom the most disregarded are women of colour. While I remain indebted to feminist theorists such as Nancy Hartsock and Dorothy Smith, I am to modify and clarify "the standpoint of women" as used by them because it tends to infer that all women can and do live within similar situations.[2] The vantage point for the present study is not selected on the basis of a supposed moral superiority based on gender, race, or class, nor is any universal applicability attributed to it. Rather, the standpoint from the margins is significant because people who are disempowered can offer critical interpretations of our society and culture that must be acknowledged and applied to rectify the distortions

---

[1]Gregory Baum theologically connects marginalization and social injustice in this way; see his "Three Theses on Contextual Theology," *The Ecumenist* 24, no. 4 (May-June 1986), 54.

[2]I am especially grateful to Ruth Smith and Deborah Valenze for their succinct statement of this issue in "Mutuality and Marginality: Liberal Moral Theory and Working Class Women in Nineteenth-Century England," *Signs: Journal of Women in Culture and Society* 13 (Winter 1988), 278, n. 4. See Nancy Hartsock, *Money, Sex and Power: Toward a Feminist Historical Materialism* (Boston: Northeastern University Press, 1983), 231-251; and Dorothy E. Smith, *The Everyday World as Problematic: A Feminist Sociology* (Toronto: University of Toronto Press, 1987).

of our own partial perspectives. The good news for those with power and privilege lies with those who struggle against the reigning definitions of success: they are willing to have us join them in creating communities for the good of all.

In this project, then, I adopt the category of "marginality" to achieve a greater specificity about the differences among us in order to name and respect our particular experiences and, thus, the unlimited grace of revelation. I also search for shared elements which, like common ground, give strength for the long haul of working and waiting for God's commonwealth. We will put in dialogue and hold in tension, then, commonalities and differences.

In order to identify the structural constraints and possibilities evident in women's lives in Canada, it is imperative for this project to consider the worlds of work and broader aspects of culture which shape women and in which women act to claim their moral agency in their everyday lives. Precisely because of the character of the experience of women who work in these culturally inscribed arenas, I will argue that it is necessary to see the bone of economic life as intrinsic to the connective tissues of culture.[1] If we ignore either economic or cultural life, our theological method is inadequate to women's experiences of victimization and agency, and to the possibilities for justice-making.

This thesis aims to be but one example of how a contextual Canadian theological method can be developed with due attention to women's experiences, especially marginalized women. If we are indeed to praise authentically the God/dess we share as divine Power and Presence among us, then we must learn to craft a theological ethic that has the capacity to shape common elements into beautiful, sturdy mosaics of our lives as people of faith. The Canadian context has abundant resources for "that eros of a thinking faith"[2] to shape into a liberative

---

[1]This sensible metaphor for the relationship between culture and social/economic analysis comes from Michael McKale, "Culture and Human Liberation," *Radical Religion* 5 (1980), 8: "The human body could not exist without tissue. Tissue and bone are dialectical in the human body. . . . They grow together and as one changes the other also changes. Culture is the tissue of human society. Culture is not simply a reflection [of an economic base], it is human praxis. . . . Culture contains its own reality and texture."

[2]Douglas John Hall, "On Contextuality in Christian Theology," *Toronto Journal of Theology* 1, no. 1 (Spring 1985), 15.

Christian theology. I shall be exploring the everyday worlds of women as apprehended in their work and culture, particularly in literature, by way of demonstrating such a method. Above all, in order to honour women's different and specific experiences, we must ask if women's experiences of concrete suffering and sources of hope in everyday life have been adequately addressed, and if feminist appeals to women's experience are accountable to differences of race and class.

This dissertation is framed by several presuppositions, especially about the meaning of moral agency, experience, tradition, and context. I will attend to these presuppositions prior to a discussion of the hermeneutical circle. First, however, I turn to some theological assumptions which inform my work.

Basic Assumptions of the Study

Contextual and Liberation Theologies

I identify the connection between liberation theologies and contextual theologies in terms of their historical genesis and interaction: liberation theologies irrupt from third world experience, and contextual theologies share with them the norm of justice but operate out of a decisive critique of first world experience.[1] While the questions that emerge from each share a common method, their respective contents relate specifically to particular social and ecclesial practices and historical contexts. Contextual and liberation theologies assume that social ethics is historically grounded; their social ethics, therefore, understand the world as transformable.

Their theological emphasis on history affirms that we encounter the divine in history, specifically in and through human beings. This affirmation, however, does not simply equate God with history. There is something "more" that happens and is an essential part of history,

---

[1]For a global mix of contextual and liberation theologies, see Virginia Fabella and Sergio Torres, eds., *Doing Theology in a Divided World* (Maryknoll, N.Y.: Orbis Books, 1985); William K. Tabb, ed., *Churches in Struggle: Liberation Theologies and Social Change in North America* (New York: Monthly Review Press, 1986); and Kenneth Aman, ed., *Border Regions of Faith: An Anthology of Religion and Social Change* (Maryknoll, N.Y.: Orbis Books, 1987).

something that allows for hope precisely within history.[1] According to Carter Heyward, this transcendent power in the world is both natural and moral. This God moves among all persons and all other creatures who struggle for power--to live, to breathe, to choose. In the power of mutual relation we experience transcendence, a "crossing over" beyond ourselves; we are made one, relative, interdependent, necessarily givers and receivers in the chain of life.[2] Liberationists, then, believe that God is Creator in nature and history. The Creator encourages humanity out of captivity into co-creating the world; women are in touch with this creative energy as they birth babies, tend gardens, and prepare food; we also meet God when we create history with All-is-Possible who empowers us to struggle for justice.[3]

The starting point of contextual and liberation theological methods is the specifics of particular historical human experience as we shape our lives as co-creators. This means, for example, that we encounter God as we participate in the process of our own liberation with others. This epistemology affirms that "the concrete truths of our lives, memories, and values are foundational to our conceptual work."[4] Both maintain that theology can only be "the second act,"[5] reflection upon what people experience in the concrete praxis of their living. Larry Rasmussen states that "Ours is a time of 'ethical theology,' rather than ethics as an implication trailing at some distance after a presentation of beliefs established on other grounds."[6] The aim of these theo-

[1]For this interpretation of history in a liberation method, see Jon Sobrino, *Christology at the Crossroads* (Maryknoll, N.Y.: Orbis Books, 1978), 386-87.

[2]Carter Heyward, "Crossing Over: On Transcendence," in *Our Passion For Justice: Images of Power, Sexuality, and Liberation* (New York: Pilgrim Press, 1984), 243-44.

[3]Dorothee Sölle names God this way in *To Work and To Love: A Theology of Creation* (Philadelphia: Fortress Press, 1984), 45-46.

[4]The Mudflower Collective, *God's Fierce Whimsy: Christian Feminism and Theological Education* (New York: Pilgrim Press, 1985), 161.

[5]Gustavo Gutiérrez, *A Theology of Liberation: History, Politics and Salvation*, trans. and ed. Sister Caridad Inda and John Eagleson (Maryknoll, N.Y.: Orbis Books, 1973), 11.

[6]Larry Rasmussen, "New Dynamics in Theology: Politically Active and Culturally Significant," *Christianity and Crisis* 28, no. 8 (May 16, 1988), 180.

logical modes, therefore, is not to deduce from doctrine the principles for pastoral life, but rather to clarify inductively, from their actual contexts and struggles, the strategies necessary to overcome human suffering and to become rightly related persons in self-determining cultures.[1]

A contextual method in theology, then, focuses on people in their struggles for justice and for authentic life. Because all aspects of a particular context are "not equally strategic for the *Missio Dei* in the working out of [divine] purpose through history," a normative stance of not just exposure to poverty and oppression but of active commitment to the struggles of the oppressed and marginalized, characterizes contextual theologizing.[2] God is known as a Presence who sides with the weak and who is with and often hidden with the powerless, and who nudges or torments the apathetic or indifferent into action.

To set the stage for the examination of the radical social gospel movement in Canada in the next chapter, and to indicate the urgency of our agenda, I will present a thumb-nail sketch of the global picture of contextual theologies dedicated to liberative praxis.

In the last two decades, new voices have irrupted in theological discourses from Latin America and Black and feminist movements in North America, and are now emerging around the world out of struggles for self-determination in Africa and Asia, and among other marginalized peoples, especially lesbians and gay men, in North America. These voices have identified how the theological problem of the dominant western theological tradition has been shaped by the confrontation with modernity of the white, male elite of Europe and North America. The central problematic of this Enlightenment theology focused on "the unbeliever" amidst the process of secularization. Out of the political liberation struggles of peoples of the so-called third world, and those marginalized in the first and second worlds, however, a different theo-

---

[1]Arguing for an inductive theological method, George Casalis reminds us that "it has nothing to do with working out a theoretical definition of a new type of theology; it means working at praxis and, very precisely, at revolutionary praxis, the primary prerequisite for the elaboration of a popular theology"; see his *Correct Ideas Don't Fall from the Skies: Elements for an Inductive Theology* (Maryknoll, N.Y.: Orbis Books, 1984), 25.

[2]Roger Hutchinson, "Contextualization: No Passing Fad," in *A New Beginning*, eds. Theresa Chu and Christopher Lind (Toronto: Canada China Programme of the Canadian Council of Churches, 1983), 69.

logical problematic has arisen: the problem of massive suffering, of the discarded non-person, of the oppressed and the marginalized.[1]

Liberation theologies sparked a renewed self-critical process within the church by working for radical social transformation with those at the bottom of their society. Because of their focus on concrete human suffering, liberation theologians discovered that to minister among the battered and forgotten, whose real needs were for a very different future based on tangible prospects for hope, they had to follow a process of analyzing and identifying those forces and dynamics that subverted or sustained human hope. Salvation's most concrete name was liberation, but the specific content had to be discerned within flesh-and-blood, everyday experiences of co-creation in the world.

Third world liberation theologians have challenged white, first world Christians to sharpen our critique of the social relations of power in our own countries, the operations of which saddle the world with interlocking structures of domination and subordination. For example, a "hermeneutics of suspicion" asks critical theological questions about power: "How is meaning constructed? Whose interests are served? What kind of worlds are envisioned? What roles, duties, and values are advocated? Which social-political practices are legitimated?"[2] In an affluent nation like Canada in which the total picture cannot be compared to the misery in three quarters of the world, we therefore have to raise our own issues particular to this context: What does it mean to be about "liberation" in a context that both perpetuates and benefits from oppression and exploitation? Who are "the poor" among us? What does "solidarity with the victims" mean in the Canadian context?

This study is rooted in my own commitments to justice that have developed through my experience as a white anglophone Canadian

---

[1]Gustavo Gutiérrez, *The Power of the Poor in History: Selected Writings*, trans. Robert Barr (Maryknoll, N.Y.: Orbis Books, 1983), 17. For an excellent analysis of the historical roots of the problematic of the nonperson in theology, see Curt Cadorette, *From the Heart of the People: The Theology of Gustavo Gutiérrez*, (Oak Park, Ill: Meyer-Stone Books, 1988); also Rebecca Chopp, *The Praxis of Suffering: An Interpretation of Liberation and Political Theologies* (Maryknoll, N.Y.: Orbis Books, 1986).

[2]Elisabeth Schüssler Fiorenza, "The Ethics of Biblical Interpretation: Decentering Biblical Scholarship," *Journal of Biblical Literature* 107, no. 1 (Winter 1988), 14.

woman in a range of contexts--in Central Africa, Sri Lanka, and New York, in economic development and adult education in Canada's Atlantic provinces, in Toronto's inner city with women in crisis, and in lifelong association with the United Church of Canada, to name only a few formative experiences. Because of my active and ongoing commitment to women's well-being, I continue to learn about the suffering caused by contradictions of class and race, as well as gender and sexuality.

In this thesis I must take seriously my own social location; a contextual method insists that, if we aim to be in solidarity with the victims of our society, practitioners of theological ethics must claim both our privilege and the fact that we are often denied access to power. I have certain privileges as a middle-class Canadian woman who is also white, heterosexual, and has had long years of formal education. Such factors enable me to write this dissertation with those working for justice and peace in mind. My audience in this thesis includes those who are on the "unbeaten path"[1] towards justice and peace. My social location and commitments, however, do not entitle me to write to or for the struggling poor. Rather, I understand my task as one of responding to the good news of the invitation from the margins to "hear and know"[2] present reality from the voices of those who suffer outrageously and who struggle to transform the world beyond its widespread bondage and oppression. Attention to *this* theological subject raises the deep hermeneutical suspicion necessary for an adequate understanding of the interconnections of our currently ordered social relations. Indeed, "the critical interpretations of the most marginated must also be accepted as 'correcting' the subjective blind spots in our own experience."[3] While

---

[1]This is the name of the newsletter of the Saskatchewan Christian Feminist Network.

[2]From Mercy Amba Oduyoye, *Hearing and Knowing: Theological Reflections on Christianity in Africa* (Maryknoll, N.Y.: Orbis Books, 1986). I follow her insistence that theology and ethics is for living, that there is no one standpoint or uniform system, but that theology reflects awareness of the horizon toward which all believers move. In this sense we are unsystematic but thoroughly methodical, dedicated to hearing and knowing how God is with us empowering liberation/salvation.

[3]Harrison, "Theological Reflection in the Struggle for Liberation: A Feminist Perspective," in *Making the Connections*, 250; see also Nancy Hartsock, "Rethinking Modernism," *Cultural Critique* (Fall 1987), 187-206.

I am not writing this thesis for the poor, I do want to join their cries against the lies of dominating systems and to embrace a common vision for awakening and inspiring the captive middle class church. Hence, this study shares with a liberation theological stance a deep and unqualified commitment to the empowerment of the silenced and oppressed. My starting point is with the lives of women struggling to claim their own lives in contexts that regularly ignore, undermine, despise, and harm them. As noted above, our primary theological question is the problematic of the non-person. How can we be faithful to the God of Abundant Life when structures of injustice systematically thwart human lives as fully valuable co-creators?

The task of theology in a contextual/liberation paradigm to participate in the forging of historically liberative social relations. Theology is a second order activity predicated upon the prior commitment to make justice-in-relation in the here-and-now: "Theology is reflection, a critical attitude. Theology *follows*; it is the second step. . . . Theology does not produce pastoral activity; rather it reflects upon it."[1] James Cone characterizes this method shaped by liberation theologies as "a critical reflection upon a prior religio-cultural affirmation and political commitment to solidarity with the oppressed of our continents."[2]

Because we *begin* with concrete human experience of struggles for right-relation, what we do, that is, the choices and decisions we make, the responsibilities and rights we claim--our moral agency--influences the way we come to perceive and know the world. The point of departure for all theological work aimed at solidarity for justice is *praxis*, "a reflective political action that includes cultural identity."[3]

The concept of praxis is predicated on the thesis that all knowledge, including theology, emerges from human experience comprised of integrated thought and action. A critical epistemology will thus place the theological tradition itself under scrutiny, as well as society and culture. Liberation perspectives insist that knowledge of reality becomes distorted under conditions of uneven power relationships,

---

[1]Gutiérrez, *A Theology of Liberation*, 11.

[2]James Cone, "Black Theology," in *Doing Theology in a Divided World*, eds. Fabella and Torres, 99.

[3]Ibid.; cf. Beverly W. Harrison, *Our Right to Choose: Toward a New Ethic of Abortion* (Boston: Beacon Press, 1983), 94-96.

whether it be in a biblical or any other community of interpretation. This methodology, according to Juan Luis Segundo, presupposes that

for reasons of convenience the mechanisms of social reality normally remain hidden from human awareness even though they are operative and determinative. And among those mechanisms we naturally find those which, gradually and unbeknownst to us, go on shaping our theology so as to uproot it from its base in divine revelation and place it in the service of social interests.[1]

Those mechanisms which elevate theology above its rootedness in historical process and subordinate theology to serve dominant group interests construct a situation of "ideological captivity." Thus,

if the praxis of a person or group is devoted to maintaining the order of the world as it is, then the group's reading of the "facts" [i.e., what is the case] will always support the status quo. By contrast, if a person's or group's praxis aims to overcome what thwarts their common life in the present, they will know the world in a different way, and "official truth" will appear as the distortions of the powerful who are in control.[2]

Ideology thus functions to mystify experience by distorting actual social relations of domination and exploitation. The result is alienation which reveals itself in "false consciousness," the internalization of a view of the world as pre-ordained and static. In this way ideology encourages attitudes of inferiority, passivity, and subservience towards the people and structures with which power is lodged. When people accept the world as "naturally" structured in hierarchical order, their perceptions and capacity to mobilize for social transformation are blunted.

Ideological suspicion is perhaps the most crucial presupposition of a liberative ethic. It assumes that we are all moral agents and approach the world from our particular avenues of activity and power. It thus raises critical questions which unmask the myth of the neutrality and universality of all knowledge, and it reveals that knowledge is actually politically constituted and mediated within complex, historically structured social relations of power.[3]

[1]Juan Luis Segundo, *The Liberation of Theology*, trans. John Drury (Maryknoll: Orbis Books, 1982), 47.

[2]Harrison, *Our Right to Choose*, 95.

[3]See Michel Foucault, *Power/Knowledge: Selected Interviews and Other Writings, 1972-1977*, ed. C. Gordon (New York: Pantheon, 1977), 78-133.

We can describe the link between liberation and contextual theological methods, then, as "emancipatory practice for justice." This practice entails employing a new hermeneutics, one of suspicion and rupture with the dominant norms; its practice shapes new content. People's lives and stories, rather than abstract ideas or theory, form the substance for theological reflection; public suffering informs a distinctive theological content and questions of human and divine power demand particular attention. It is within this paradigm of theological ethics that I work.[1]

Feminist Ethical Principles

The method of all liberation theologies assumes that our primary transformations as persons come from *conversion and commitment to the other*, to those deemed insignificant and pushed to the margins of our society and to marginated and oppressed peoples of the world. By "the other" I mean specifically those outside the circle of significance in a dominant society and culture, for example, those who are impoverished and unemployed, lesbians and gay men, women, and racial/ethnic people. We can, of course, also objectify and treat ourselves as objects and thus stand in need of conversion to ourselves as subjects, rather than as objects of someone else's creations.

Proceeding from this assumption of the need for *conversion to the Other*, some key principles of a specifically feminist theological and ethical agenda which inform this project must be elucidated here. These principles are moral agency, embodiment, and accountability.

Moral Agency

According to Bruce Birch and Larry Rasmussen, moral agency

is a way to name that which is necessary to make sense of ourselves as creatures who act "morally." It is a tag for describing human experience, and especially human action, from a moral point of view. It means we are those kinds of creatures who are able to perceive various courses of action, weigh

---

[1] See Karen Lebacqz for a helpful discussion of these new methods and contents in "Getting Our Priorities Straight: Theological Education and Socially Responsible Ministry," in *Theological Education for Social Ministry*, ed. Dieter Hessel (New York: Pilgrim Press, 1988), 66-82.

them with a view to various considerations, choose among the actions on the basis of the considerations, and act on the choices. It also means we can be held accountable for our choices and actions. "Agency" encompasses both character and conduct, both our moral "being" and our moral "doing". . . .[1]

This definition outlines the contours of the holistic venture to live as self-defining, accountable persons. To many trained in moral theory, however, several assumptions outlined here may be unfamiliar in my treatment of moral agency. Moral agency is not co-terminus with an existent individual. By moral agency I mean a capacity that is developed as an ongoing project within specific conditions of possibility and constraint. Moral agency is based on the value of human persons and their sustainable environments, aiming at "the enhancement of personhood, defined as the capacity for responsible self-direction."[2]

Dehumanization and loss of conditions to create full life are, then, evil. In feminist ethics the critical task is to uncover the massive social denial and distrust of women's moral agency, particularly evidenced in the maneuver of the perceived invisibility of actual moral domains in women's lives so that often women do not even recognize themselves as moral agents! The aim of ethics in a feminist mode is the deepening of moral agency understood as taking responsibility for our own lives within community. At the heart of feminist theological ethics, then, stands the norm of women as complete, fully valuable, moral persons in their own right without mediation through men.[3]

As in other liberative ethics, solidarity with those who suffer injustice is the starting point of feminist ethics. The hermeneutics of a feminist ethics is one that aims to involve all people in taking active responsibility for the state of the world. To specify the conditions of

---

[1]Bruce C. Birch and Larry R. Rasmussen, *Bible and Ethics in Christian Life*, rev. ed. (Minneapolis: Augsburg Fortress, 1989), 40.

[2]Carol Robb, "Introduction" to Harrison, *Making the Connections*, xvi. I am indebted to Pamela Brubaker for calling my attention to the work of Daniel Maguire on the value of human beings in relation to their social-material contexts; see *The Moral Choice* (Minneapolis: Winston Press, 1978), 72.

[3]Ruth Smith, "Feminism and the Moral Subject," in Andolsen et al., eds., *Women's Consciousness, Women's Conscience*, 235-50. Kathryn Pauly Morgan discusses four maneuvers in ethical theory and moral practice that deny women's moral agency in "Women and Moral Madness," *Canadian Journal of Philosophy* Supplementary Volume 13 (1983), 210-26.

moral agency involves a multi-dimensional investigation of the causes of suffering; and if we are not to blame ourselves and other women and act with the kind of sustained energy and discipline needed to oppose oppression, we must think of ourselves as unfinished, capable of change, and capable of gaining power over our own lives. In other words, unless we believe we have some power over our lives, it makes no sense to think of ourselves as responsible for our own welfare. Initially, we affirm ourselves as women in terms of acknowledging our own specific struggles for liberation from public invisibility; then from this concrete engagement with our own agenda we join with others on common projects in church and society, for instance, organizing for adequate day care and medical coverage, working to repeal oppressive and unjust policies and laws, or learning to be a survivor of incest.[1]

Embodiment
        Feminist theologies are sensual. They begin with experiences of "epistemological rupture" from dominant, dualistic ways of seeing and living in the world which devalue the body and the material world, overemphasize the mind, and define spirituality in opposition to eros.[2]

---

[1]For the development of feminist ethics, see Eleanor Haney, "What is Feminist Ethics? A Proposal for Continuing Discussion," *Journal of Religious Ethics* 8, no. 1 (Spring 1980), 115-24; and Carol Robb, "A Framework for Feminist Ethics," in *Women's Consciousness, Women's Conscience*, eds. Andolsen et al., 211-34; for continuities with mainstream ethics, see Carol S. Robb, "Introduction" to Harrison, *Making the Connections*, xi-xxii. I am indebted to discussion of the dynamics of agency under conditions of oppression by Susan Wendell, "Oppression, Victimization, Choice and Responsibility," (Paper submitted to Department of Philosophy, Simon Fraser University, Burnaby, B.C., 1987) [Photocopy].

[2]Dorothy Smith, "A Sociology for Women," in *The Everyday World as Problematic*, 49-104, discusses women's experience of epistemological rupture, using the metaphor of a line of fault across which women are constrained to treat ourselves as strangers, as Other, and explores socially organized ways which structure the rupture of women's experience, between our experiences and the available forms by which experience becomes "experience." Cf. George Casalis, "Methodology for a West European Theology," in *Doing Theology in a Divided World*, eds. Fabella and Torres, 106, who contends that practice as the theological point of departure becomes the principle of epistemological rupture. I have articulated this principle from a feminist perspective. See also Rosemary Ruether, *Sexism and God-Talk*, 72-92, who discusses the development of dualism in Christianity whereby false consciousness, based on a hierarchical system of domination and alienation which denies the reciprocal relationship between humanity and nature, renders nature, like women and other oppressed groups, subordinate to male control.

Women's experience of trivialization and subjugation, as "the other" ensconced in the private sphere, is reproduced by theologies which maintain the mind/body, subject/object split. Female history of living as "the other" under various social arrangements is being reconstructed as the ground for critical feminist theological reflection. Hence, it is out of a deep "epistemological rupture" with the dominant exclusionary modes of knowing, premised as they are on a mind/body split, that the work of feminist theologies emerges. We affirm that we are whole, historical beings.

In order to confront the rupture we experience through being objectified and treated as less than fully credible moral subjects, I stand among those women who are affirming a different non-dualistic epistemology where, as described by Beverly Harrison,

> the human body [is] the integrated locus of our perception *of all reality*. Through it, by touch, sight and sound we experience our relations to the world. Through our deep responsiveness, our passion, we experience longing for connectedness to the whole. But our passion is more than this. *It is also the source of our energy*, which is to say, *our power to act*.[1]

Not only is the ultimacy of the subject/object split challenged, "but we also insist that our mode of knowing God/dess/Godding--our mode of knowing that which is Holy--is the same as our *mode of knowing all things*. And that mode is *sensuality*!"[2] This epistemology of radical embodiment serves as the foundation of feminist ideological suspicion which operates from the margins of male supremacist cultures; it challenges their reductionist tendency to engage in objectivist rationality. In other words, women are claiming that only an embodied rationality can adequately mediate divine-human wisdom.

The significance of taking *women's experiences* as a starting point in a liberation perspective rests on the insistence that the mind/body, subject/object, public/private split must be overcome. As we shall see from examining women's lives in Canada, bodily integrity and rational embodiment are imperative sources of women's moral agency:

---

[1]Beverly Harrison, "The Dream of a Common Language: Towards a Normative Theory of Justice in Christian Ethics," *Annual of the Society of Christian Ethics* (1983), 20; and "The Power of Anger in the Work of Love: Christian Ethics for Women and Other Strangers," in *Making the Connections*, 12-15.

[2]Ibid., 43.

without control over our bodies our moral agency is severely constrained. We begin this project, then, by embracing a methodology that is adequate to *the relationality of all human experience*, and hence to its integration and intrinsic wholeness.

Accountability

The affirmation of our "power in relation" recognizes the finite nature of human existence and our moral accountability for our world, within the limits set by our relatedness to others and to our environment.[1] Beverly Harrison states the implications of this presupposition:

> From this theological perspective, faith is understood chiefly as the power (and it is power, a shared or communal power) to live one's life fully, genuinely engaged in receiving and communicating a sense of life's joy and possibility. To live by faith means to accept one's own power, always partial and finite, always power-in-relation, but nonetheless real, to engage with others and to tenderly shape the processes of nature/ history for genuine human and cosmic fulfillment.[2]

I believe we are accountable for our actions and lives within a web of relations that includes the different resources of power which are available within the particularity of our lives and the ongoing ways we achieve a balance with ourselves, our neighbours, and God. We are morally creative and responsible when we declare to whom we are accountable and, in this process, assess who is implicated in and who bears the cost of our decisions and actions.

An essential aspect of taking responsibility for our lives as moral agents is battling the oppression which exists under our own skin: How have I internalized a demeaning view of myself? How have I oppressed others? Audre Lorde encourages a process of accountability to our neighbours beyond the white, heterosexual elite: "I urge each one of us here to reach down into that deep place of knowledge inside herself and touch that terror and loathing of any difference that lives there. See whose face it wears. Then the personal as the political can

---

[1]See for example Carol Christ, "Reverence for Life: The Need for a Sense of Finitude," in *Embodied Love: Sensuality and Relationship as Feminist Values*, eds. Paula M. Cooey, Sharon A. Farmer, and Mary Ellen Ross (San Francisco: Harper & Row, 1987), 51-64.

[2]Harrison, *Our Right to Choose*, 93.

begin to illuminate all our choices."[1] If we are to listen carefully to those in the margins, we must link our choices in solidarity with them rather than with the powerful. To do so, we must struggle with our own suffering never to forget how we have been hurt; from this emotional connection we can begin to identify, understand, and feel with the oppressed rather than simply to maintain our own privileges, for example, my privilege as a white woman. Then we can hope to build bridges with difference as a creative spark. Difference can then weld a common movement in resistance to oppression and in recognition of the God who surprises us with the colour purple in a field.[2]

A Feminist Hermeneutical Circle of Praxis

> The human struggle for liberation is precisely the struggle to create the material, spatial, and temporal conditions for all to enjoy centered, self-determined social existence.[3]

I uphold this vision as the basis of this study. While reconstructing a feminist liberation method *in toto* is not my project, I will briefly review the methodological backdrop which informs this thesis.

Social ethics in a feminist mode joins with other liberative theologies in appealing to a hermeneutical circle of praxis.[4] This circle is an interpretive process based on struggles for social justice. It involves an array of base points or stages, never as easily distinguishable as they

---

[1]Audre Lorde, "The Master's Tools Will Never Dismantle the Master's House," in *Sister Outsider: Essays and Speeches* (Trumansburg, N.Y.: The Crossing Press, 1984), 113.

[2]Alice Walker, *The Color Purple* (New York: Simon and Schuster, 1982), 203; her writings inform my vision of incarnation. On naming and respecting diversity, see The Mudflower Collective, *God's Fierce Whimsy*, 158.

[3]Harrison, "Theological Reflection in the Struggle for Liberation," in *Making the Connections*, 241.

[4]The classic and succinct statement of the hermeneutical circle is in Segundo, *The Liberation of Theology*, 9; for a feminist critique of Segundo's formulation, see Elisabeth Schüssler Fiorenza, "Feminist Theology as a Critical Theology of Liberation," in *The Challenge of Liberation Theology: A First World Response*, eds. Brian Mahan and L. Dale Richesin (Maryknoll, N.Y.: Orbis Books, 1981), 91-112. Beverly Harrison, "Theological Reflection in the Struggle for Liberation," in *Making the Connections*, 249-59, presents an in-depth feminist critical appropriation and construction of a liberationist method.

will appear on paper, which are incorporated in tackling concrete social conflicts. In brief, the first methodological stage is the crucible of human struggle for justice. Here we name how we experience the world. The second stage is the application of ideological suspicion to the way we experience reality in order to name the sources of oppression. Third, loyalties and solidarities must be clarified in order to establish priorities for more effective resistance and solidarity. Within this process norms and goals for action must be scrutinized in relationship to strategies being planned, and then these strategies must be assessed in relationship to the communities they are designed to serve. Accountability to specific social groups is thus built into this method.

The final phase of this hermeneutical method is explicitly theological. Our theological work within the Christian tradition is both critical and constructive. These two tasks involve ritualizing and celebrating the sources of hope for our pilgrimage, even as we denounce all that destroys life as sin. This theological phase requires locating cultural resources that empower us, as well as identifying how knowledge, including theology, arises out of our lived-world activity and is controlled by those in centers of power. Hence, at this point, we can recognize how every theological stance is relative to a particular context. The entire process continues afresh with new action, critiques, theological insights, and ritual elements to enable the next steps of the journey. I will now explain the four phases of the hermeneutical circle in relation to the feminist hermeneutics at work in this study.

Arising from Experience

A specifically feminist liberation hermeneutic maintains that the starting point of our theological work is women's experience as *lives-in-relation*. "Experience" as a source for theological reflection is not a neutral, universal lump of events; "experience is the crucible out of which theologies arise."[1] Beginning with experience involves appreciating that we are "social selves" actively engaged in reflecting upon the specifics of our lives. In the face of external versions of our lives, women have developed a healthy suspicion that what we are told about ourselves is *not* what we experience. The first stage of a feminist hermeneutical process, then, is a commitment to discover "how the per-

---

[1]Collins, *A Different Heaven and Earth*, 34.

sonal is political." This work of discovery heralds women's entrance into the hermeneutical circle. Because in most cultures women have been confined to silence and powerlessness as "the other," critical consciousness initially develops by sharing our stories and hearing each other into speech.[1] Women's experiences are thus shared through narration and these stories give the unique ingredients and tastes to a feminist theological feast. One way of understanding women's experience, significant especially for this study, is through narrative.[2]

Experience and Narrative in Feminist Theology

As Beverly Harrison describes it, women's story telling for critical consciousness involves

> recognition that what we have experienced, in isolation and silence, as private pain is in fact a public, structural dynamic. *My* life is now perceived in a new way in light of *your* stories. Together we slowly re-vision our reality so that what appeared, originally, to be an individual or personalized "problem" or even a human "failing" is exposed as a basic system or pattern of injustice. The reality of oppression, exploitation, or subjugation becomes clear as we "learn together" to grasp the common meaning of our lives.[3]

Feminist ethics, then, relies on stories, oral and written, to define our experience as female persons. I will approach fiction in keeping with this insistence on the centrality of women's stories. A key value in employing narrative as a resource for feminist ethics is its capacity to defy the objectivism rampant in much theological practice, be it of the "otherness of man" style of characterising the divine-human relationship, or in theological reflection about "the poor." Narrative can aid us in breaking down the elevation of mind over body, rich over poor, male over female, culture over nature, white over black which is rooted

---

[1]This process is beautifully articulated by Nelle Morton in her essay "Beloved Image," in *The Journey is Home* (Boston: Beacon Press, 1985), 127-29. On the goal and process of feminist theologizing, see her work "Toward a Whole Theology," in ibid., 62-85.

[2]For a ground-breaking study of women's religious experience in terms of literature, see Carol P. Christ, *Diving Deep and Surfacing: Women Writers on Spiritual Quest* (Boston: Beacon Press, 1980).

[3]Harrison, "Theological Reflection in the Struggle for Liberation," in *Making the Connections*, 243.

in the mind-body split of the dominant culture. Narrative can insist on the concreteness of lived experience; it keeps us engaged in the tangibles of our daily worlds. In narrative we can look at how moral relations are portrayed imaginatively, in terms of power relations specific to particular cultural dynamics presented by the authors. Narrative also offers imaginative visions of alternatives to how life is currently being lived, visions which are vital to our naming of sources of hope. Indeed, without narrative in the work of justice-making and worshiping God, our passions for each other as persons sharing the struggle to be fully human dry up. If we forget to engage narrative as a central resource in doing theological ethics, we ignore a valuable resource for learning what women have to teach us about survival in the face of disordered power in relation. We also lose a source of personal transformative power for sustaining with compassion our struggles for justice.

Defining the Agenda

Naming the oppression that women experience is the second step in this process by which women may seek justice. We use the tools of social analysis to explore how racism, sexism, compulsory heterosexuality, capitalism, and militarism have been disguised as benevolent, unchangeable givens but operate instead as interconnected structures generated by relations of ruling.[1] In this phase of the circle, we discover how existing power-in-relation has shaped our praxis/awareness.

The effort to overcome our own and others' suffering--poverty, pain, denial, and self-hate--pushes us to understand how the sources of oppression have been produced and reproduced and how they function in our particular social relations. We develop the sense of suspicion (i.e., that things are not the way they are represented or meant to be) into a more adequate, critical social analysis and appropriation and reconstruction of history. For example, within the Canadian context, we begin to ask "Where were the women and what were they doing? How did the native women respond to the immigrant groups?"

By giving voice to our own stories in our own words, women become involved in conscious political action. Recognition that contra-

---

[1]The term is from Dorothy Smith; see her "A Sociology for Women," in *The Everyday World as Problematic*, 49-104 for an excellent critique of ideological formations as they effect gender relations.

dictions in our personal lives are shaped by broader political dynamics raises "questions of identity, the retrieval of lost history, the destruction of self-deprecation, and liberating self-affirmation."[1] The central moral task in feminist liberation theology is to become the subjects of our lives. "We cease, thenceforth, to be defined by the men who run our churches, by the corporations who project our images, or by men in [government] who seek to control our destinies."[2] While critical consciousness begins our journey of praxis for liberation, in and of itself this dynamic awareness will not save us. We must continually relate our lives to ongoing strategies for transformation, which means we must understand, and act our way into, our own power.

Analysis of Power Relations

The third stage is clarifying our solidarities and loyalties: who says this praxis is good, and whom is it actually benefiting? At this point, we stop to assess the norms and goals for action as well as to evaluate our strategies in terms of how they affect our communities of accountability. Hence, as we work on behalf of our own well being in relation to the concrete well-being of particular peoples, the issue of accountability must be explicitly addressed.[3]

In this study I argue that taking women's experiences seriously entails giving value to our everyday lives as the arena for comprehending how public realities shape our lives.[4] Thus, "human experience" in feminist theology indicates who we are in all our relational power and

---

[1]Pauli Murray, "Black, Feminist Theologies: Links, Parallels and Tensions," *Christianity and Crisis* 40, no. 6 (April 14, 1980), 86-95.

[2]Sheila Collins, "Reclaiming the Bible through Storytelling," in *Must We Choose Sides? Christian Commitment for the 1980's* (Oakland, Cal.: Inter-Religious Task Force for Social Analysis, 1979), 99. Ada-María Isasi-Díaz and Yolanda Tarango, *Hispanic Women: Prophetic Voice in the Church* (San Francisco: Harper & Row, 1988) articulate this process as expressed in their community; see 94-103 for their theoretical observations.

[3]See The Mud Flower Collective's reflections on this process in *God's Fierce Whimsy*, 23.

[4]For an elaboration of this point in terms of power/knowledge configurations, see Larry Rasmussen, "The Near Future of Socially Responsible Ministry," in *Theological Education for Social Ministry*, ed. Dieter Hessel (New York: Pilgrim Press, 1988), 20.

how we have been able to shape and name our environment. This process uncovers both conflict and complicity through the recognition of power dynamics that shape our lives. The commitment to struggle against dependency, invisibility, and exploitation, and to join others in shaping a *different* version of reality is born out of the painful struggle to take our own lives seriously and to claim full responsibility for them. The crucial agenda for feminist theology and ethics is attention to the specificity of women's experiences. In order to further the work of a liberative praxis, we must privilege and hear the voices of those suffering from conditions of injustice, especially those most silenced and denied. Karen Lebacqz insists on this epistemological position:

> If justice begins with the correction of injustices, then the most important tools for understanding will be the stories of injustice as experienced by the oppressed and the tools of social and historical analysis that help illumine the process by which those historical injustices arose and the meaning of them in the lives of the victims.[1]

Lebacqz attempts to deal with the realities of being both oppressed and oppressor in her work and encourages solidarity, initially based on connection by way of hearing the stories of oppression. Those who experience invisibility, not only in the mainstream but also in liberative theological ethics and other justice-based discourses, insist on privileging a relationship between our stories of suffering and those on the margins. This thesis aims to take seriously this critique and to be in dialogue with the suffering and wisdom of those on the margins.[2]

---

[1]Lebacqz, *Justice in an Unjust World: Foundations for a Christian Approach to Injustice* (Minneapolis: Augsburg, 1987), 150. In "Getting Our Priorities Straight," in *Theological Education for Social Ministry*, ed. Hessel, 71-72, she discusses connections to be made among various experiences of pain and suffering (e.g., stories from white women oppressed in their own culture, from gay men and lesbians about sexual discrimination and oppression, as well as written stories from oppressed peoples).

[2]Recent work by third world women that treats this issue includes: Letty Russell, Kwok Pui-Lan, Ada-María Isasi-Díaz, and Katie Geneva Cannon, eds., *Inheriting Our Mothers' Gardens: Feminist Theology in Third World Perspective* (Philadelphia: Westminster Press, 1988); Virginia Fabella and Mercy Amba Oduyoye, eds., *With Passion and Compassion: Third World Women Doing Theology* (Maryknoll, N.Y.: Orbis Books, 1988); and John Pobee and Barbel von Wartenberg-Potter, eds., *New Eyes for Reading: Biblical and Theological Reflections by Women from the Third World* (Geneva: World Council of Churches, 1986).

Hearing the Voices from the
Margins of the Margins

> Does the liberating word that feminist theology addresses to women who
> view the world from the underside of history (white women) have the same
> liberating effect for those women who view the world from *the underside of
> the underside* of history (black women)?[1]

In a liberationist hermeneutic it is necessary for the justice agenda to engage each cultural context from the position of the most invisible and to include in its definitions and strategies the issues raised there. For instance, how do I as a white women read narratives by women of colour? How can I not reproduce what Katie Cannon explicates as typical of white ethical discourse in its provision of truncated and distorted views of women of colour?[2] It is not a matter of "explaining" the simultaneity of oppression; instead we seek to know how this oppression happens in the lives of native, black, and third world women through their own articulation.[3]

Bell Hooks testifies to the enlarged vantage point among black people in a white racist world:

> Living as we did--on the edge--we developed a particular way of seeing reality. We looked both from the outside in and from the inside out. We focused our attention on the center as well as on the margin. We understood both. . . . [Black women] often have a lived experience that directly challenges the prevailing classist, sexist, racist social structure and its concomitant ideology.[4]

---

[1]Delores Williams, "Black Women's Literature and the Task of Feminist Theology," in *Immaculate and Powerful: The Female in Sacred Image and Social Reality*, eds. Clarissa W. Atkinson, Constance H. Buchanan, and Margaret R. Miles (Boston: Beacon Press, 1985), 103.

[2]Katie Geneva Cannon, *Black Womanist Ethics*, American Academy of Religion Series (Atlanta: Scholars Press, 1988), 167-68.

[3]Arthur Brittan and Mary Maynard, *Sexism, Racism and Oppression* (Oxford: Basil Blackwell, 1984; reprint ed., 1985), 6-7, argue that simultaneous oppression is what is left out of so much white radical literature. I concur and attempt to take heed so that the experience of oppression in a multiplicity of sites is voiced by those who live it.

[4]Bell Hooks, *Feminist Theory: From Margin to Center* (Boston: South End Press, 1984), 1, 15.

To privilege the readings of history by those in the margin is not justified on the basis of "natural" categories of race or gender but because the very concrete everyday experiences of the lives of "women, and other marginated people, are less cut off from the real, material conditions of life than [are the experiences of] those who enjoy the privileges of patriarchy."[1] Being the ones who have the most to gain from justice-based social relations, those at the margins may also have less invested in maintaining the current social order.

This vantage point from the "margin of the margins" has many contributions, two of which I will emphasize. First, from this position, women can see the interconnections of power structures and they have particularly high stakes in criticising them. Second, these voices of outsiderhood can envision, and are essential for, the creation of any lasting counter-hegemony by liberative movements. Bell Hooks clearly demonstrates that consciousness is formed by experience, bound up as it is with concrete relationships of power. Those at the margins of society who struggle to survive with dignity and worth can offer their critical interpretations of the way peoples' real interests and hopes are falsified by the distortion of power in warped social relations.[2] In short, we can listen for the different articulations of women's struggles for authentic personhood; we can learn of their inner longings, and the kinds of cultural codes women use to claim their own well-being.

Reading narratives written out of different cultural, class, age, and sexual experiences can also function to test our participation in a "politics of diversity."[3] I therefore approach narrative as relevant for feminist theological ethics in two specific ways. First, in order to link up with other women in genuine solidarity, it is vital to know one's own context with its particular set of struggles. Second, narrative

---

[1]Harrison, "The Power of Anger in the Work of Love," in *Making the Connections*, 6.

[2]On the necessity of listening to the voices of the marginalized, see Lee Cormie, "The Epistemological Privilege of the Oppressed: Liberation Theologies, Biblical Faith, and Marxist Sociology of Knowledge," *Proceedings of the Catholic Theological Society of America* 33 (1978), 155-81.

[3]This is the title of a recent collection of essays addressing the question given priority on a feminist agenda: can we properly apprehend the differences among women without losing a common political purpose? See Roberta Hamilton and Michele Barrett, eds., *The Politics of Diversity* (London: Verso, 1986).

opens up windows into the lives of women who have different struggles and who venture to claim their own lives against quite different odds.

Because of these possibilities, I look to narrative as a privileged source for informing a practice of self-criticism and a vehicle for hearing the voices of variously marginalized women. We need the knowledge gleaned both at the margin and the centre if we are to render faithfully the wholeness of women's experience, which a feminist sensibility must do in its task of making justice among us. Delores Williams, womanist theologian and poet, beautifully images the graceful capacity of such a vision as table fellowship, "the welcome table," where women can stop on their journeys to share in the promise of life abundant.[1]

Just as the importance of a broad based social analysis cannot be minimized, so too we must attend to the experiences out of which our discursive practices occur. Through narrative we can better explore the world of emotions, of political and moral values, of individual and collective identity, of social and historical particularity and thus better feel and, it is to be hoped, understand the relationships between these commitments and experiences, and the broader social dynamics.

The "margin," as we shall see, is not a static category. It is meant to indicate some tendencies that are structurally determined by nation, region, ethnicity, age, sexuality, race, gender, and class, but which cannot be reduced to these. In today's political climate "the others" include people of colour, homosexuals, the poor, feminists, socialists, and even left-liberals![2] The point is that we need the voices from the margins if we are to know what damage is being done, what interests are being served by maintaining business as usual, and how better to resist the causes of the wounds so that we may be healed.

If the key for a liberative theological practice is solidarity with those who suffer injustice, we learn, with others whose experience is very often different from our own, to forge communities out of common purpose and vision. Liberation strategies and priorities for action can never be accomplished in isolation from shared commitments to particular projects. While justice is the stated norm, we must clarify

---

[1]Delores Williams, "What are Women Theologians Saying?" (Auburn Theological Seminary Conference, New York, 1988).

[2]Asoka Bandarage, "Women of Color: Towards a Celebration of Power," *Woman of Power* 4 (Fall 1986), 13.

how specific principles and norms are articulated in relation to more effective actions and solidarity. All options for action must also be scrutinized, then, for how well we have attended to commonalities *and* differences--of race, culture, class, sexual orientation, and religion --and thus remain open to other communities of accountability.

Theological Work and Ritual in the Midst of Our Struggles

This brief sketch of the hermeneutical circle is completed by a final step, the intrinsic music which sustains the motion of the circle: the ritualizing of our struggles and celebration of our sources of hope for the journey. This element of ritual and celebration is a continual and intrinsic aspect of struggles for justice. The process, as should be obvious, is never neat and tidy, nor is it necessarily followed in the logic presented. Each step of the hermeneutical circle should be used, however, as a tool for self-criticism and evaluation of shared struggles.

This stage aims to recover communal traditions of resistance, to create a genuine historical perspective in order to recover our connections with the struggles of our forebears, to comprehend not only how the past has been shaped by specific conflicts and associations but also how historical structures are *not* objectively "out there" but alive and well and forming the *ongoing* dynamics of the present.[1] The goal of this step is empowerment for the continuing journey. We will first explore the role of tradition in more detail, and then briefly address theology, culture, and image in the context of this final stage.

The Role of Tradition

As was pointed out earlier, the fundamental feminist hermeneutical principle is the primary importance of contemporary struggles for the full, concrete emancipation of women around the world. Elisabeth Schüssler Fiorenza insists that the authority of canon, including tradition, must come from the current praxis of women and the vision shaped by women's experience.[2] In light of this commitment, we con-

---

[1] Harrison, "Theological Reflection in the Struggle for Liberation," in *Making the Connections*, 249.

[2] Elisabeth Schüssler Fiorenza, "Feminist Theology as a Critical Theology of Liberation," *Theological Studies* 36 (1975), 616.

tinually ask: How have our faith traditions functioned to oppress different groups? What are the particular consequences for women in all their diversities? While it is generally true that the value of tradition lies primarily in its relationship to the present moment, we appropriate a tradition by using the strands that allow moral creativity and accountability in our pilgrimages towards right-relation in the future. Hence, if we claim, as I do, that faith is trust in the enduring process of liberation, the Christian tradition, when critically appropriated, is a vital resource for contemporary liberation.[1]

The value of church tradition in a feminist hermeneutic lies in a tradition of prophetic writings, the life of Jesus, and the most liberating theologies we have inherited over the centuries; all of these articulate a call to serious immersion in real, concrete human suffering. We give authority to this tradition because it provides us with an "authorizing past," an authority which generates the courage to help us ground ourselves in faithful action in the present.

This tradition, however, cannot bear the entire weight of defining truth or moral action for our *contemporary* involvement in faithful praxis. The norm of a feminist interpretation of scripture and tradition is derived from the experience of women's struggles for self-identity, survival, and liberation in a patriarchal society and church; authority does not rest with the Bible and tradition as divine revelation, simply as given. In the development of a feminist theological hermeneutic we adopt an "advocacy stance," one that has the ability to account not only for women's experience as victims of varied forms of oppression but also for women's agency and power as the locus of revelation. The goal of this hermeneutics is "not simply the 'full humanity' of women, since humanity as we have known it is male-defined, but also women's religious self-affirmation, power, and liberation from all patriarchal alienation, marginalization, and oppression."[2] Granted these presup-

---

[1]See Segundo, *The Liberation of Theology*, 118-20 for his understanding of faith as deutero-learning, a process of "learning how to learn."

[2]Elisabeth Schüssler Fiorenza, "The Will to Choose or Reject: Continuing our Critical Work," in *Feminist Interpretation of the Bible*, ed. Letty Russell (Philadelphia: Westminster Press, 1985), 126; see also her *Bread Not Stone: The Challenge of Feminist Biblical Interpretation* (Boston: Beacon Press, 1984), x, xvii; and *In Memory of Her: A Feminist Theological Reconstruction of Christian Origins* (New York: Crossroads, 1983), 29 and 32 ff.

positions regarding a feminist appropriation of Christian tradition, we now move beyond this source to address the role of cultural resources in feminist theological practice.

Theology, Culture, and Image

Feminist theologians actively incorporate cultural resources and theological critique into the regular ritualization and celebration of our struggles to seek a world of well-being of all creation. We look at culture as an essential theological source, as did the Canadian preacher, Salem Bland, a Canadian radical Christian who fervently believed that:

> Culture is an enlargement of experience. It is power gained to enter into other lives and modes of thought foreign to our own. . . . God's truth comes to us in fragments and people need to share these fragments with each other. [In 1913 he still believed that the church was still the hope for the world]--but novelists, not preachers, are stating the new ethical standards of our age.[1]

While I approach culture as an inherent dimension of all social life, as the realm of symbolic-expressive activity that is interwoven into the fabric of our everyday lives,[2] I will argue for a dynamic reading of culture that connects cultural practices conveying meanings and purposes, ideas and values, with broader social relations. Culture, then, is viewed as a way of life *and* how this way of life is experienced, understood, and interpreted. I will present critical cultural theories of everyday life which explore how we understand ourselves in relation to others. Culture in this reading is, therefore, capable either of oppressing or of liberating. Because we rely upon the resources available in our lived experience to express our journeys theologically, culture, critically appropriated, is a crucial avenue of investigation in a liberative theological ethic for access to women's lives.

---

[1]Cited by Richard Allen in "Salem Bland and the Spirituality of the Social Gospel: Winnipeg and the West, 1903-1913," *Prairie Spirit: Perspectives on the Heritage of the United Church of Canada in the West*, eds. Dennis L. Butcher, Catherine Macdonald, Margaret E. McPherson, Raymond R. Smith, and A. McKibbin Watts (Winnipeg: University of Manitoba Press, 1985), 222-23.

[2]This definition of culture is the work of cultural critics Robert Wuthnow, James Davison Hunter, Albert Bergesen, and Edith Kurzweil; see their *Cultural Analysis: The Work of Peter L. Berger, Mary Douglas, Michel Foucault and Juergen Habermas* (Boston: Routledge and Kegan Paul, 1984). I return to this issue in detail in Chapter 4.

Whereas dominant theologies appeal to our rational faculties and dogmatic formulations, feminist theologies appeal not only to discursive communication but also to the role of images, myths, and rituals in the continuing process of conversion.[1] Indeed, the primary feminist protest against the underlying dualism of the mind/body split in the western theological tradition is to be found in its challenge to the notion that the basic category of theological envisagement is the concept. "Concepts function to explain reality. Theological language evokes reality . . . . [T]he *primal and irreplaceable mode of theological discourse is the image* and relatedly, *the metaphor*, . . . those fundamental images that put us in touch with life through vision."[2]

Metaphorical images do not set out abstract ideals and doctrines but rather generate a world view and infuse our lives with meaning and nourishment for empowered, fruitful lives. For liberation theology, moral vision plays a vital role: it aids resistance to the alienation and dehumanization of the current situation. The fullest approach to moral life, according to philosopher Dorothy Emmet, is a kind of purposive activity where the manner of achieving that goal is an integral part of the end.[3] Vision functions to inspire our task of linking the realistic means of our empowerment to the goal of all-inclusive community.

It is explicitly in the process of creating ritual that we actively critique scripture and our faith traditions, and celebrate our sources of strength and hope. Rituals are forms for ceremonies which often involve patterned behaviours. They involve deep sharing and are a crucial source of emotional and spiritual power; rituals focus our energies, allow us to be renewed, help us forge bonds of community and inspire us toward action beyond ritual. In short, rituals are the symbolic actions which enable us to envision how the world could be different, and to imagine the means of social and personal transformation.[4] Through

---

[1]See Kwok Pui Lan, "Discovering the Bible in the Non-Biblical World," *Semeia* 47 (1989), 36, on the sacred status of women's stories of struggles for humanhood.

[2]Harrison, "Restoring the Tapestry of Life," 42-43.

[3]Dorothy Emmet, *The Moral Prism* (London: Macmillan, 1979), 6-7.

[4]I am grateful for the work of Charlotte Caron, especially her work in religious ritual; see "Qualitative Methods: An Experiment in Feminist Theological Method," (Paper submitted at Carleton University, Ottawa, 1988), 7 [Photocopy].

rituals and vision we are especially reminded of, and invited into, our immediate experience of God/dess and our connection with all life. Thus, in the process of critical reappropriation of our traditions, we construct new images and metaphors that give life to our collaboration, diversity, shared struggle, and vision of wholeness-in-relation. And thus renewed, we continue to engage in emancipatory practice within our communities of commitment.

Method and Scope of the Study

My search for the voices of women in theological ethics, especially those most marginalized, has emerged from my deep commitment to women's lives as autonomous sources of moral knowledge and theological imagination. My commitment to this task has deepened with the recognition that the direct abuses of power in social relations are known particularly well by impoverished women who struggle to survive. I will attend to those at the margins because, as I have argued, such attention is necessary for an adequate methodology for normative theological ethics. I will thus make substantive, not simply procedural claims on its work.

In chapter two, I will place this feminist project in its historical framework. Here I will do the preliminary work of examining the radical Christian tradition as a source for the methodological roots of this project, before investigating the amplifications required. This tradition, as we shall see, holds remarkable resources for a contemporary liberative ethics. In particular, I will engage with the lively concern of the tradition for economic justice and radical social analysis. I will also discuss in more detail the limitations of this tradition from the perspectives of women. My provisional hypothesis is that two amplifications are needed to render women's experience visible and to make marginalized women's reality central within Canadian theological ethical developments. The first is illumined by political economic theory; the second by modes of cultural analysis such as literary criticism.

Chapter three will address the initial weakness of the faith-and-justice tradition, particularly its inattention to women's work. I will develop the first amplification necessary within this tradition, a feminist social analysis of Canadian reality intended to portray a broader spectrum of women's lives. A deeper problem, however, requires another methodological step beyond the amplification of the political economic sources. If we are to hear women's own voices as they suffer and hope, struggle and dream, we must attend to the cultural dimension of the Canadian context.[1] In chapter four, I will again critically appropriate the radical Christian tradition and amplify a critical cultural analysis and theology of culture to give access to the particularity of women's lives. The distinctive contribution of this thesis lies in this second amplification: in the engagement of the cultural dimension from a feminist standpoint and in the effort to integrate both the social-analytic and the cultural sources in a distinctively feminist theological ethics.

To accomplish this cultural analysis, in chapter five I will apply a critical cultural hermeneutic to selected Canadian women's narratives. Having identified the importance of specifying women's experience for a feminist theological ethic, I will listen to three stories about marginalized women's voices in order to recover their sufferings and sources of hope. I have chosen three narrative voices from the Canadian prairies: Beatrice Culleton's Native Canadian voice in the novel *In Search of April Raintree*; Joy Kogawa's novel of Japanese-Canadian experience, *Obasan*; and Margaret Laurence's *The Diviners*, written from a white, rural, anglophone perspective. To clarify the significance of these narratives for theological ethics, I will use a hermeneutics requiring examination of specific moral themes represented in them: the ethics of survival of peoples and of constructing female identities, women's agency and suffering, and resources for the regeneration of persons in community. The concluding chapter will present significant implications of listening to the voices of marginalized women for liberative theological ethics in the Canadian radical Christian tradition.

---

[1]Douglas John Hall and Gregory Baum cite the importance of the cultural base for doing theology, but do not give sufficient attention to this reconstructive resource. For example, Hall, *The Canada Crisis: A Christian Perspective* (Toronto: Anglican Book Centre, 1980), 90 ff., uses the metaphor of midwives for the function of Canadian literature and art in the creation of a new national identity, but again this source is not fully developed in his method; see also Baum, "Three Theses on Contextual Theology," 49-59.

CHAPTER TWO

CANADIAN RADICAL CHRISTIANITY: STRENGTHS AND LIMITATIONS OF ITS METHOD FOR THOSE AT THE MARGINS

Contextualization of Theological Ethics in Canada

I will now identify and colour in some of the key resources for honouring the particularities of women's lives in Canada. I will explore the discussion in Canada on "contextualization" in theology and ethics, and consider how a feminist liberationist hermeneutic shapes the task and appropriation of theological tradition. From this perspective, I will explore in some depth the resources for accountability to marginalized women in Canadian Radical Christianity in the 1930s and 1940s. The purpose here is to ground this project in the soil of the radical "social passion"[1] with which it is continuous. My critical appropriation of this movement will focus on its theological norm of mutuality in the creation of community, and will suggest the methodological steps needed to place women at the centre of a "social gospel" praxis.

What does it mean to do "contextual theology"? Canadian theologian Douglas Hall argues that in

---

[1]This phrase is from Richard Allen, *The Social Passion: Religion and Social Reform in Canada: 1914-1928* (Toronto: University of Toronto Press, 1971).

> that mode of reflection we call Christian theology, there is a meeting between two realities: on the one hand the Christian tradition, namely, the accumulation of past articulations of Christians concerning their belief, with special emphasis upon the biblical testimony; and on the other hand, the explicit circumstances, obvious or hidden, external or internal, physical or spiritual, of the historical moment in which the Christian community finds itself. . . . [T]heology means the *meeting* of these two realities. It is the *struggle* of imagination-intellect which occurs in that meeting, the *ongoing* encounter between the claims of the tradition and the lived experience of the present.[1]

This definition affirms the modern discovery of the historical nature of all knowledge, including knowledge of God, and thus the conviction that all theology is fundamentally shaped by particular social relationships and under specific historical conditions. Our deepest experiences of the divine are thus within our lived-world contexts of everyday life.

A genuine contextuality does not mean ladling out superficial answers to people's questions from the stockpot of Christian doctrine; it means authentic involvement in the concrete struggles of one's own groups so that all theological expression tastes uniquely spiced by the actual dilemmas, sufferings, and joys of particular historical situation. Indeed, as James Cone states, it is impossible to separate theology from the community it represents. Only through profound sensitivity to our genuine needs as diverse people, and to the cultural resources for an embodied theology, can there be an adequate response to actual suffering and possibilities for wholeness. Only from a strong base of identity and conviction can we relate to others who are committed to living out their faith within their own unique contexts.[2]

Canadian social ethicists and theologians have been discussing contextualization for more than a decade. While the nomenclature of this discussion has evolved from "political" to "contextual" theology, the concern with concrete issues, rather than theoretical analysis for its own sake, remains. "The point of departure for political ethics is the way *power* is exercised in an 'unjust, non-participatory and unsustain-

---

[1]Douglas John Hall, "On Contextuality in Christian Theology," *Toronto Journal of Theology* 1 (Spring 1985), 3-4.

[2]James Cone, *A Black Theology of Liberation*, 2nd ed., (Maryknoll, N.Y.: Orbis Books, 1986), 30. See also Samuel Rayan on theology as praxis of salvation, "Indian Christian Theology and the Problem of History," in *Asian Christian Theology: Emerging Themes*, ed. Douglas J. Ellwood (Philadelphia: Westminster Press, 1980), 130.

able society.'"[1] The key element in defining a contextual approach, then, is attention to the question of power.

"Power" is the ability to act on and effectually shape the world around us, particularly through collective action and institutional policy. To have power means to have access to physical resources and wealth, to knowledge, and to the loci of social decision making and to be able to impact institutional and social policy.[2]

In social terms to be *marginal* means to live outside the dominant locations of power, subordinated and often silenced. As I will demonstrate, however, alternative forms of power to power-over exist on the margins of society. Feminist and womanist theological paradigms are built on the premise that the *only legitimate form of power is shared power*. Given that power is wielded differently according to historical context, all experiences of marginality are not the same. Indeed, the notions of margin and centre must not be understood as standing in opposition to one another but rather as working in dialectical relation. Thus, gender, race, class, and nation create different experiences of marginality with distinctive effects on our moral and political agency.[3]

Contexts, then, are in large measure determined by various economic, political, ideological, and cultural structures which shape our social relations. Basic to Canada's context are certain facts: while dominating the original, native peoples of Indian and Inuit cultures, this nation was founded by two groups, the French and the British, and has

---

[1]Roger Hutchinson, "Conclusion," in *Political Theology in the Canadian Context*, ed. Benjamin Smillie (Waterloo, Ontario: Wilfred Laurier University Press, 1982), 251; emphasis added. For examples of this discussion, see Gregory Baum, "Three Theses on Contextual Theology," 49-54; Douglas John Hall, "On Contextuality in Christian Theology," 3-16; Roger Hutchinson, "Contextualization: No Passing Fad," in *A New Beginning*, eds. Chu and Lind; Christopher Lind, "An Invitation to Canadian Theology," *Toronto Journal of Theology* 1 (Spring 1985), 17-26; and Smillie, ed., *Political Theology in the Canadian Context* .

[2]Harrison, *Making the Connections*, 290, n. 5.

[3]See Smith and Valenze, "Mutuality and Marginality: Liberal Moral Theory and Working Class Women in Nineteenth-Century England," 282; also, Elisabeth Schüssler Fiorenza states: "It seems to be methodologically inappropriate to speak in generalized terms about oppression or about liberation theology in the singular." See her "Toward a Feminist Biblical Hermeneutics: Biblical Interpretation and Liberation Theology," *The Challenge of Liberation Theology*, eds. Mahan and Richesin, 93.

remained on the edge of empire, first the British and now the American; its national character has been dominated both by its colonial status, in which major decisions regarding economic and political interests were often made elsewhere, in London or now in collusion with Washington; and by the struggle to survive, in a land dominated by the vast Canadian shield, numerous rivers and lakes, and an inhospitable climate; its official cultural policy is one of multicultural mosaic rather than melting pot, because, in order to survive under harsh conditions, people of diverse cultures had to depend on one another and to create community. The Lone Ranger was no hero here.

In a global perspective Canada holds an ambiguous place. It has power as a first world capitalist nation, yet its resource-based economy with a small manufacturing base creates a state of dependency, particularly on the United States. Within the country, a history of uneven and dependent development can be traced from before confederation itself. The domination of Canada's politics by the collusion of powerful business, church, and state interests began well before the nation's inception in 1867 and continues to this day with even greater tenacity.[1]

Gregory Baum, the much-lauded Canadian Christian ethicist and theologian, has rightly described society as a conflictual construct wherein Christians must take sides, and he has done a compelling analysis of what he terms "the perspectival commitment" which initiates the "faith-and-justice" stance of contextual theology.[2] Reflecting from his location in the northern hemisphere on the "preferential option for the

---

[1]For background on Canadian history and political economy I recommend Harold Cardinal, *The Unjust Society: The Tragedy of Canada's Indians* (Edmonton: M. G. Hurtig, 1969); George Manuel and Michael Poslins, *The Fourth World: An Indian Reality* (New York: Macmillan, 1974); Tobique Women's Group with Janet Silman, *Enough is Enough: Aboriginal Women Speak Out* (Toronto: The Women's Press, 1987); Susan Mann Trofimenkoff, *The Dream of Nation: A Social and Intellectual History of Quebec* (Toronto: Gage, 1983); Veronica Strong-Boag and Anita Clair Fellman, eds., *Rethinking Canada: The Promise of Women's History* (Toronto: Copp Clark Pitman, 1986); Michael Cross, ed. *The Consolidation of Capital: 1846-1924* (Toronto: McLelland and Stewart, 1978); and Michael Cross, ed., *Modern Canada: 1930-1980* (Toronto: McLelland and Stewart, 1983). Classic studies include J. M. Careless, *Colonists and Canadiens* (Toronto: Macmillan, 1971) and Ramsey Cook, *Canada: A Modern Study* (Toronto: Clarke Irwin and Co., 1963).

[2]Gregory Baum, "Option for the Powerless," *The Ecumenist* 26 (November-December 1987), 5-11.

poor," Baum identifies a double movement intrinsic to a critical contextual approach. First, the perspectival stance expresses the view of society from the vantage point of the people at the bottom and on the margins. Second, the contextualization of theology must be based on active solidarity that gives public witness to common struggles. Thus, theology must be contextual in these two very particular senses: it must correspond to the culture and country that produced it, and it must especially express and live a conscious solidarity with the people in society who suffer injustice.[1] In short, the gospel in this vein is understood as "a judgment on social sin, on the structures that marginalize the majority, and as a promise of new life for the people."[2]

An explicit normative stance is implied in the term "contextual": it indicates a partisan or advocacy stance. It rejects all approaches which claim a universal validity of scriptural and doctrinal norms where "Christian" truth has the same content regardless of historical experience. Given the norm of justice, the inductive approach of contextual theology is not relativistic but *relational*. It confronts specific sin and suffering in particular contexts while facing the future as a common historical project.[3]

To construct an integrated and solid theological framework in the Canadian context, we must begin to define our lives from the inside out, to take our lives and struggles seriously rather than to cut off the roots we need to claim as genuine theological material. Roger Hutchinson reminds us that the main problem is not whether our methodological categories are imported or indigenous, but whether the strategic moralities developed are grounded in actual Canadian conditions.[4]

Benjamin Smillie, eminent social gospel theologian, articulates a contemporary faith-and-justice stance rooted in an awareness of social injustice and Canadian church complicity in it and points to the conditions shaping the "theological ferment in the churches," noting that

---

[1]Gregory Baum, "Political Theologies in Conflict," *The Ecumenist* 22 (September-October 1984), 84.

[2]Baum, "Three Theses on Contextual Theology," 56.

[3]See Letty Russell, "Universality and Contextualism," *The Ecumenical Review* 30 (1979), 23-26.

[4]Hutchinson, "Summary Statement," in *Political Theology in the Canadian Context*, ed. Smillie, 254.

what makes the prodigality of our life style even more offensive is that our relative affluence is bought at the price of the structural inequalities in our society. If we are Indian or Metis, single parents, live in rural areas of Northern Quebec, Northern Ontario, Northern Manitoba, Northern Saskatchewan or Northern B. C., or if we are a family from the Atlantic Provinces, or the head of a family sixty-five years or older, then we are likely to be poor.[1]

Smillie identifies the origins of political theology in "the socialist alternative for Canada found in the movement politics of the Agrarian Revolt, the British idealism of the Cooperative Commonwealth Federation--New Democratic Party, and the Marxist socialism."[2]

While these are resources for theological work grounded in our specific context, they are inadequate for addressing the realities of women's lives. Further, a salient source of indigenous critical theology --the social gospel movement known as "Radical Christianity" --is missing, not to mention the sources I will explore below in chapters four and five, the cultural dimension rooted in women's everyday lives.[3] I will, then, next examine the theological tradition most conducive to feminist commitments--Radical Christianity in Canada--in order to confront its oppressive elements and embrace its liberative elements for a theology predicated on the full personhood and well-being of women.

A Feminist Contextualization

Women's contemporary struggles for wholeness include the creation of "a usable past." In the context of a society where religion has become so privatised, the importance of reclaiming marginalized traditions cannot be overstated. Loss of public memory has contributed to

---

[1]Smillie, "Introduction: Theological Reflections on the Canadian Context," in *Political Theology in the Canadian Context*, ed. Smillie, 6-7.

[2]Ibid., 28-33; see also Gregory Baum, "Discussion," in the same collection, 136 ff., on the features of Canadian socialism. In this thesis I accept this premise of class analysis, but will argue for inclusion of analytic categories of gender and race so that we may adequately account for women's experience.

[3]The Radical Christian movement of the 1930s and 1940s is well represented in the collection of essays by R. B. Y. Scott and Gregory Vlastos, eds., *Towards the Christian Revolution* (Chicago: Willett Clark and Company, 1936).

apathy and our inability to make connections with ourselves and our neighbours, whether near or far.[1] Mary Hunt has defined "tradition" for a feminist paradigm as:

> the cumulative stories of a person and a people which ground their self-understanding and invite their participation in a future which is *connected* to the past. Tradition in a narrow sense refers to the tradition of the Church. . . . But here we mean it in a broader sense including the lost history of women and the passed over experiences of marginalized people. Tradition helps us to ground theology in an ongoing quest for meaning and value. It helps us to understand that we are asking/answering questions in continuity with the people who profess belief in many of our presuppositions.[2]

A Canadian theological movement that combines elements of tradition in *both* senses above is the indigenous social gospel strand know as "Radical Christianity," which flourished in the 1930s and into the 1940s. I will examine its norms and strategies through a feminist re-reading and consider whether it offers fertile ground for doing theology in a Canadian liberative mode, where the work of social ethics includes "an evaluative hermeneutics of history."[3] I aim to test this resource for its potential to hear the voices of marginalized women in Canada by using the following approach: first, I will present the theological and ethical norms of the movement; second, I will examine the role of women in this social gospel tradition; and third, I will reevaluate this data in light of contemporary criteria.

---

[1]For this approach to history and tradition that is at once responsible and usable, see Eleanor L. McLaughlin, "The Christian Past: Does it Hold a Future for Women?," *Womanspirit Rising: A Feminist Reader in Religion*, eds. Carol P. Christ and Judith Plaskow, (New York: Harper & Row, 1979), 94.

[2]Mary Hunt, "Feminist Liberation Theology: The Development of Method in Construction," (Ph. D. dissertation, Graduate Theological Union, Berkeley, 1980), 164-65.

[3]Roger Hutchinson, "Mutuality: Procedural Norm and Foundational Symbol," in *Liberation and Ethics: Essays in Honor of Gibson Winter*, eds. Charles Amjad-Ali and Alvin Pitcher (Chicago: Center for the Scientific Study of Religion, 1985), 107. I am indebted Hutchinson's groundbreaking study, which has amply demonstrated the validity of this tradition for the work of Christian social ethics. For historical background and an overview of Canadian Christian socialism in the 1930s, see chapters one and two of his "The Fellowship for a Christian Social Order: A Social Ethical Analysis of a Christian Socialist Movement," (Th. D. dissertation, Emmanuel College, Toronto School of Theology, 1975).

Radical Christianity of the
Thirties and Forties

Social gospel Christians in the 1930s faced a crisis in democracy brought about by the rise of totalitarian states overseas and of economic malaise at home. The radical social gospel movement is privileged in this project because it took seriously the day-to-day suffering of common people, responding with the question "What is to be done?" To illustrate this commitment, I will briefly explore and assess the relationship of Radical Christianity to women's work and experience as "social gospelers," both in terms of the former's stated norm of solidarity and of contemporary feminist criteria in theological ethics.

A strong minority of Christians sought social justice as the best expression of their faith in the 1930s. The 1935 report of the National Council of the Student Christian Movement (SCM), for example, envisaged ways of forming "a new social order." It aimed to study social situations through personal contact in social service projects and political activity, as well as by reading and discussing books, "the object of which is to understand the causes of social evil and the nature of Christian action in the redemption of society."[1] This direction took root in the unique learning contexts of the SCM "work camps" begun in the 1940s. In the SCM National Council reports of 1937 and 1939, recommendations which provided the foundation for such work advocated that the SCM's ministry with students include seeking a just and equitable peace and opposing racial prejudice. The SCM sought the support of Canadian religious activists such as Gregory Vlastos, King Gordon, Eugene Forsey, and Agnes McPhail, as well as American visitors such as Harry Ward and Reinhold Niebuhr.[2]

In the early 1940s a deep rift developed between liberal social gospelers and a growing body of neo-orthodox students. A radical alternative, however, developed through the renewal movement in the churches and focused on ethical and religious dimensions of the social crisis. Roger Hutchinson has argued that the most viable theological

---

[1] Student Christian Movement of Canada, *Student Christian Movement: A Brief History, 1921-1974* (Toronto: SCM, 1975), 86.

[2] Ibid., 87, 94; see especially "The Report of the Commission of the Student Christian Movement and the World Crisis, 1939."

base, and an alternative to both the culturally accommodated "Christ of culture" of the earlier liberal social gospel theology and the "Christ and culture in paradox" of neo-orthodoxy, was formulated in the Fellowship for a Christian Social Order (FCSO). The Fellowship created a unique theology from its socialist perspective that anticipated in its normative stance liberation theologies that emerged two decades later.[1]

The FCSO manifesto of 1934 stated the following aim:

> This Fellowship is an association of Christians whose religious convictions have led them to the belief that the capitalist economic system is fundamentally at variance with Christian principles; and who regard the creation of a new social order to be essential to the realization of the Kingdom of God.[2]

This theological affirmation was developed along with certain ethical implications. An analysis of the capitalist system demonstrated how it affronted and negated the Christian ethic. By elaborating this Christian ethic, the FCSO gave articulate form to a movement which was already a dynamic force throughout Canada.

In 1936 the FCSO published a collection of essays, under the title *Towards the Christian Revolution*, which laid out its theoretical foundations.[3] The agenda was to detail the most adequate Christian response to the social and economic crisis of the day. "Whether

---

[1]Hutchinson, "The Fellowship For a Christian Social Order," 25 and 311. For an overview of the pioneer scholarship on this movement, see Hutchinson, "The Canadian Social Gospel in the Context of Christian Social Ethics," in *The Social Gospel in Canada*, ed. Richard Allen (Ottawa: National Museum of Man, 1975), 286-316. For an assessment of its ecclesial and historical context, see Ted Reeve, "The Church and the Economic Crisis: A Study of the United Church's Continuing Concern for Social Justice" (M. Th. thesis, Emmanuel College, Toronto School of Theology, 1986). The most thorough introduction to the roots of the social gospel in Canada is Allen, *The Social Passion*.

[2]Cited by J. King Gordon, "A Christian Socialist in the 1930's," in *The Social Gospel in Canada*, ed. Allen, 137.

[3]Scott and Vlastos, eds., *Towards the Christian Revolution*. This volume includes essays by both editors, who were, respectively, professor of Old Testament at United Theological College, Montreal, and associate professor of philosophy at Queen's University, Kingston; John Line, professor of history and philosophy of religion at Victoria College, University of Toronto; Eugene Forsey, lecturer in economics and political science at McGill University, Montreal; and J. King Gordon, then the traveling secretary and lecturer of the FCSO and occasional professor of Christian Ethics at United Theological College, Montreal.

FCSOers used as a starting point for their theology the religion of the prophets and Jesus, or an interpretation of man's [sic] nature and situation, the underlying emphasis was on developing a theological stance which [1] had adequate depth and scope to make sense out of what was actually happening, [2] to guide action, and [3] to sustain a vision of a more just and humane world."[1] This volume characterized the early position of the FCSO "that *the content and focus of the Christian faith are disclosed in the struggle for justice and right relations in man's [sic] actual historical existence.* Beliefs about God, church, world and self were all rooted in this central insight."[2] This continuity between faith and everyday experience was grounded in the very structure of human life itself, which the radical Christians identified as *mutuality*.

Mutuality as Norm

The starting point of this radical theological paradigm was human experience, understood as essentially social, communal, and mutually responsible. "Human life is human relatedness," and real personality was based on the material facts of co-operative community.[3] Aided by John Macmurray's work, FCSOers developed a revolutionized anthropology--*the social self*--as the best middle path between the distortions of liberal individualism and totalitarianism.

> There are therefore two things to be remembered in considering the individual in his [sic] social *milieu*. They are the dependence of the individual on the social environment, and equally his [sic] unique individuality. We can construct from these a criterion for judging both the present social system and proposals for social change, for it seems to us a sufficient test of any such proposal or system whether, on the one hand, it recognizes the part played by the environment in determining the individual, and whether, on the other, its tendency as affecting the individual is towards quickening and furthering, not deadening and obstructing, his [sic] unique capabilities.[4]

Hence, the Christian ethic of love can only be discerned in conjunction

---

[1] Hutchinson, "The Fellowship for a Christian Social Order," 182.

[2] Ibid., 58-59; emphasis added.

[3] Gregory Vlastos, "The Ethical Foundations," *Towards the Christian Revolution*, eds. Scott and Vlastos, 63 and 68-69.

[4] John Line, ibid., 16-17.

with the norm of justice. If the self is essentially communal as well as free, account has to be taken of both elements in the social milieu that human beings have created. The principle of mutuality was a radical reformulation of the traditional Christian assumption that love, on the one hand, was altruistic and self-sacrificing, a tender suffering of the violation of personal rights, while justice, on the other hand, was a hard, rational compromise resting on imposed duty.

Gregory Vlastos argued adamantly against the Niebuhrian view that the world, incapable of love, was quite capable of justice, claiming instead that the basis of justice was to be found in

> community of purpose and reciprocity of service. Is there any sure founda-
> tion of justice save a recognition of mutual need and mutual respect, a sense
> of unity, partly existing, partly to be realized in the common future? The
> imperative of justice is: Do not exploit. The imperative of love is: Admit
> all to the community of ends.[1]

The correct understanding of the religion of Jesus inhered in the creation of community, and thus in right living rather than right belief, because love is ultimately recognized in community. God is love, a pattern of life described as mutuality. "Thus the ethic of love is the ethic of the co-operative community. And just because it is that, it is also the ethic of free and mutual personality. The two ideas, community and personality, are strictly correlative."[2] The inalienable connection between love and justice had its source in mutuality:

> Where the two are separated justice becomes legalistic and love sentimental:
> justice becomes a defence of the established order, and love a weapon of the
> will to power. Both love and justice will fail, unless grounded together upon
> material community. . . . They call for no sacrifice, save that which will
> promote the growth of mutuality itself. They tolerate no surrender of rights,
> save for the one purpose of achieving rights more secure and more equitable
> for all.[3]

The valuation of human well-being is clear in the insistence on ending all sacrifice except that which is chosen to repair and sustain mutuality.

---

[1]Vlastos, "Justice and Love," *The Canadian Student* 50 (1937), 6.

[2]Vlastos, "The Ethical Foundations," in *Towards the Christian Revolution*, 69.

[3]Vlastos, "Justice and Love," 6.

The Nature and Reality of Sin

Radical Christianity's effort to reconstruct the social order included a clear definition of sin: that which broke relations of mutuality and hindered the creation of community. People were not inherently sinful, but they were responsible for developing exploitative power relations which produced sinful structures. Sin included "all acts and processes that yield affluence, or even sufficiency, to some while impoverishing others, or that cause power to be used in unreciprocal ways over the will and freedom of others."[1] Capitalism was understood to be the world's major sinful structure. In recognition of this evil, one could enjoy the fruits of repentance by taking an active part in transforming those conditions of injustice.

Theological Vision of Community

The Fellowship interpreted the gospel imperative, then, as working towards a more inclusive mutuality. The love commanded by Jesus was to be embodied "in a community of interest effective in protest and concerted endeavour towards social justice."[2] Jesus' ethic of love and mutuality was conceived in embodied, material terms.

> If love exists at all, it exists as a material activity: the material interaction of separate beings recognizing each other's interests and seeking common fulfillment. The spiritual meaning of love is only the felt meaningfulness of this "brute," material fact, directing cooperation, anticipating its further development, celebrating its present reality. Love does modify my consciousness. . . . But it modifies my behaviour just as much. I no longer act alone but with and for another. . . . The first maxim of the ethic of love, therefore, is concern for material values. Without material values there can be varieties of conscious experience but no co-operation; without co-operation there can be no community, no genuine love. The test of our sincerity in the pursuit of spiritual values will come back to the question: How seriously do we take their material conditions?[3]

Who is Jesus? He is the advocate for the poor and the disinherited. "In the very forefront of the vision of the Kingdom is the abolition

---

[1]Line, "The Theological Principles" in *Towards the Christian Revolution*, eds. Scott and Vlastos, 47.

[2]Nicholas Fairbarn, "The Evangel of the Kingdom," in ibid., 185.

[3]Vlastos, "The Ethical Principles," in ibid., 59-61.

of poverty, oppression and economic injustice, because these stand as stubborn obstacles to the free spiritual life of man [sic] in fellowship."[1] The Biblical testimony of covenant undergirded this preferential option for the marginated in society. Eugene Forsey concluded from his economic analysis of capitalism that "[u]ntil Christians learn to understand and apply the lessons of Marxism they cannot enter into the Kingdom of Heaven--nor, probably, can any one else."[2]

Divine-Human Relationship

This commitment to community and solidarity was based also on a view of the divine-human relationship which was an alternative to "the Barthian irrationalist projection of the divine order."[3] The image of God was not the sum of human moral ideas, but rather "the patterned ground of value in the world itself. He [sic] is the structure of reality which men [sic] must discover and express in their ideas, in order to conform to in their actions."[4]

In this theology human beings were created to cooperate with divine activity in history in the creation of community, mutuality, and solidarity. The Fellowship named "revolutionaries, workers together with God"[5] those Christians who were dedicated to ending strife and injustice, and thus to transforming society into a divine commonwealth of righteousness and love. It further designated all who were excluded from the basic requirement of what was necessary to be fully human-- i.e., community--as co-workers with those of Christian faith. How one lived according to these norms was the test of one's faith, and one knew God as the One who judges and takes sides with those people and classes to whom the essentials for authentic life had long been denied;[6] thus, one knew God not in right belief, but rather in the creation of community.

---

[1]Scott, "The Biblical Basis," in ibid., 89.

[2]Eugene Forsey, "A New Economic Order," in ibid., 139.

[3]Line, "The Theological Principles," in ibid., 45.

[4]Vlastos, "The Ethical Foundations," in ibid., 70.

[5]Line, "The Theological Principles," in ibid., 50.

[6]Ibid., 48.

"The Cultus of Community"

The final point in this review of Radical Christianity's norms is
its emphasis on "the cultus of community"[1] as an integral element in
the reconstruction of social relations. It recognized the power of symbolic ritual in the creation and sustenance of religious community.
"The idea of the Kingdom is only a skeleton, until it is clothed with
emotion rooted in reverence and understanding. An idea or faith which
lacks 'incarnation' or dramatic embodiment will remain ineffective."[2]
Elements of the ritual life of the community of faith included assembly,
celebrations of the significance of religion for personal and social life
generally or of its meaning for particular crises, and significant and
appropriate action by the assembled.[3] The cultus then embodied and
exhibited the meaning of the Christian culture it was helping to create.

> If religion be defined as a way of living, determined by conviction about and
> reverence towards the Ultimate Reality, worship is the reaffirming of the
> conviction and the deliberate expression of that reverence. . . . Reverence,
> affirmation and vision call for utterance which at once expresses and con-
> firms them. And since men [sic] come to their full human stature only in fel-
> lowship, their worship is supremely a social matter.[4]

The rite of common bread and drink betokens a life given up that Life
may triumph over the forces that would destroy it.

> Here men [sic] see and know in their inmost being that love is stronger than
> evil and the way of the Kingdom more satisfying and enduring than the
> world's way of conflict and possession, domination and exploitation. Here
> faith in God, the Father [sic] of all, verges on sight. Faith in one's fellow
> man [sic] and love of neighbour, with new hope in the coming Kingdom, are
> kindled like a flame that cannot be put out.[5]

This statement summarizes well the interconnection and relatedness of
all life--communal, spiritual, human and divine--which are symbolized
and sustained in celebrations of this solidarity.

---

[1] This term is from R. B. Y. Scott, in ibid., 190.

[2] Scott, "The Church's Role," in ibid., 196.

[3] Ibid., 192.

[4] Ibid., 191.

[5] Ibid., 195.

Adequacy to Women's Experience of the Period

Bringing this Radical Christian heritage under scrutiny in light of women's experience of the same period enables us to ask some probing questions regarding its theological adequacy. While its mixed-theory approach to the task of a theology based on the norms of love and justice is to be applauded, a hermeneutic of suspicion must be applied to this tradition if we are to reclaim and extend it without reproducing its oppressive elements. Also, this hermeneutic reflects the concern of the movement itself, that "the validity of [the theology on which faith is grounded] had constantly to be tested and reveal its meaning in social practice."[1] An immanent critique of Radical Christianity will use Radical Christianity's own categories of mutuality and sin to assess the limitations of the movement's own *application* of its theological vision.

Whose experience informed Radical Christianity's theology?[2] The use of androcentric formulations and language reveals the actual power relations that existed between women and men. In the established literature on the Canadian social gospel movement, women's work and experience are conspicuously absent. One reason for the invisibility of women was that "women's participation in the social gospel movement was at the practical, and not primarily the leadership level."[3] Similarly, as Carol Lee Bacchi shows in her study of the links between women's role in the suffrage and moral reform movements (including the social gospel), the social gospel played an important role in the political awakening of women, who, as people of faith, saw their call as mission and reform work. At the same time, Bacchi shows how the church upheld the traditional social structure based on the ideology of domesticity: the restriction of women's "proper" activities to the

---

[1]J. King Gordon, "A Christian Socialist in the 1930s," in *The Social Gospel in Canada*, ed. Allen, 122.

[2]A growing body of literature by feminist historians in Canada makes women not only visible but central in their work. Susan Mann-Trofimenkoff, Alison Prentice, Jennifer Stoddart, Veronica Strong-Boag, and Sylvia Van Kirk are among those active in this endeavour.

[3]Elizabeth Anderson, "Women Workers in the Methodist Church, 1889-1925," Paper submitted at Emmanuel College, Toronto School of Theology, 1985, 13. (Photocopy.)

home. She concludes that "while the social gospel encouraged a degree of political activism, it constrained women by keeping them tied to their traditional roles."[1] Her research also shows that radical feminists who challenged sex-role stereotyping usually moved outside the church.

The period of this early social gospel has been typified as an era when the ideology of domesticity or "maternal feminism" held sway. Elizabeth Anderson's research on the work of women in the deaconess, missionary, and Student Christian movements, however, has provided an alternative minority tradition to this dominant one. Anderson gives credit to the work of women tending the bonds of community in a wide variety of settings.

> [Women] could be found across the country in small towns and large cities, teaching English to new immigrants; organizing mothers' meetings to teach nutrition and offer support; visiting families with food and clothing to try and soften the impact of poor wages or none at all; stationed at railway stations and ports to meet new immigrants and direct them to services, or meet rural girls moving to the city and directing them to housing and jobs; running homes and schools for girls in the city, or boys and girls in Indian reservations; running Sunday schools in large churches; working as church secretaries; doing the pastoral visiting for a congregation; nursing the sick; taking children and mothers to the countryside for a week of rest, good food and fresh air.[2]

Such varied examples of social gospel practice reveal the largely ignored work and struggles in which women engaged.

When we thus bring into focus women's concrete experience, different images emerge which give substance to the Radical Christian claims for relationships of communal mutuality. Indeed, an adequate Christian moral theology "must be answerable to what women have learned by struggling to lay hold of the gift of life, to receive it, to live deeply into it, to pass it on. . . . [W]omen have always been immersed in the struggle to create flesh-and-blood community of love and justice."[3] The experience of women can also be witnessed in social

---

[1]Carol Lee Bacchi, *Liberation Deferred? The Ideas of the English Canadian Suffragists, 1877-1918.* (Toronto: University of Toronto Press, 1985), 59.

[2]Anderson, "Women Workers in the Methodist Church, 1889-1925," 11.

[3]Harrison, "The Power of Anger in the Work of Love," in *Making the Connections,* 8.

gospelers' own accounts of their work: for example, circuit lecturing in sex education; staffing settlement houses, using all their practical skills in making ends meet; organizing a Labour Women's Social and Economic Conference which, by the time that the Cooperative Commonwealth Federation was formed in 1933, had held sessions in every major centre in western Canada.[1]

When the radical social gospel is considered from the standpoint of women, new insights also emerge about their participation in mission work. It is no exaggeration to suggest that the very definition of the radical social gospel is altered. The presence of women in mission work at home and abroad widened the scope of evangelism from saving souls to caring for people's physical and communal needs. Because women were denied ordination, they were sent as teachers, doctors, nurses, and social workers, rather than as preachers; these new mission needs actually inspired women's professional education.[2]

Many women also participated in the Student Christian Movement, unique in the university and church because it supported and required the participation of women. The SCM's recognition of the equality of women and men, formally and informally, deepened its debates on, for example, women's roles in human relationships, the purpose of university education, and the possibility of combining career and marriage. In every SCM generation, women brought "private" concerns into the public arena for debate, so that contemporary issues from women's lives emerged as legitimate for the work of the SCM.[3]

Attention to women's experience makes clear that women in the social gospel pioneered many kinds of "social service" work and educa-

---

[1]See for example Beatrice Brigden, "One Woman's Campaign for Social Purity and Social Reform," and Ethel Parker, "The Origins and Early History of the Presbyterian Settlement Houses," in *The Social Gospel in Canada*, ed. Allen, 36-62, 86-121.

[2]Elizabeth Anderson, "'Not by Might, nor by power but by my spirit, saith the Lord of Hosts': Women Missionaries as Women of Faith, 1880-1935," Paper submitted at Emmanuel College, Toronto School of Theology (n.d.), 11. (Photocopy.) In 1936, Lydia Gruchy became the first woman ordained in the United Church of Canada.

[3]Elizabeth Anderson, "Women in the Student Christian Movement: 1921-1949," Paper submitted at Emmanuel College, Toronto School of Theology (n.d.). (Photocopy.); see also, Student Christian Movement of Canada, *A Brief History of the Student Christian Movement*.

tion. Their work can rightfully be claimed as the basis of a faith-and-justice activism which is committed to *living the vision* of community that underlies the good news witnessed in the lives of those who followed Jesus' passion in relation. Inclusion of women's concrete experience, then, is crucial to fleshing out the moral meaning of the norm of mutuality, and to ensuring that it does not deteriorate into, for example, a personalistic sentimentality that avoids the very issue of power in relation it was designed to address. While further research is needed, the above review of what women as social gospelers accomplished is evidence for the thesis that mutuality as described by radical Christians is a socially-constructed, interdependent activity with which women have long been associated.

Not to be forgotten, of course, the influence of race and class on women's exclusion from public power arenas; middle class white women historically have had access to the privileges of education and training available to many social gospelers. Despite differences in the degree of marginality, however, one reality common to most women can be identified from the evidence gathered: women's agency has primarily involved creating and tending the bonds of community, those concerned with real human need, development of personhood, and subsistence. This common social-cultural task can only be addressed if *both* public and private spheres are interrelated and taken into full account. The Radical Christian norm of mutuality helpfully confronted the legacy of liberal social theory and its stress on the autonomous, isolated individual.[1] Including women's lived-world experience history, however, opens up new possibilities for forging a *shared* destiny without reproducing alienation.[2]

---

[1] Line criticises laissez faire philosophy and liberal theology in his essays "The Philosophical Background" and "The Theological Principles," in *Towards the Christian Revolution*, eds. Scott and Vlastos, 1-25 and 26-50.

[2] On feminist historiography, see Joan Kelly, *Women, History and Theory: The Essays of Joan Kelly* (Chicago: University of Chicago Press, 1984); Elizabeth Fox-Genovese, "Placing Women's History in History," *New Left Review* 133 (May-June 1982), 5-29.

A Critical Appraisal of Radical Christianity

From the foregoing discussion of Canadian Radical Christianity, we can identify several theo-ethical emphases that are important for the church's continuing work of justice-making. All, however, require revision and amplification before we can appropriate them for the task at hand. With these amplifications, the strengths of this tradition that might fruitfully be employed in doing feminist theological ethics are its emphases on: first, mutuality and moral agency; second, social sin; and third, economic justice and for solidarity with the exploited. My aim here is to discern not only the common ground between Radical Christian and feminist theologies, but also to indicate specific ways in which feminist insights may deepen these emphases.[1]

Amplification of Moral
Agency as Mutuality

The first strength is Radical Christianity's emphasis on human relatedness and agency, on the experience of mutuality and the theological vision of community. Creative love and work for mutuality in relationship characterized the experiential base of the radical tradition which gave birth to its theological formulations. Its norm of mutual relationship also affirms the unity of spiritual and material life, indeed of all creation. While this theoretical assumption is shared in the feminist commitment to overcome all dualisms and to understand the interconnectedness of all oppressions, we must incorporate a commitment to the feminist theological basepoint of *embodiment* if Radical Christianity's criticism of social relations is to be deepened.

This concern to ground mutuality in embodied relationality is absent in the literature I have discussed. Greater recognition of the norms of embodiment and bodily integrity as basic to the work of love and justice would redirect this theological tradition into a contemporary Radical Christianity dedicated to supporting the conditions for mutuali-

---

[1] For the development of my analysis here I am indebted to Ruth Evans; see her "Behold, I Am Doing a New Thing: Canadian Feminist Theology and the Social Gospel," in *A Long and Faithful March: "Towards the Christian Revolution," 1930s/1940s*, eds. Harold Wells and Roger Hutchinson, (Toronto: United Church Publishing House, 1989), 153-65.

ty by, for example, creating safe places for abused women and children, giving active care to persons with AIDS, and respecting sexual expressions of mutuality regardless of sexual orientation.

The conception that human agency is rooted in mutuality provides us with a strong theological resource for shaping concrete bonds of community. Here the dynamic of faith takes on new life as we perceive ourselves as co-workers with God. Radical Christian theology claimed that love is most alive in relationships of justice. Since all moral relations are social relations, we human beings are responsible for the shape of God's good creation. The Radical Christian insight that mutuality is the core of life means that *all* images of the divine and human are *relational*. Thus, patriarchal images of the divine that denounce or destroy our capacity for mutual relationship are unacceptable. If love of neighbour and love of God are as totally intertwined as Radical Christianity believed, then images of divine power are also those which communicate the power of co-relation in sustaining our lives as co-creators of a just and loving world.

This radically relational vision of a just community dovetails, then, with current feminist attention to the issue of moral agency and power in relation. Radical Christian affirmation of a good use of power concurs with feminist theological principles: the locus of power *is* in mutual relationship. The Radical Christians' norm of genuine mutuality is astonishing for its time and place, especially in its insistence on the foundational importance of justice to the Christian ethic of love. By itself, however, the restricted scope of mutuality as applied by Radical Christianity would perpetuate sexist and racist oppression because it never addressed power relationships in concrete *interpersonal* terms. While Radical Christians maintained that their commitment was with the dispossessed, their own social location and gender and race privilege limited their deeper self-criticism about the nature of real differences in human experience, for example, between women and men.[1]

Hence, in order to be specific about *whose* experience defines theological discourse, we base feminist theological ethics on an analysis

---

[1]The Student Christian Movement of Canada more consciously attempted to deal with race and gender oppression, but its access to church courts was limited; its historical function perhaps has been to keep an agenda of race and gender equality alive, as a minority radical tradition, and to train progressive leadership for national and international struggles.

of power dynamics as constituted inter-personally *and* globally. In light of this understanding, we transform our images of the divine-human relationship such that God is described not as "the structure of reality which men [sic] must discover and express in their ideas"[1], but as the experience of the Beloved, of All-Is-Possible or of the Power-To-Act-Each-Other-into-Well-Being.[2]

Amplification of Conception of Social Sin

The second strength of Radical Christianity is its understanding of sin as that which breaks the bonds of relationship. This concept grows out of a recognition of the nature of moral life as a human project. Because the Radical Christian exposition of mutuality reflected privileged male experience, however, it was a construct that illuminated evil primarily in the *public* sphere. Thus, while Radical Christians addressed sin as social, arguing against privatised religion or a totally transcendent deity who denied the validity of human agency, what they regarded as social sin took account only of the public arena and ignored the existence and sociality of relations in the private sphere.

Capitalism was identified as the main social evil and the overriding cause of broken bonds of community. Biblical study and economic analysis provided a criticism of the social relations produced under capitalism, and class struggle was advocated in the effort to construct a more just society. The subject of these efforts remained the image of the male worker, and the "private" realm of the family and everyday life were consigned to invisibility and their moral adequacy assumed.

The type of "conflict theology" advocated by Radical Christianity correctly addressed economic relations as a deeply significant locus of oppression within its historical context. Its strategies of coalition building with those most affected by economic injustice are certainly legitimate today. Its analysis assumed, however, that the effect of its proposed move to a socialist economic order would be equally beneficial to

---

[1]Vlastos, "The Ethical Principles," in *Towards the Christian Revolution*, eds. Scott and Vlastos, 69.

[2]These images come from Carter Heyward, Dorothee Sölle, and Beverly Harrison. For other examples, see Virginia Ramey Mollenkott, *The Divine Feminine: The Biblical Imagery of God as Female* (New York: Crossroad, 1983).

women and men. By contrast, feminists contend that this will not occur until structures of domination and exploitation that predate and in-
tersect with capitalism have been named and eradicated as well. In
short, Radical Christianity's analysis of sin is limited in terms of what
sustains specific injustices as barriers to mutual relation.[1]

To apply this theological insight effectively, we must reshape the
conception of sin as a breaking of power in relation and contest the
separation of the public from the private, the arena of impersonal relations of institutions from the arena of interpersonal, emotional, physical
relations. Radical Christians began to challenge this separation by calling for a relational conception of human nature and a social ethics of
mutuality which aimed towards a socialist society. By confronting only
the public sphere, however, they failed to address the root of the problem: the grounding of the separation of private and public existence in
mind/body dualism. Because the public/private distinction was not
challenged, the conception of sin as lack of mutuality, and thus the uni-
lateral exercise of power over others, obscured women's experience.

Radical Christianity named the creation of relationships of justice
as the prophetic task. If we are to realize this vision and acknowledge
how all moral goods are *inter*related possibilities,[2] then women's experience both as victims and moral agents must be given central place
as primary data for a contextual theology. Sexuality, family life, and
domestic labour must therefore be considered to be just as historically
constituted and socially constructed as is "public" economic life, *and*
just as urgent a focus for theological reflection.

A feminist assessment of sin recognizes the structural character
of evil not only in relations of economic production, but also in all disordered power relations. All of these become historically embedded in
social structures as complex dynamics of oppression and exploitation.
Beverly Harrison elaborates her understanding of sin in this way:

---

[1]As in liberation theological method, an intelligible, demystified faith uses
social analysis as "neither causal/predictive nor critical/descriptive but evaluative/
transformative; it aims to assess how our actions may affect a situation for the better, not how a historical process will proceed if no intervention occurs." Harrison,
"The Role of Social Theory in Religious Social Ethics," in *Making the Connections*, 65.

[2]Harrison, "Sexism and the Language of Christian Ethics," in *Making the
Connections*, 39.

> The deepest tragedy of human life is that evil, the wrong that we do each other under God, plays itself out and is felt over time in the very ways social systems develop. . . . Social structure, the patterned ways communities and groups related to each other, generates dynamics of power that shape our communal and personal identities, including our sense of self-worth and self-esteem. . . . Evil is the consequence of disparities of power because where disparity of power is great, violence or control by coercion is the predominant mode of social interaction. Evil . . . is the active or passive effort to deny or suppress another's power-of-being-in-relation.[1]

If we are to begin to comprehend the extent of sin and evil in our lives and the world, in order to stand against them, we must understand how personal circumstances are related to broader structural realities.

Amplification of Concern
for Economic Justice

A third theme of Radical Christianity that unites it with a feminist liberation theological ethic is its emphatic concern for righting economic injustice in solidarity with the dispossessed. On the basis of their work for economic justice, Radical Christians considered it faithful activity to take sides with "those who by reason of unjust economic conditions or for whatever cause sit in despair and in the shadow of death."[2] From this perspective, Radical Christians focused on the human Jesus and the related Christian mandate to expose the barriers which divided the poor, the needy, the widows and orphans from the comfortable and the rich. "It [theology] will show how these barriers prevent the development of the mutuality wherein life consists. It will unite also the dedicated into a fellowship which is stronger than the ties of blood."[3]

Obviously, there are similarities between this commitment and the feminist conception of solidarity as continuous and loyal relationship. Feminist liberationists emphasize the need for accountability to the particularities of women's lives; for them "an understanding of jus-

---

[1]Harrison, "The Older Person's Worth in the Eyes of Society," in *Making the Connections*, 154 and 156; see also Rosemary Ruether's chapter on evil in *Sexism and God-Talk*, 159-92.

[2]Line, "The Philosophical Background," in *Towards the Christian Revolution*, eds. Scott and Vlastos, 27.

[3]Vlastos, "The Ethical Principles," in ibid., 56.

tice as making right relations incorporates the insights of the Hebraic tradition that 'doing justice' entails not merely advocacy *for* those marginalized and excluded but solidarity *with* them in the form of mutual accountability."[1] As we shall see, however, a traditional class analysis does not open the way to the lives of the most marginalized.

Weaknesses of the Radical Christian Tradition

Radical Christianity has been dominated by men's experience and the public sphere, and has consistently neglected women's experience and the private sphere. These weaknesses reinforce the underlying white patriarchal values in its theological utterances. Another weakness is its culturally monolithic character. Its cultural perspective has been limited by its exclusively middle-class view of Canadian reality. Hence, the analytic method of the radical social gospel movement has remained oblivious both to the integrity of non-dominant cultures (including the culture of the working classes), and to the sub-cultures of class, gender, and ethnicity in which women's lives are met. The assumption that their class-based strategies for change would be as beneficial for women as for men limited their vision of radical social transformation. As we will see, these assumptions still operate today in "progressive" church documents and theological reflection.

A Lively Concern For Economic Justice in Canadian Theological Ethics

Political economy is . . . the science of the management of the public household, the community. The essential economic problem which any community has to solve is the same as that which confronts a private household: our wants are unlimited, our means of supplying them limited.[2]

If we are to develop more fully the Radical Christian concern for the material conditions of our everyday lives, we must identify both its strengths and limits. I will examine the economic ethics of Radical

---

[1]Harrison, *Our Right to Choose*, 115.

[2]Forsey, "The Economic Problem," in *Towards the Christian Revolution*, eds. Scott and Vlastos, 99.

Christianity, including its contemporary incarnation in faith-and-justice ecumenical work, to assess how adequately it deals with the economic reality and well-being of women. While the social analysis of women's realities and needs is a necessary basepoint of a liberative social ethic, it is as yet insufficiently developed.

A brief review of three of the most critical and constructive works in Christian theological ethics on economic justice in Canada will provide a basis for this reconstruction: first, the Fellowship for a Christian Social Order's 1936 position in *Towards the Christian Revolution*; second, the Canadian Conference of Catholic Bishops' 1983 statement, "Ethical Reflections on the Economic Crisis"; and third, the United Church of Canada's 1984 economic justice policy statement, "The Church and the Economic Crisis."[1] While these documents emerge from different ecclesial traditions, there is a common concern to speak forthrightly about the fundamental structural roots of the Canadian economic crisis and to interpret it in ways relevant to a Christian justice agenda and to the broader social context of Canada.[2]

---

[1]United Church of Canada, "The Church and the Economic Crisis," (Toronto: United Church of Canada, 1984), hereafter cited as UCC 1984. The text of "Ethical Reflections on the Economic Crisis" is found in *Ethics and Economics: Canada's Catholic Bishops on the Economic Crisis*, (Toronto: James Lorimer, 1984), eds. Gregory Baum and Duncan Cameron, 1-18, hereafter cited as CCCB 1983.

[2]Economist William Tabb has lucidly addressed various aspects of the economic crisis that are pertinent to my discussion here, especially the global nature of restructuring. He demonstrates how economic needs lie at the heart of political moves to the right and argues that the original meaning of "incorporation" defies such practices. He suggests making the criterion *the social cost of economics* central to the current debates over policy direction. He therefore presses for a different strategy of combining politics and economic democracy. See "The Economic Crisis of the Present Economic System: A Restructuring," in *Theology in the Americas: Detroit II*, eds. Cornel West, Caridad Guidote, and Margaret Coakley (Maryknoll, N. Y.: Orbis Books, 1982), 12-32. On the relationship between the contemporary economic crisis and Christian social ethics see Lee Cormie, "The Churches and the Economic Crisis," *The Ecumenist* 21 (March-April 1983), 33-38.

The Fellowship for a Christian
Social Order Position, 1936

For the FCSO, economic democracy was the goal of a Christian social vision. The central chapters of their book deal specifically with the nature of capitalism. They place economic reality at the heart of their concerns because for them religion involves the whole of life, and thus it is imperative to understand the dynamics of social existence.

> Christian character does not develop in a vacuum. It is forged in the struggles of daily life; and most of the daily life of most people is spent in the effort to satisfy economic wants. The struggle for bread is not the only thing in life, nor the highest thing. But it is basic, for without bread there is no life.[1]

Eugene Forsey, then teaching economics at McGill University, wrote two chapters to outline "The Economic Problem" and "A New Economic Order" for the nascent radical Christian fellowship. He sought not to polemicise but rather to investigate what was ultimately at stake in the economic order and then to put economic life in the service of the co-operative community which he believed necessary in accordance with Christian covenant. In the mid-1930s his indictment of capitalism was based on an assessment of the logic of the system as it actually functioned. It was clear, he argued, that those who could afford to pay supposedly controlled the production process by their demands; production was not concerned with meeting human needs because the aim of those in control of the political economic system was to make profits. "The supplying of needs, or 'service to the public,' was purely incidental," he insisted. In short, "if it 'pays' we get it, if it doesn't we don't."[2] Forsey was quick to assure the reader that this was not an ethical judgment but a *fact*, one that held true irrespective of the moral qualities of individual capitalists.

In addition to the goal of profit-making, this study described the character of industrial capitalism as monopolistic, the result of the disappearance of the free market. The problem with this concentration of

---

[1]Forsey, "The Economic Problem" in *Towards the Christian Revolution*, eds. Scott and Vlastos, 98.

[2]Ibid., 101.

capital lay in its irresponsibility, and in the state's collusion with it.

> Governments register the results of battles and bargains among economic interests of unequal strength. Under capitalism, whether fascist or democratic, the strongest interests are capitalist interests. . . . [F]or the most part *government is business.*[1]

It follows that the defects of capitalism included not only ill-gotten profit, but also a lack of effective accountability to social good which could be achieved by adequate planning. The solution to this problem could not be "controlled capitalism," because its very system was diseased, as evidenced by the government's compliance with a laissez faire model of regulation suitable to business interest. Writing in the 1930s, Forsey observed:

> What the gradual evolution of capitalism has given us is *state-capitalist* public ownership: ownership by the state for the benefit of capitalists. . . . Not even government ownership of all industry would necessarily mean socialism. If the former private owners are given, and allowed to keep, full compensation, industry will still be run mainly on capitalist lines. . . . In other words, the essential thing about controlled capitalism is that it is still capitalism, and as such, whether in the form of self-government in industry or state-capitalist public ownership, inevitably a scarcity economy [which] cannot solve the economic problem.[2]

In sum, the fundamental evil--the "devil of social injustice"--was capitalism: "It is the very system of private ownership and control of the materials and means of production which renders exploitation possible, indeed inevitable."[3] For Radical Christianity, social reconstruction which would build communal well-being began with a clear recognition of this reality. Their challenge for Christians to join sides with those marginalized by the capitalist process was a response to their reading of the "signs of the times" and to the biblical prophetic mandate to struggle for right relationships.

The contemporary meaning of "the mind of Christ" for the church was to work for a classless society. The ethic of solidarity and

---

[1]Ibid., 120.

[2]Ibid., 122-123.

[3]Martin Estall, a.k.a. Propheticus, "The Marxist Challenge," in ibid., 205.

of confrontation with the existing structure of society was derived from Marxian principles. The dialectical nature of social change was translated into terms more familiar to Christians: doctrine of sin, repentance, atonement and reconciliation.[1] Marx's theory had the capacity to analyze the social order as unjust, and also to disclose Christian sanctioning of it. Following John Macmurray's elaboration of persons as social creatures in relation, FCSOer Martin Estall concluded that the immediate task of Christians under conditions of inertia and unreal religion was a religious revolution. "It therefore appears that the Marxist challenge is simply, but momentously, a challenge to Christianity to fulfill its appointed task, to make real its own gospel."[2] The implications of this proclamation for an indigenous liberation theology were expressed in its hopeful title, *Towards the Christian Revolution.*

The Canadian Catholic Bishops' Position, 1983

On New Year's Day of 1983, the Canadian Catholic Bishops presented their "Ethical Reflections on the Economic Crisis." This document represented the culmination of fifteen years of ecumenical analysis of social issues based on a deep-seated criticism of the dominant economic development model, one that in Canada is capital-intensive, energy-intensive, foreign-controlled and export-oriented.[3] The Bishops spoke as pastors responding to the "scourge of unemployment that plagues our society today and the corresponding struggles of workers in this country."[4]

---

[1]Ibid., 200.

[2]Ibid., 223-24; John Macmurray's influence in Radical Christianity in Canada was well acknowledged by groups such as the FCSO and the SCM; Estall's source in this instance was Macmurray's *Creative Society*, 147.

[3]CCCB 1983, 15.

[4]CCCB 1983, 4. See Gregory Baum, "Shift in Catholic Social Teaching," in *Ethics and Economics*, eds. Baum and Cameron, 19-93; Christopher Lind, "Ethics, Economics and Canada's Catholic Bishops," *Canadian Journal of Political and Social Theory* 7 (Fall 1983), 150-66; and for a contextual guide to, and review of, the development of Christian social research and teaching, see Lee Cormie, "The Economic Crisis is a Moral Crisis," in *Justice as Mission: An Agenda for the Church*, eds. Terry Brown and Christopher Lind (Burlington, Ontario: Trinity Press, 1985), 183-95.

Two principles important to contemporary Roman Catholic moral theology guide their study. The first, consistent with Latin American liberation theology, is the preferential option for the poor, and is considered necessary because "[a]s Christians we are called to follow Jesus by identifying with the victims of injustice." The Bishops articulate a methodology that enables Christians to meet this commitment: "analysing the dominant attitudes and structures that cause human suffering, and . . . actively supporting the poor and oppressed in their struggles to transform society."[1]

The second principle, consistent with papal social teaching since *Rerum Novarum*, identifies the special value and dignity of human work in God's plan for creation. John Paul II's recent encyclical, *Laborem Exercens*, is cited in particular as the basis for this second principle.

> [I]t is through the activity of work that people are able to exercise their creative spirit, realize their human dignity, and share in creation. By interacting with fellow workers in a common task, men and women have an opportunity to further develop their personality and sense of self-worth. In so doing, people participate in the development of their society and give meaning to their existence as human beings.[2]

Undergirding this theological perspective is a conception of human labour analagous to Marx's aspiration for non-alienated labour.[3]

These two fundamental theological principles have been violated, the Bishops charge, by structural economic changes wherein "capital," with its single stress on the accumulation of profits, has been reasserted as the dominating organizing principle over the people who do the actual work.

An analysis of the dominant strategies used to combat the Canadian economic crisis reveals the deep contradiction between corporate assessments of the causes of the crisis and the Catholic Bishops' position. The corporate goal is to restore profitability and competitiveness in the private sector because inflation, rather than unemployment, is

---

[1]Ibid.

[2]Ibid., 5.

[3]For a discussion of the dehumanization of labour under capitalism, see Harry Braverman, *Labor and Monopoly Capital: The Degradation of Work in the Twentieth Century* (New York: Monthly Review Press, 1974).

identified as the major problem. "The causes of inflation are seen as workers' wages, government spending and low productivity rather than monopoly control of prices."[1] In keeping with this diagnosis of the roots of the crisis, the solution for business, and for its ally, the Canadian state, has been austerity programmes, corporate tax reductions, and direct investment incentives.[2] As the Bishops contend, those most hurt by the economic crisis are expected to make sacrifices for the sake of an economic recovery which will not bring them any rewards for their suffering.

In keeping with their primary emphasis on combating unemployment, the Bishops argue for an alternative economic model. Their strategy is one of stimulating socially useful forms of production, creating permanent jobs in basic industries that are labour intensive, using appropriate forms of technology, and a greater use of renewable energy sources in industrial production. This strategy attempts to be comprehensive. It aims to develop more balanced and equitable programmes for curbing inflation, to maintain health care and social security, and to create self-restraint models of economic development and new forms of worker managed and owned enterprises.

The Bishops have determined the economic crisis to be fundamentally a moral one. Its meaning is found in the general standpoint of the victims of the crisis--namely, the unemployed, the welfare poor, pensioners, Native peoples, women, young people, small farmers, fishermen, some factory workers, and small business men and women. The values embedded in current policies for economic recovery contradict the Christian commitment to the well-being of the marginalized, and to the meaning and dignity of labour.[3] The voice of Christ, the Bishops assert, is heard in the voices of the poor and powerless. Their statement concludes with study/action guidelines intended to continue the ethical process of dialogue with the victims, analysis of the basic causes of unemployment, and advocacy of alternative strategies.

---

[1]Ibid., 11-12.

[2]A few results of this strategy have been weakened unions, rapid technological change, deregulation, and privatisation of publicly owned enterprises.

[3]Ibid., 6.

The United Church of Canada Position, 1984

The United Church of Canada's National Working Group on the Economy and Poverty drafted the denomination's policy document, "The Church and the Economic Crisis."[1] This group discerned that radical measures were needed, and prevailed upon the church to work for the transformation of capitalist economic structures. As in the crisis of the 1930s, Canadians in the 1980s faced growing poverty and social disruption. In the 1984 document, the terminology of "household management" explicitly echoes the 1936 position of the FCSO.

> The church's policy on the economic crisis is not unique. It is the latest in an historic series of initiatives in which the people of the United Church have addressed themselves to issues of justice in Canadian society. The prophetic work of our tradition in raising issues of full participation and equality of women, public health care, the extension of social services and the restructuring of our economy according to principles derived from our faith goes back beyond the formation of the United Church of Canada in 1925. These initiatives continued through the Great Depression and the post-war period.[2]

According to this faith stance, we and our home, planet earth, are created for good, and creation should continue to be the source of life "until the end of time." The three aspects of stewardship developed by the World Council of Churches are adopted here as norms for economic life: justice, participation, and sustainability.

> This stewardship [economics] is to be *just*: it is to strive for equal access, equity, and privilege for all people and not only for one or some. It is to respect the economic and cultural base of all people and peoples. It is to be *participatory*: the planet is a shared facility or gift which is to be held for the economic good, and the use of which is to be a common heritage. Therefore, decisions affecting the use of land and resources are to arise from a broad base of the people, and not from elites. . . . The environmental base of life

---

[1] For an in-depth assessment of a broader spectrum of United Church social teachings, see Ted Reeve, "The Church and the Economic Crisis: A Study of the United Church's Continuing Concern for Social Justice." Chapter 4 is devoted to background history, sources, and analysis of the document under review here; see 69-103. While Reeve's study is valuable for historical comparison and a methodology for assessing how far the church was accommodated to, or critical of, the social order, my interpretation, while much briefer, differs in its criteria and overall purpose of investigation.

[2] UCC 1984, 2.

is to be protected and nurtured to ensure health and enjoyment for all the created order "as long as earth lasts." Our economy must be sustainable.[1]

On the basis of these criteria, the study examines the record of performance of Canadian society in relation to justice, and finds it flagrantly wanting. It acknowledges the current crisis and indicates that "the policy resolution on the church and the economic crisis is [but] one serious effort to let our immediate problems be enlightened by that vision [of a new heaven and earth]."[2]

The core analysis of the crisis was written by John Foster, a long-time activist and leading intellectual in the tradition of Radical Christianity. In his discussion of unemployment, a central impetus for this document, he states that Canadians are "*more likely* to be unemployed if we are women, if we are young, if we are involved in one of Canada's old stand-by resource industries. If we are older we are likely to be unemployed longer."[3] This central problem presumes a theosocial understanding about where the value of human life is created, in what Marx called "sensuous, human labour." The document recognizes that the context is a *global* crisis of capitalism which takes a particular form in Canada due to its historically specific conditions, and identifies five sources of the crisis in Canada.

First, the Canadian economy is dependent upon the economy of the United States.[4] Because of this dependence, Canada has also wit-

---

[1]Ibid., 2.

[2]Ibid., 3.

[3]Ibid.

[4]The theory of dependency formulated by A. G. Frank has been common currency in Canadian political economy since the 1970s; variations on this thesis have been explored in attempts to account for Canada's peculiar combination of dependency on empire and domination by it; staples-tied resource production; a strong finance sector; and uneven internal development of regions--a sort of hybrid position between overdeveloped imperialist and underdeveloped colonial economies globally. The best brief overview is "Introduction: The Coming of Age of Canadian Political Economy," in *The New Practical Guide to Canadian Political Economy*, eds. Daniel Drache and Wallace Clement (Toronto: James Lorimer, 1985). The bibliographies in it and Patricia Marchak's excellent article, "Canadian Political Economy," *Canadian Review of Sociology and Anthropology* 22 (1985), 673-709, contain comprehensive resources. On the international origins and debate, see Catherine Hyett, "Theories of Dependency," *The Ecumenist* 25 (March-April 1987), 37-44.

nessed a similar disintegration of the ideological consensus of welfare capitalism. Examples of this breakdown are increasing numbers of food pantries and the escalating crisis in the welfare system. Second, given this dependency, the manufacturing sector of the Canadian economy is weakened by foreign ownership and management, by minimal investment in research and development, and by integration into an increasingly competitive global market. (The globalization of capital has produced similar ideological and political shifts in many countries.) Third, freedom of capital, "the ability of investors to transfer funds along with new technology to less-regulated, cheap labour centres, for example, in south-east Asia" has had a devastating effect in Canada. "Thus words like 'runaway shops,' 'deindustrialization,' have become familiar to unemployed people in old Ontario manufacturing towns."[1] Fourth, the legacy of poor management by state and business of traditional resource industries is now taking its toll. The fifth cause is the government's use of monetarist deflationary policies. This final factor has been called a "crisis by design," where the state deliberately adopts such measures *knowing* the results would be severe unemployment.

How have these four factors affected Canadian social formation? The following list of "failures to meet the demands of our faith in care for the earth and human society" specifies the character of social sin:

A. The native populations have been sidelined out of the mainstream of Canadian life, and in far too many places, dispossessed of their heritage of land and resources.
B. Two million Canadians do not have access for themselves and their families to a meaningful and healthy life through employment.
C. Wealth and economic management have become concentrated in the hands of a few.
D. Women have been thwarted from full participation in decision-making and leadership.
E. The economy is without priorities to allow for renewal, and has run on as if there is no tomorrow.
F. Canadians participate in the international war machine which globally drains $1,000,000 a minute from useful productivity.[2]

The conclusion, with which I concur, is that these social costs add up to a moral crisis.

---

[1] UCC 1984, 4.

[2] Ibid., 3.

This United Church of Canada document explicitly confirms the pronouncements on the economic situation made by the Catholic Bishops' 1983 "Ethical Reflections on the Economy." It shares the Catholic Bishops' emphases on commitment to the poor and the priority of labour over the rights of property and the freedom of capital. In keeping with these norms, the United Church statement speaks of ideological critique (especially of "classical 'liberal' free market economics") and empowerment of the church in its task of making visible the choices and alternative values available in the context.[1]

The theo-social assumption and norms at work here are outlined in the document's last pages, in conjunction with a list of resolutions designed to put them into action. The document reiterates the global nature of the crisis, and the concern with unemployment as the main consequence of reigning economic policies. It also makes recommendations for change, such as a guaranteed adequate annual income, full employment, and adequate housing.[2]

Two features of the actual resolution approved as official policy of the United Church are the primacy of action for justice, and a special section entitled "Women and Poverty." It would appear that the action for justice recommended is premised on the principle of increased public planning, particularly by means of democratic participation in investment decisions, ownership, and control of economic resources in Canada. A perception of the social order as conflicted and divided over its fundamental ethical orientation undergirds the entire document. It is from this standpoint that the statement acknowledges that women are the most vulnerable victims of poverty. Resolutions addressing women's particular economic situation were adopted, including more equitable tax laws and measures to prevent further cutbacks in programmes such as Family Allowance.[3] The adequacy of these measures for alleviating women's specific burdens will be assessed in the next chapter.

---

[1]Ibid., 5-7.

[2]Ibid., 8-11.

[3]Ibid., 11.

Summary

The constructive contributions of each of these documents to Christian ethics are three key assumptions which these Catholic and Protestant radical social teachings on the economy invoke.[1]

First, the biblical norm of creation, and human involvement in this task via *work*, is common to all. This norm provides a global vision of human nature and destiny, and assures that the notions of a social self and of authentic development, understood as development of the whole person and the common good, are posited as necessary grounds for the theological task of creating justice in community.

Second, the positions examined make explicit an advocacy stance as the starting point of Christian involvement in economic affairs. The standpoint of the marginalized and exploited is theologically privileged, and sin is understood as intrinsically social or structural. Using radical social theoretical tools, all three positions attribute a major source of oppression to the economic system of capitalism. The chief evil of this system in all these analyses is unemployment. While the language used to address this systemic manifestation of evil differs among these documents, the norms of "labour over capital," "integral human development," and "justice, participation and sustainability" indicate a similar moral stance toward the economic crisis. The strategies proposed in these teachings also indicate clearly the fundamental common ground on which their criticisms are based: all advocate a major transformation of the existing economic system in favour of public participation in and significant control of economic priorities, and a significant decrease in foreign dependency.

Finally, each document emphasizes that the value to be embodied in social relations is the realization of the *imago Dei* as full humanity, the good of whole persons in community. Each radically confronts the dominant moral climate of destruction of the value of all created life by the rich at the expense of the vast majority of the world's poor.

It is important not to understate the significance of radical social statements from the churches in the midst of widespread backlash and

---

[1] I am drawing here on Lee Cormie's apt assessment of the basic shift in values he locates in recent Catholic social teachings; see Cormie, "The Economic Crisis is a Moral Crisis," in *Justice as Mission*, eds. Brown and Lind, 185-86.

reactionary agendas within church and state. We are indebted to this Radical Christian tradition because it challenges the existing disorder in social relations. This tradition engages in critical and normative readings of scripture and Christian tradition, and attends to the social power dynamics operative in specific contexts and eras. Taking into account the specific location of Canada, this tradition envisions a common future that is jointly created, and encourages solidarity with the marginalized themselves, who must be key agents of social transformation.

Women will only come into focus as historical agents and subjects of their own lives within particular contexts if our theological ethics make women visible. Social power is predicated upon economic power, and women are increasingly vulnerable in their capacity to provide adequately for themselves and their families. A further analysis of how these documents help or hinder the assessment of *women's* experience, by examining the reality of women's political economic lives, will be part of the work of the next chapter. This analysis will enable us to see how much stronger our economic ethics can be with a feminist social theoretical analysis. This analysis not only requires us to provide a stronger reading of women's experience, but it also gives us tools for doing that.

CHAPTER THREE

A FEMINIST CRITIQUE OF RADICAL CHRISTIAN ECONOMIC ETHICS IN CANADA

Introduction

> Work is at the centre of our lives. It provides the means of life itself, the goods and services essential to our survival and our well-being. Good work enables us to use our gifts, to develop our skills, to become proud and confident of our abilities. It fosters responsibility and cooperation among us, a sense of community with co-workers. Few of us have good work by this definition.[1]

Defining the work of women's everyday lives *is* a task of value in a misogynist, sexist, and homophobic culture. While economic ethics cannot be reduced to material life because of the reality of transcendence, the experience of "crossing over" the chasms which divide us, economic life is instrumental to social values. Material life, in turn, stands under the judgment of a broader vision of *shalom* or embodied mutual relations of wholeness.[2]

Creative human work stands at the heart of both a Radical Christian and a feminist ethical vision. In this chapter I will build on the

---

[1]Jennifer Penney, *Hard Earned Wages* (Toronto: Women's Educational Press, 1983), 9.

[2]I am grateful for Carter Heyward's development of this understanding of a theological construct often used against the goodness of our embodied existence in *this* world; see *Our Passion for Justice*, 243-47.

theoretical concern with political economic analysis in evidence through-out the radical social gospel tradition in Canada. This Radical Christian tradition sought to understand the roots of the economic crisis that had beset the nation, to articulate a Christian social vision, and to discover in that process strategies for its amelioration. As we have seen, their method employed certain theological norms and sources-- mutuality and justice, the option for the dispossessed and solidarity with them, a critical philosophical framework, and socio-economic analysis to illuminate the causes of poverty and oppression.

As noted above, however, the Radical Christian tradition in its struggle for justice rendered the personal sphere and women's experience invisible. Its inattention to women's relations and contributions to the economy through their work, whether paid or unpaid, meant a correspondingly truncated notion of human labour. I have examined the political economic perspective developed in three representative positions of Radical Christianity to assess how adequately it dealt with economic reality and well-being of women. While this political economic work is a necessary resource for theological ethics, it is insufficiently developed for doing ethics accountable to women's experience. I demonstrated that the existing economic ethics must be critically employed if marginalized women's experience and well-being are to be placed at the heart of theological social ethics.

In order to extend critically the Radical Christian tradition's work in economic ethics, I will explore the realities of women's economic lives. The resources used must be appropriate to critical theological norms, and adequate to women's experience, particularly the most marginalized. To further specify *whose* experience counts in this theological reflection, we can add two basic criteria: first, does the socio-economic analysis illumine everyday reality and the roots of oppression; and second, does it formulate effective strategies for social amelioration of the roots of oppression?[1] I will employ, therefore, a hermeneutics of suspicion: What does "the preferential option for the poor" mean for Canadian women, especially poor women of colour? Is

---

[1]Gita Sen and Caren Gown also stress the necessity of formulating and testing economic strategies from women's actual experience of them. See *Development, Crises, and Alternative Visions: Third World Women's Perspectives* (New York: Monthly Review Press, 1987.)

the social theory of the Radical Christianity in Canada adequate to describe and address the everyday realities of women? Before examining the economic realities of Canadian women's lives, I will briefly review the feminist theoretical criteria formulated earlier.

Our theological ethic must take seriously the indispensable relationship of human *social* justice to *personal* well-being and affirm that the way to corporate well-being is aided by personal relationships of mutuality. That is, a personal or so-called private ethic is bound up with a political or so-called public ethic. We cannot split one from the other. Without recognition of the structures of injustice operative in all areas of our lives, in our bedrooms and kitchens as well as in boardrooms and pool halls, we will not identify the dynamics of power in social relations accurately, and thus not be accountable to those most broken by reigning structural arrangements.

According to Beverly Harrison, an adequate social theory must have certain characteristics.[1] First, attention must be given to concrete conflict and suffering. It must be assumed, however, that the existence of widespread social exploitation can be confronted and resisted through people's creative capacity as historical subjects to forge alternative modes of production to those of exploitative political economies. Second, political economy is understood as a socio-historical reality, and thus is in principle transformable. If *people* are the center of moral value, then the goal of involvement in the project of social transformation is justice for all. Third, because its method is historical, this social theory is more likely to hold itself answerable to and accept responsibility for concretely illuminating our experiences of everyday life. Because it is responsive to our agency as constitutive of being human, the sphere of moral action is thus located in concrete, daily experience (rather than in an abstract dynamic such as the business cycle). Here the issue of appropriate policies and strategies for radical transformation of socio-economic relations must be laid out. Fourth, an adequate social theory must show that all economic activity is related to the overall cultural and institutional matrix of social life.

---

[1] Harrison, "The Role of Social Theory in Religious Social Ethics: Reconsidering the Case for Marxian Political Economy," in *Making the Connections*, 76-80. See also her "Agendas for a New Theological Ethic," in *Churches in Struggle*, ed. Tabb, 89-97.

It is the goal of radical economists to translate the presumed mysteries of political economy, to help people understand what is going on and how it affects their lives. . . . When a social theory helps people experience their presumed private troubles as actually grounded in the way the social world works, that theory is theologically and morally apt.[1]

I follow these criteria because they insist upon the moral agency of those marginalized and excluded by relations of domination and exploitation. In other words, if our solidarity is not to objectify "the poor" and reproduce those very structures we are fighting to overcome, *their* voices, sensibilities, and histories of resistance must be heard.

We must begin by identifying the social relations of power and structural sources of exploitation that effect women's work and condition the material reality of their everyday lives. The work of political economists is essential to provide an overview of the experience of women's work--what women do everyday to survive and flourish. We will discover some details of how unjust social structures cement some women in positions of dependency on men, on the state, or on both.

To assess the historical roots of oppression of women in Canada with respect to the particularity of their lives, I will employ both feminist and political economic theory that aims to understand society in a multidimensional and holistic manner.[2] I will give primacy to feminist resources that make visible women's everyday struggles to survive, though they too must be examined for their adequacy to the lived experience of the most marginalized women. The chapter will conclude

---

[1]Harrison, "The Role of Social Theory in Religious Social Ethics," in *Making the Connections*, 79; see also ibid., 282, n. 55: "In sum, *social theoretical* formulations are to be judged by how well they clarify the sources of oppression of poor black [and indigenous] women. *Theological* formulations are to be judged by how profoundly they give voice to the source of hope such women experience."

[2]An examination of themes and the development of Canadian political economy is beyond the scope of this study. For an excellent overview and bibliography, see Marchak, "Canadian Political Economy"; a useful companion piece is Deborah Harrison, *The Limits of Liberalism: The Making of Canadian Sociology* (Montreal: Black Rose Books, 1981). The most complete interdisciplinary bibliographic resource is Drache and Clement, eds., *The New Practical Guide to Canadian Political Economy*. Heather Jon Maroney and Meg Luxton have collaborated to produce the most illuminating discussion on the relationship between malestream liberal and Marxist traditions, and gender analyses in Canada; see "From Feminism and Political Economy to Feminist Political Economy," in *Feminism and Political Economy: Women's Work, Women's Struggle*, eds. Maroney and Luxton (Toronto: Methuen, 1987), 5-30.

with an identification of key implications for the work of a Christian ethics that is committed to addressing the suffering of women.

A Survey of Canadian Women's Economic Realities

Why focus on women's work?

> . . . because work not only provides meaning and identity in our lives but also shapes our resources, our social contacts and our opportunities, because the subordinate position of women is located in the work they do, and because the overwhelming majority of clients . . . and workers in the social service sector, where the current crisis is most clearly reflected, are women.[1]

Without attention to the experience of women, particularly those most marginalized, the depth and pervasiveness of human alienation and oppression can be neither named nor addressed.

In what follows I will survey women's work, first in the household and then in the labour force, to establish more clearly what the economic crisis means for women. I will then present the theoretical resources in feminist analysis which go furthest in accounting for women's current economic realities. I will then assess these accounts in light of the contributions of racial and ethnic minority women who analyse the roots of their oppression and formulate their priorities and economic strategies. In the final sections of this chapter, I will evaluate the Radical Christian economic tradition in terms of feminist economic criteria, and suggest basepoints necessary for an adequate Canadian Christian economic ethics informed by women's realities.

Women's Domestic Labour

How is it that whole areas of life that are necessary for the very existence of society, and that consume much of women's time, energy, and imagination, are located *outside* the field of economic legitimacy and hence of moral gravity? In his book *Gender*, Ivan Illich describes

---

[1]Hugh Armstrong and Pat Armstrong, "Looking Ahead: The Future of Women's Work in Australia and Canada," in *Feminism and Political Economy*, eds. Maroney and Luxton, 214.

the fundamental assumptions of economics as ones pertaining to scarcity and competition, with the result that "economics only recognizes that labour which is paid a wage as 'economic activity' and contributing to the value of a good, a 'commodity.' All unwaged labour is ignored."[1] Because large portions of women's work are unpaid or unreported--babysitting, cleaning other people's homes, prostitution, caring for the elderly--their labour is ignored and seen as economically insignificant.

Meg Luxton argues that women's work in the home is one of the most important labour processes of industrial capitalist society. This task confronts powerful myths surrounding the family and household work. The first and most tenacious myth, that "woman's place is in her home," grips human imagination and practices worldwide.[2] Hence, the assumption that domestic labour is rightfully women's domain and responsibility is common to women's experience worldwide.[3] This myth is based on the assumption that women's biological capacity to bear children determines that women are also created to take care of

---

[1]Cited by Nancy Hannum, "Gender Based Economic Activity," paper prepared for the National Working Group on the Economy and Poverty, United Church of Canada, March 9, 1989, 3.

[2]Meg Luxton, *More Than a Labour of Love: Three Generations of Women's Work* (Toronto: The Women's Press, 1980), 13. I am also indebted to Meg Luxton and Harriet Rosenburg for their concise presentation of the most common myths sustaining the gendered division of labour. I develop only those pertinent for my purposes of portraying women's everyday experience. See their "Introduction" to *Through the Kitchen Window: The Politics of Home and Family* (Toronto: Garamond Press, 1986). For a cogent discussion of the historical roots of the myth behind women's "special nature," and the consequent increased economic vulnerability and political powerlessness, see Beverly Harrison, "The Effect of Industrialization on the Role of Women in Society," in *Making the Connections*, 42-53. On the Canadian historical background of the structural formation of the gender division of labour, see Paul Phillips and Erin Phillips, *Women and Work: Inequality in the Labour Market*, (Toronto: James Lorimer, 1983), 1-32.

[3]*The State of the World's Women 1985* (Oxford: New Internationalist Publications, 1985), 3. While my project focuses on Canadian reality, I want to point to the fact that there are significant commonalities as well as differences in the diverse positions of women. It is beyond the scope of this dissertation to establish or to elaborate on these connections. Other initial resources for global comparisons include the following: Gita Sen and Caren Gown, *Development, Crises, and Alternative Visions*; Maria Mies, *Patriarchy and Accumulation on a World Scale: Women in the International Division of Labour* (London: Zed Books, 1986); and Swasti Mitter, *Common Fate, Common Bond: Women and the Global Economy* (London: Pluto Press, 1986).

them; thus, the logic of this ideology goes, women are "naturally" inclined to cook, clean, nurture others, and manage the household.

A second myth maintains that the family/home is "a haven in a heartless world." In the privacy of the household, refuge from outside hazards and protection from danger is supposedly promised "by the power of love, reciprocal human feelings, and kinship obligations. But the home is not really a private fortress: it is a sieve, open to all the excesses of industrial development," and all the pain of multiple conflicts that surface especially in times of crisis as in the contemporary welfare state.[1] This myth sustains the fiction that the social world is divided into two separate and unrelated spheres, "the 'public' world of industry, commerce and politics--a world of competition and danger, which is exciting but also somewhat unsafe and hostile--and a 'private' world of the family/household which is safe and loving."[2] The norm of this myth, indeed its sole legitimate ground, is the "natural" heterosexual marriage with a male breadwinner and a dependent housewife.

A third prevailing myth is that women who are at home full time do not "work." Behind the phrase "women's work" hang both the deadening weight of social stigma and the negative implications of the myths in concrete social practice.

> "Only women's work," like "just a housewife," implies that not only is it useless labour but somehow not *work at all*. All too often there has been a distinction made between "labour" and "work" in our everyday usage of these terms. Any kind of effort, preferably grinding, that people put out to accomplish some goal may be seen as labour, but only labour that results in direct money payment is dignified work. . . . [T]he importance of the productive efforts of women has been denied and, in some cases, even the existence of this work.[3]

---

[1]Rosenburg, *Through the Kitchen Window*, 84. I employ her metaphor of the home as sieve to emphasize that the "private" sphere is the place where all human problems are ultimately poured and from which healing is sought. See below for a brief overview of the construction of the gendered division of labour.

[2]Luxton and Rosenburg, "Introduction," *Through the Kitchen Window*, 9. See also Dorothy Smith's analysis of the public-private split, and the construction of women's invisibility and the family as an object for display, "Women, the Family and Corporate Capitalism," in *Women in Canada*, ed. Marylee Stephenson, rev. ed. (Don Mills, Ontario: General Publishing, 1977), 14-48.

[3]Marylee Stephenson, "Women's Work," in *Women in Canada*, ed. Stephenson, 127.

That women are "hidden in the household"[1] is underscored by the fact that their domestic labour is unpaid, undervalued, and deemed less real than what goes on outside the home.

While household work is consistently rendered invisible, women's lives are concretely shaped by its demands. Unraveling the "combination of menial labour, often involving long hours, boring repetitive housework, and very complex emotional work with children, husbands and dependent elderly people" has not been easy.[2] The vast majority of Canadian women devote at least some their lives to work as housewives or homemakers, at least five million women work full time in their homes, and most of the rest work part-time in the home in addition to paid work in the labour force.[3] Studies by Statistics Canada estimate that if a monetary value were attached to the unpaid work of women in the household, the Gross National Product (the combined value of goods and services produced nationally) would increase by 40 to 50 per cent.[4]

Historically, the relegation of women to the private sphere resulted from structural changes in the Canadian economy by industrialization, urbanization, and immigration.[5] Industrialization brought about the separation of paid work and home life. By the turn of the century, family production was all but a memory as agriculture was increasingly mechanized, commodities were being manufactured for the market, and the cash economy was well established by the importance of trade relations. For women this meant that their economic labour in the fields

---

[1]This is the title of a collection of articles edited by Bonnie Fox, *Hidden in the Household: Women's Domestic Labour Under Capitalism* (Toronto: The Women's Press, 1980).

[2]Hilary Rose, "Women's Work, Women's Knowledge," in *What is Feminism?*, eds. Juliet Mitchell and Ann Oakley (New York: Pantheon, 1986), 164.

[3]Pat Armstrong and Hugh Armstrong, *The Double Ghetto: Canadian Women and their Segregated Work* (Toronto: McLelland and Stewart, 1978), 90. See also Luxton and Rosenburg, *Through the Kitchen Window*, 9.

[4]Women's Research Centre, "Women and the Economy Kit," quoted in "Women and the Economy: Grounding Assumptions," United Church of Canada, *Women's Concerns Newsletter* (Spring 1987), 4.

[5]I am drawing on the historical overviews in Armstrong and Armstrong, *The Double Ghetto*, 58-60, and in Caroline Andrew, "Women and the Welfare State," *Canadian Journal of Political Science* 17 (December 1988), 671-73.

and their production of basic necessities--such as butter, candles, soap, and cloth--were replaced by production external to the home.

Women's work was rapidly transformed also by the compulsory education that accompanied the introduction of increasingly sophisticated production techniques. Children were less involved at home and required more care because they remained dependent longer. Most significantly, women became economically dependent on the wages of men for their survival. But despite changes in the kind of domestic labour, the number of hours spent in housework has not changed.[1]

Beverly Harrison evaluates the relationship between the two modes of production, domestic and waged, as the subordination of the household sphere to the economic sphere, and points to its effects.

> [One] social dynamic in society involves the productive system, which is determined by how we organize ourselves to produce goods and services for survival out of the material resources available. . . . In modern society . . . especially since the development of a distinctively capitalist mode of production, the power of reproductive and cultural systems to shape society has been displaced by the overriding power of the productive system, which now generates change and overrides the values of the intimacy system. This creates incredible strains in society--*incredible* strains.[2]

In short, the process of industrialization which moved production out of the household resulted in the separation of "home" and "work," impos-

---

[1]In 1978, Canadian theorists working on an integrated approach to women's work summarized the status of women's domestic labour: "Not only are women segregated into a predominantly female workplace, the home, but this workplace is becoming increasingly privatised and isolated from those of all other workers. Over the last 30 years, technological advances have served to lighten some of the more strenuous household tasks. Declining birthrates and growing educational, health and other social institutions have influenced the nature of child care in the home. However, the time devoted to housework and child care has not diminished significantly. Rising standards, the limited effect of technical development, privatisation, and the increasing complexity of the world outside the home have all contributed to the lack of change in hours spent in the home. Finally, in spite of the rapidly growing proportion of married women in the labour force, . . . domestic work continues for the most part to be their responsibility." See Armstrong and Armstrong, *The Double Ghetto*, 90. That women's work has in fact become *more* burdensome since this analysis was recorded will be demonstrated later in a discussion of the economic crisis and its worsening effects on women.

[2]Harrison, "The Older Person's Worth in the Eyes of Society," in *Making the Connections*, 157.

ing upon the family the new primary economic role as a centre for con-sumption. The family became defined as a unit organized around edu-cation and protection of children, emotional fulfillment, and consump-tion. From this point on, the family has had increased importance as an institution vital for maintaining the cohesion of social well-being amidst a rapidly changing society.

Women's place in the broader society became defined in terms of the family. For middle class women, industrialization and the conse-quent ideology of the family meant removal from the sphere of produc-tion to a role as "creatures of leisure"; for working class women, it meant long hours in poor working conditions and inadequate housing in urban slums. "This family-centred and family-bounded definition of women's activity corresponded to the reality of the bourgeoisie in the latter part of the nineteenth century, but certainly not to the lives of the working class women who were moving into industrial employment. But they, too, were influenced by the new view of the family and the increased social importance given its role."[1]

The split in the labour process resulted in two seemingly separate spheres--one, formally recognized paid work (dominated by the notion of the breadwinner/ husband/father), the other, socially necessary but unrecognized domestic work (the preserve of the economically depend-ent housewife/mother). While the separation did not produce the same economic burdens among women, the implications of this designation have left women uniformly responsible for the sphere of domestic life. The study of "domestic labour" has brought into visibility the distinc-tive labour of women in four specific areas: one, reproduction of day to day human resources, including emotional work;[2] two, procreation and socialization of children; three, housework; and four, survival management, or skills in making ends meet.[3]

---

[1]Andrew, "Women and the Welfare State," 671.

[2]For an excellent study of women's caring labour, see Hilary Rose, "Women's Work, Women's Knowledge"; on the difference between the production of people and of things, see her "Hand, Brain and Heart: A Feminist Epistemology for the Natural Sciences" in *Sex and Scientific Inquiry*, eds. Sandra Harding and Jean F. O'Barr, (Chicago: University of Chicago Press, 1987), 265-82.

[3]See Luxton, *More Than a Labour of Love*, 18-19; and Pat Armstrong, *Labour Pains: Women's Work In Crisis* (Toronto: Women's Educational Press, 1984), 99-119.

Fundamental to the analysis of women's domestic work is documentation of the crucial role it has for social sustenance and the well-being people experience. Women do *not* have a choice about whether to take responsibility for this work; invisible and unrewarded as it is, women *must* do housework unless they can pay someone else to do it or share it with a partner or other household members.[1] Hence, it is women who manage the household. This involves a variety of tasks; responsibility for food involves budgeting, planning, shopping for and providing meals; further, preserving food, and planting and maintaining a garden can help stretch household resources. Women maintain the home year-round, including organizing and doing seasonal cleaning, repairs, and regular chores such as laundry, ironing and mending, washing dishes, and budgeting for all expenses, in order to insure a comfortable environment for all who live in and visit the home.

Another key area of women's responsibility, perhaps the most taken for granted, is the delivery of personal care and management of tension in the household. This emotional work demands a great deal of time and energy, and includes supporting and encouraging others in the household; acting as liaison between various members' experiences at work, community, and home; and caring for family/household members when they are ill. Women also generally have the responsibility of caring for children, including feeding, clothing, cleaning, and transporting them, as well as supporting them emotionally and keeping them safe, throughout all stages of their dependent lives. Women are also usually responsible for arranging child care and other activities, from visits to the dentist to after-school programmes.

In short, women maintain the material conditions necessary for life. The work is endless because it is not time-bound, as is a paid job, but task-oriented. "Because it is the labour of ensuring human subsistence, the production time of domestic labour can never be reduced; it can only be shared or redistributed."[2]

---

[1] In this overview of household labour, I am relying on the synopsis provided by the Women's Research Unit, "Women and the Economy Kit," as quoted in "Women and the Economy," United Church of Canada, *Women's Concerns Newsletter* (Spring 1987), 3.

[2] Luxton, "Time for Myself: Women's Work and the 'Fight for Shorter Hours,'" in *Feminism and Political Economy*, eds. Maroney and Luxton, 172.

In sum, while women do not experience the same demands in domestic labour across racial/ethnic and class lines, an important consideration that I will take up below, all work done in the home is consigned outside the parameters of politics and official inquiry by the label "private." Domestic work, therefore, is predicated on an historic splitting of the labour process into public and private spheres, such that the family and household are subordinated to the public and relegated to invisible or, at best marginal, status.[1]

Women's Participation in Waged Labour

That women's work in the household is rarely thought of as carrying social value is illustrated again by the fact that women's waged work is generally an extension of what they have been socialized to do in the home, and for which they continue to be underpaid.

> In 1911 the average wage of employed women stood at 53 per cent of the average male wages. In 1931 it was 60 per cent. By 1978 the average earned income of women who worked the entire year was 58 per cent of men's full-year earnings, while the average annual income of women was only 49 per cent of the male average--though this includes part-time workers. For every occupational group, for every age group, for part-time and full-time workers, for every educational level and every region of Canada, men received higher average incomes.[2]

Myths regarding "women's work" lurk within social statistics, policies, and conventions--for example, that women's contributions to

---

[1]While women usually have no choice about taking on the increased "shadow work" necessary for economic survival, different classes can shift the burden from themselves onto those in lower social strata. The term "shadow work" is Ivan Illich's designation for work that transforms a purchased commodity into a usable good. Nancy Hannum, "Gender Based Economic Analysis," 4-5 points out the *increasing* marginalization of women's economic activity with the rise of shadow work. In industrial society more and more unwaged labour or "shadow work" is required to support the existence of reported economic life. Although both men and women do shadow work, most is done by women in the home and the neighbourhood. For example, in any North American city this unreported labour includes raising children, maintaining the health of the wage-earner, self-tutoring and planning, paying bills, negotiating with creditors, etc. For rural people, it is even more onerous.

[2]Phillips and Phillips, *Women and Work*, 52.

economic production and survival is minor; that women work for pay to supplement the family's income; that women receive equal pay when equally qualified; that women have moved into all occupational areas in society. These myths perpetuate injustice against women.[1]

The composition of the labour force has dramatically changed over the last fifty years. "In 1946, only one-quarter of Canadian women were employed or looking for employment. By 1966, just over one-third were in the labour force. What started as a trickle in the early 1950s has, since the mid-1960s become a flood. Yet rather than signaling a fundamental shift in women's work, the rapid movement of women into the labour force has meant more of the same kind of work. "Paid or unpaid, women scrub floors, serve food, sort laundry, mind children, make coffee or clothes, answer the telephone or wait on people. . . . Most women now work for pay, but most still do women's work."[2] In fact, in Canada today women comprise 51 percent of the population and over half of them, 51.6 percent, participate in the paid work force. Women are 41.2 percent of the entire labour force and earn roughly 60 percent as much as male full time workers. Women in two parent families who work for pay contribute an average of 28.7 percent to family earnings.[3] How are we to explain such statistics? Certain features of the Canadian economic context must be defined before exploring further women's participation and experience in it.

Similar to other capitalist economies, Canada's development has been dominated by the rise of the giant transnational corporations. Three sectors of the Canadian economy can be identified.[4] The first is the monopoly sector. It is shaped by foreign-owned corporations, although a few Canadian-based companies in primary resource extrac-

---

[1] I rely here on Ruth Leger Sivard, *Women . . . A World Survey* (Washington, D.C.: World Priorities, 1985); Sivard's work is a unique resource for specifying women's global economic reality.

[2] Pat Armstrong and Hugh Armstrong, *A Working Majority: What Women Must Do for Pay*, Prepared for the Canadian Advisory Council on the Status of Women (Ottawa: Ministry of Supply and Services Canada, 1983), 7.

[3] Women's Research Centre, "Women and the Economy Kit," as quoted in "Women and the Economy: Grounding Assumptions," United Church of Canada, *Women's Concerns Newsletter* (Spring 1987), 3.

[4] Armstrong and Armstrong, *The Double Ghetto*, 20-23.

tion also exist. Because the emphasis is on high capital investment, and thus labour productivity, strong unions have been created to protect the workers and push for decent pay. (This does not include their clerical and sales staff who are underpaid.) Industries in this sector, notably mining, oil and gas, forestry, utilities, and parts of manufacturing, command the best paying jobs, maintain the lowest percentage of new jobs, and offer the fewest jobs, if any, to women. The second is the competitive sector, where service and trade industries are primarily located. This includes retail sales, construction, agriculture, and fishing and trapping. These industries are characterized by relatively low capital investment per worker and thus have relatively low productivity, low wages, and low union activity. The third is the state sector, well known for its rapid growth in the postwar years.[1] Here employment has dramatically increased, and is often better paid than work in the private sector. Although clerical and hospital workers continue to be poorly paid, rates of salary increase have been higher.[2]

Occupational Segregation

There are three basic characteristics of women's experience in the labour force in this economic context. First, and most obvious, is occupational segregation. Women's participation in a limited portion of the labour force has been facilitated by the bureaucratic and commercial revolution of the 20th century. "This has given rise to a steadily increasing demand for workers who are literate, and who have accurate bookkeeping skills, office machine skills, administrative ability and pleasant personalities."[3] Since women have not found jobs in the

---

[1] See Leo Panitch, "The Role and Nature of the Canadian State," in *The Canadian State: Political Economy and Political Power*, ed. Leo Panitch (Toronto: University of Toronto Press, 1977; reprint 1983), 3-27 (page references are to reprint edition).

[2] In part this is because increased taxation allows labour costs to be more easily passed along than in the competitive sector, but there has also been phenomenal growth in the size and militancy of state sector unions in Canada. See the section below, "The Economic Crisis and the Particularities of Women's Lives," for a critical look at women and the welfare state.

[3] Patricia Marchak, "The Canadian Labour Farce: Jobs for Women," in *Women in Canada*, ed. Stephenson, 148.

monopoly sector, they have been disproportionately hired in service and trade industries that form the low-productivity, low-pay competitive sector, and in the state sector.

Pushed into the labour force by economic necessity, women have also been drawn into the labour force by the growth in demand for female workers. For instance, in 1980, there were more than a million more jobs available than there had been in 1975, and the majority of these were taken by women. Most of the new jobs created were in female job ghettos, and one in four provided only part-time work. In other words, more of the jobs were women's jobs, and women took them because they needed the income.[1]

Patricia Marchak has aptly called this situation of women's work "the Canadian labour farce."

> In 1980, half of all Canadian women were in the labour force. By occupation, they were concentrated in clerical, sales, and service jobs, making up 78 percent, 40 percent, and 54 percent respectively of all employees in these jobs; and they were employed mainly in the service industries, the public sector, trade and finance.[2]

In their humane and thorough study of "what women must do for pay," one team of researchers has breathed life into such statistics. They combine statistical research with experiences of working women surveyed in personal interviews across Canada. Whether secretaries, cashiers, waitresses, babysitters, mail sorters, factory workers, domestics, home workers, farm workers, cleaners, bank tellers, telephone operators, hairdressers, clerks, or sales women, their experiences revealed a common thread: the connection between their gender and their conditions of work. This study documents the sex-specific nature of the labour force and its meaning for women from their own vantage point. The realities of women's economic lives assembled under the rubrics of the gendered-division of labour are indeed grim.[3]

---

[1] Armstrong and Armstrong, *A Working Majority*, 32.

[2] Marchak, "Rational Capitalism and Woman as Labour," in *Feminism and Political Economy*, eds. Maroney and Luxton, 198.

[3] Armstrong and Armstrong, *A Working Majority*, passim.

The Wage Gap

The second major feature of women's waged labour is the gap in wages, security, and benefits. Women perform a limited number of low-skilled and/or low-paid jobs. Women still earn roughly 60 percent of what men earn: "In 1985, women who worked all year, including full and part time workers, made 59.6 per cent of men's earnings, a decrease from 60.1 per cent in 1984."[1] Most of the women at the very bottom of the wage scale are in sales and service jobs, the fastest growing occupational categories for women. Hence, sex-segregated jobs and poor pay go hand in hand. In addition to poor pay, women's work is often boring, cramped, unhealthy, dehumanizing, unrecognized, and without opportunities for advancement or social reward.

Women's Double Day

The fact that most women who work are married and must return after their shift to their other job, domestic labour, constitutes the third and final destructive characteristic of women's work. The double day exists for all women who have entered the paid labour force because of economic need. That the participation rate of married women is rising in spite of their poor job opportunities and low wages, and in spite of the scarcity and high cost of childcare facilities, suggests that real economic pressures push women to seek paid employment. According to the National Council of Welfare, there would be a 51 per cent increase in the number of poor families in Canada if wives had no earnings.[2]

While women may have little choice about whether to work for income, they have even less choice over assuming the burden of domestic labour because, as noted, the home or domicile is considered to be the exclusive sphere of women. In a recent study of workers in a Montreal garment factory, Charlene Gannage examined the impact of the double day:

---

[1] *The Globe and Mail* (Toronto) 14 October 1987, A10, cited by Theresa O'Donovan, "On Human Work: A Feminist Critique of LABOREM EXERCENS" (M. A. thesis, St. Michael's College, Toronto School of Theology, 1988), 48.

[2] Armstrong and Armstrong, *A Working Majority*, 28-29.

> Women's paid work experience is mediated by both gender ideology and the material conditions of the double day. . . . Women's family responsibilities affected their ability to hold a job as well as their earning capacity. . . . The inability to work overtime is one major factor in accounting for the wage gap between male and female wages.[1]

In part, then, women's lesser income reflects the fact that they have fewer hours to spend at paying jobs.

The combination of paid and unpaid labour for women, as Meg Luxton and others have extensively documented, means that "married women's paid employment intensifies their total labour time dramatically, reducing the prospects for regular leisure time to virtually nil. Most studies show that employed married women with children work between 70 and 80 hours each week."[2]   And because women earn half of what men receive they will continue to be responsible for domestic chores and crises, and will be criticised for inadequate attachment to their paid employment. Thus, women are caught in an economic bind that is structurally defined, often working twice as many hours as men for half the pay.[3]

---

[1]Charlene Gannage, "A World of Difference," in *Feminism and Political Economy*, eds. Maroney and Luxton, 157.

[2]Luxton, "Time for Myself," 173.

[3]The myth of women's transient link with paid labour, often reflected in idealist economic analyses such as structural functionalism, is refuted by a variety of considerations: by the high value women place on their work outside the home, by the fact that women must earn money to survive, and by the way capitalism structures the work women do. On this last point see Patricia Connelly, "The Economic Context of Women's Labour Force Participation in Canada," in *The Working Sexes*, ed. Patricia Marchak (Vancouver: University of British Columbia, Institute of Industrial Relations, 1977). It must also be remembered that "[w]omen's current situation in the work force is qualitatively different from their position in any earlier economic crisis. Women have a permanent (if unequal) attachment to the labour force." Lynda Yanz and David Smith, "Women at Work in Canada," in *Union Sisters: Women in the Labour Movement*, eds. Linda Briskin and Lynda Yanz, (Toronto: The Women's Press, 1983), 17. On the matter of women's "failure" of loyalty, see also Hilda Scott, *Does Socialism Liberate Women?* (Boston: Beacon Press, 1974).

The Economic Crisis and the Particularities
of Women's Lives

In light of the broad structural dimensions of what most women must do to survive, it is increasingly apparent that women's work has intensified in the face of the growing economic crisis. The economic pressures that shape women's experience, both in the home and the labour force, mount as both the state and employers seek ways to balance budgets and maintain profits. The economic vulnerability of women takes on special parameters in relation to a welfare state that actively supports capitalist modes of capital formation. As women's unemployment, underemployment, and poverty continue to rise, women's position in relation to the state merits particular attention.

In a recent Presidential address to the Canadian Political Science Association, Caroline Andrew contended that the economic crisis itself could not be understood without examining the ambiguous, contradictory, but nonetheless vital relations between women and the welfare state.[1] When we examine women from the standpoint of their active roles as primary participants in both "private" life and the economy, we see three relations to the welfare state. First, women are engaged through their reform activities in the formation of the welfare state; second, they are the majority of workers within it; and third, they are the primary clients of it. Recognizing these relations provides an illuminating basis for analysis of women's increasing impoverishment.

Traditionally, Canada has been shaped by a unique form of liberalism committed to the welfare state, as well as to state intervention in the economy.[2] Women's fundamental role in shaping the modern Canadian welfare state, however, has been insufficiently recognized. It was women's organizational activities in the reform era of 1880 to 1920 that established the roots of the welfare state in the soil of the familial territory of concern allotted to women: improved living condi-

---

[1]Andrew, "Women and the Welfare State," 667-83.

[2]Linda Briskin, "Socialist Feminism: From the Standpoint of Practice" (Toronto: Social Sciences Division, York University, 1988), 32. (Photocopy.) For the historical background of the welfare state in Canada and discussion of its contradictions see Michael Cross, "Introduction," in *Modern Canada: 1930-1980s*, eds. Cross and Kealey, 11-17.

tions, education of children, social services. The state became increasingly involved in coordinating and supervising these services in the interests of "the family," to preserve and strengthen it amidst the tremendous social pressures of modern life.

To understand women as workers in the Canadian welfare state, we must recall that following the Great Depression and the two world wars, the government created the "welfare state" as a strategy for, first, protecting the country from another depression; and second, direct intervention in the economy to "smooth out" economic cycles. Programmes such as family allowances, housing subsidies, university funding, the Canada Pension plan, and hospital insurance were implemented. Overwhelmingly, it is women who have been employed in delivering these services. They are also the majority of the clients of the welfare state. The most dependent for assistance are elderly women and single mothers. Under present policies, Family Benefit Assistance, public housing, day care subsidies, and welfare programmes are increasingly needed by women but have been the first to be frozen.

In addition, employment in the state sector, which particularly affects women, is under vigorous attack. When governments introduce fiscal restraint programs, as the Canadian government has, women bear the brunt of the belt tightening because they constitute a high proportion of those receiving and delivering benefits and services. In Canada, many of the women with technical, professional, managerial, and administrative skills work directly or indirectly in government funded sectors such as education, health, and public administration. With fewer jobs, with increases in part-time employment, and with governmental efforts to limit the power of those unions that have provided women with access to better work conditions, women's political and economic strength is being, and will continue to be, significantly reduced. The present trend toward privatisation of state services also threatens women's jobs and their potential for collective strength.[1] The contradictory tendencies between the state's role as mediator of basic socio-economic inequities, and its role as a guarantor of full employment, have surfaced as conflicting goals in the crisis as the present government has heeded the requisites of private capital accumulation.

---

[1]See Armstrong and Armstrong, "Looking Ahead," in *Feminism and Political Economy*, eds. Maroney and Luxton, 220

The three sectors of the economy (monopoly, service and trade, and state) collide under pressures for sustained and increased profit from foreign capital. For example, the 1984 restraint measures of the Mulroney government were made "to create a favourable investment climate." Together with an all-out ideological war against social spending, the Mulroney government froze welfare payments and reduced public sector spending by 25 percent; withdrew funds from women's programmes; and reduced legal aid and rent subsidies.[1] Canada faces, then, a major contradiction between ideological commitment to the legal and political equality goals of its parliamentary democracy, and the actual experience of economic inequality of a growing population of dependent citizens, particularly women.

These feminist criticisms of the welfare state are essential for understanding the scale of women's particular economic vulnerability. Most policies reveal that Canadian politicians still image their society as one where the nuclear family with a male breadwinner and a dependent wife is normative. State strategies designed to resolve, or at least slow down, the growth of poverty aim to create more help for the unemployed while freezing services most relied on by women, services such as housing, day care, and transportation subsidies. At the same time, women are under increasing pressure to provide other services, such as care for children and the elderly, without pay. Even if fully functional, however, government "programmes do not respond to the real needs and to the real situation of their clients. The reality of family organization has changed greatly within the last half century, but often these programmes are designed as though the whole society were organized neatly in nuclear families." While the welfare state may minimize the worst suffering, it does so by imposing a rigid definition of family, one with which more and more women's experience simply does not correspond. Thus it "provides assistance to women but at the cost of dependency."[2]

Historian Veronica Strong-Boag makes a similar claim in her discussion of the role of the state in maintaining female inferiority. She demonstrates that wage labour has been opened to women, but only

---

[1] Carole Wallace, "Women and the Deficit," *Status of Women News* 10 (November 1984), 20.

[2] Andrew, "Women and the Welfare State," 679-80.

with powerful simultaneous pressures to preserve the "ideal" patriarchal family. For example, protective legislation such as mothers' allowance was designed to enable sole-support mothers to stay home and care for their children. These allowances, however, like a husband's wage in many families, actually subsidized women's part-time labour. Thus, even the wages of married women who lacked male support were tied to the notion that women's wage-earning is *supplemental, not essential* to family survival. State wages for mothers, while offering some immediate help to the desperate, help confirm women's over-riding responsibility for the survival of the domestic institution and offer very few long term benefits, such as skills development, for the women themselves.[1]

What is now being acknowledged everywhere as the "feminization of poverty"[2] demonstrates most clearly the impact of the economic crisis on women's position in the gender division of labour. The restraint policies of government and business increase the range of work women are expected to undertake at home, and increase insecurity in terms of work and wages.[3] As both men and women suffer deteriorating conditions at work, the tension and violence at home escalates and it is primarily women who manage this emotional suffering; who are victims, along with children, of violence; and who juggle household needs and budgets often by intensifying their own labour. Women's "art of survival" becomes strained during such times of hardship, when real wages fall or disappear, and when the purported safety net of the welfare state functions ever more like a sieve. Today it is more difficult than ever to replace income with intensified domestic labour.

---

[1]Veronica Strong-Boag, "Working Women and the State: The Case of Canada, 1889-1945," *Atlantis* 6 (Spring 1981), 8; emphasis added.

[2]For discussions of the "feminization of poverty," see: Karin Stallard, Barbara Ehrenreich, and Holly Sklar, *Poverty in the American Dream* (Boston: South End Press, 1983); Hilda Scott, *Working Your Way to the Bottom: The Feminization of Poverty* (London: Pandora Press, 1984); Ruth Sidel, *Women and Children Last: The Plight of Poor Women in Affluent America* (New York: Viking Press, 1986).

[3]It must be noted, however, that restraint policies have varied effects on different women. One indisputable fact is that restraint measures divide groups and put many groups in competition with each other, often undermining any sense of collective justice.

Recent job creation programmes offer an illustration of how state programmes affect men and women differently. When these programmes aim at men, one can safely assume that men's poverty would be solved by a job. For women, however, getting a job would not necessarily mean living above the poverty line. The state's proposed strategy of providing part time work and job sharing would, even if adopted, still leave women with responsibility for domestic labour and little opportunity for advancement. "Job creation schemes in Canada, then, have done little to create or even maintain employment, but when they have been successful, more of the benefits have gone to men."[1]

Other indicators of the worsening position of many women can be detailed by tracing the incursion of the new technology in the workplace. "The effects of the crisis are being complicated by the rapid introduction of microtechnology, which threatens to eliminate between one and two million Canadian jobs by 1990."[2] This technology is designed chiefly to increase productivity and managerial control, particularly in the field of information processing, which is already radically altering the clerical work where one third of all women are employed.[3] The impact of microelectronic technology will create some new jobs, but it will destroy many more.

In sum, the economic crisis has a harsher impact on women, given their position as workers and clients in the welfare state, and because responses to the crisis by state and business add up to a "combined strategy of cuts in social welfare and the rationalization and flexibilization of labour."[4] Hence, the present Canadian welfare state per-

---

[1] Armstrong and Armstrong, "Looking Ahead," in *Feminism and Political Economy*, eds. Maroney and Luxton, 222. Women's unemployment rates are obscured by the absence of large layoffs, the transformation of full time jobs into part time jobs, and discouraged workers, who have temporarily ceased looking for work. The global structural changes described in the churches' economic teachings have been difficult to assess in relationship to women's unemployment, regardless of whether their unemployment is the consequence of technological changes, underemployment in part time or seasonal work, or unregistered in-house work.

[2] *The Globe and Mail*, (Toronto) 4 May 1983, A1, cited by Briskin and Yanz, *Union Sisters*, 15.

[3] Armstrong and Armstrong, "Looking Ahead," in *Feminism and Political Economy*, eds. Maroney and Luxton, 222-24.

[4] Mies, *Patriarchy and Accumulation on a World Scale*, 17.

forms a contradictory role in the lives of women, offering some basis for autonomy and yet restricting them to a dependent status on the grounds of family ideology. The limitations of current state policies for women's well-being stand out starkly through statistics on the rising rates of the unemployed; of the untended elderly; and of the impoverished divorced and single mothers living below the poverty line.

I have assembled various historical, economic, and political science materials to make visible the positions of women in the Canadian economic context. In this process I have identified various tendencies to ignore or trivialize women's participation in communal survival, and have examined perspectives that focus on women's lived experience. Missing, however, from many sympathetic political-economic analyses of the current crisis is attention to other issues that *compound* women's economic suffering. Some feminist theoretical critiques of political economy can lead us to a more adequate account of the concrete differences in women's economic reality. Here we must especially see the faces of Native Canadians, immigrant women, working class women, and women of colour for whom life options are bleaker still. Therefore, while it is a significant step to make gender central to the analysis of Canadian economic realities, we must take another step by incorporating a multi-dimensional assessment of the roots of oppression, and by evaluating its effect on feminist priorities and strategies.

Towards a Multi-Dimensional Analysis of the Roots of Oppression, Priorities, and Strategies

The Problem: Invisibility and Distortion of Marginalized Women's Lives in Some Feminist Theory

Feminism has played an important role in showing that there are not now and never have been any generic "men" at all--only gendered men and women. Once essential and universal man dissolves, so does his hidden companion, woman. We have instead, myriads of women living in elaborate historical complexes of class, race, and culture.[1]

---

[1] Sandra Harding, "The Instability of the Analytical Categories of Feminist Theory," in *Sex and Scientific Inquiry*, eds. Harding and O'Barr, 285.

As we have seen, the most lively and adequate discussions of women's economic lives have attempted to build on the structural analysis exposing the public-private dichotomy. Even the focus on the interconnections rather than the differentiation between the public and private spheres, however, has not always clarified how the family, the state, and the economy dynamically interact across races, cultures, and sexual orientations. While this feminist materialist perspective treats women's economic reality explicitly, the distinctiveness of the lives of Native women and women of colour is not adequately treated.

As I have insisted from the outset, a feminist framework of normative and empirical claims must be accountable to those marginalized by ethnic prejudice, racism, and heterosexism.[1] Despite marginalized women's integration into wage labour, their position remains extremely disadvantaged, not only due to the gender division of labour, but also to racist and heterosexist oppression. To identify that a range of configurations is operative in women's specific everyday life, our language needs to address this issue, for instance, by identifying the structural oppressions as straight-white-capitalist-patriarchy, and thus indicating how the effects of the current crisis have different impacts on particular women and, in some cases, on specific men.

In the foregoing survey of women's economic realities in Canada, I was exploring an approach that attempts to demonstrate the uneven gender effects of the crisis across industries, occupations, households, and within the formal economy. For example, while the crisis has initially and most obviously hit with massive layoffs the primary and manufacturing sectors, the areas where men work, their unemployment is concentrated in a limited range of industries and occupations.[2] These jobs, however, will reappear if a recovery takes place. Such is not the case in the labour-intensive service sector, which is being threatened in a variety of ways by the new technology, where women are concentrated. The assumption that "a job equals escape from poverty for men," however, obscures the racial oppression operative in social relations. Work is increasingly unavailable for Black and

---

[1]While attention to the overarching problematic is beyond the scope of this project, it bears stating here: How do we explain white male power and economic exploitation?

[2]Armstrong, *Labour Pains*, 174.

Native men, and other men of colour. As Linda Burnham states: "The deepening impoverishment of Black women has not been accompanied by a rise to affluence on the part of Black men."[1] Here is a good example of how the implications of race are lost when subsumed under a feminist class analysis. In addition, the very terms by which unemployment is defined in official statistics obscure the actual numbers, and the effect of lack of work for women is thus not registered in state statistics and policies.[2]

The economic vulnerability of women must also be specified by particular women's racial and ethnic realities so that adequate strategies can be constructed. For example, it is clear by now that women's work in the household, including child care, is undervalued and unpaid, and that this responsibility significantly contributes to women's increased economic vulnerability, and therefore to their political and social marginalization from the power to make decisions affecting their own lives. In short, we need a dialectic between macro theories of oppression and the lived experience of women in order to discern the operations of power relations in everyday life.

The importance of carefully analysing the links among class, race, and gender categories must be emphasized. For many women, poverty may be a condition of the downward mobility into which some are shunted after divorce, or the price paid for living outside the traditional heterosexist family. Sometimes socialist feminists argue that class is the determining factor in women's oppression, so that

> shared class experiences override other differences, such as ethnicity. While ethnic differences continue to be important, they are not the determining factor. Hence, all women have about the same amount of money to spend on food [in the one-company mining town under study]. What they spend it on

---

[1]Linda Burnham, "Has Poverty Been Feminized in Black America?," in *For Crying Out Loud: Women and Poverty in the United States*, eds. Rochelle Lefkowitz and Ann Withorn (New York: Pilgrim Press, 1986), 74. We must remember that for men of colour unemployment is compounded by race: e. g., thirty per cent of Black men in the United States are unemployed, discouraged, or unaccounted for, as compared with eleven per cent of white men.

[2]Ibid., 75. Pamela Sparr also contends with assessments of women's poverty that take gender as the primary or only cause of women's oppression. Such an approach obscures both the poverty of men of colour and the common base of class exploitation across racial groups at the heart of capitalism. See Sparr, "Reevaluating Feminist Economics," in ibid., 61-66.

reflects personal and cultural choices but these differences are virtually insignificant to the organization of domestic labour.[1]

While such a claim may be true in one study, it is not wise to presume
this as a generalizable criterion. Theoretically any neglect of race,
class, and sexual diversity should be critically scrutinized to avoid ob-
scuring the realities of any group of women. For example, Daria Stasiulis sharply points out that

> Black feminists have unearthed a double standard implicit in white feminist
> writings whereby the entry into waged labour is regarded as emancipatory for
> Third World, migrant and native women, but subjugating for white, non-mi-
> grant women. Such Eurocentric reasoning is built upon common mispercep-
> tions regarding economic roles of Third World and aboriginal women as neg-
> ligible, non-productive and completely dominated by the dictates of
> menfolk.[2]

Another example of how generalizations apply differently across
racial and cultural barriers can be observed in some feminist critiques
of the family.[3] A common white feminist criticism of the nuclear family assumes that it creates and shapes women's subordination and dependency on men. Male domination, enshrined in the family, is perceived as the problem. For women of colour, however, the family may

---

[1]Luxton, *More Than a Labour of Love*, 25. As a socially constructed category, race is a term that relies both on self-definition and the definition of others.
Ethnicity in principle differs from race; it refers to differences that exist between
peoples in culture, traditions, history, beliefs, habits, and practices. "Individuals
have choice about their ethnic identity in a way that they cannot have about their
race." See Michele Barrett and Mary McIntosh, "Ethnocentrism and Feminist Social Theory," *Feminist Review* 20 (1985), 28.

[2]Daria K. Stasiulis, "Rainbow Feminism: Perspectives on Minority
Women in Canada," *Resources for Feminist Research* 16 (March 1987), 5.

[3]For an extended critique of the nuclear family as a source of women's
oppression, see Michele Barrett and Mary McIntosh, *The Anti-Social Family* (London: Verso, 1982). On the experience of women of colour, see Rose Brewer,
"Black Women in Poverty: Some Comments on Female-Headed Families," *Signs*
13 (1988), 331-39; Delores Williams, "The Color of Feminism," *Journal of Religious Thought* 43 (Spring-Summer 1986), 42-58; Charlene Gannage, "A World of
Difference," in *Feminism and Political Economy*, eds. Maroney and Luxton, 139-
66. Also Arthur Brittan and Mary Maynard provide a good summary of the family
as an ambiguous context of oppression cross-culturally in *Sexism, Racism and Oppression* (Oxford: Basil Blackwell, 1984; reprint ed., 1985), 178-79 (page references are to the reprint edition).

function as a primary site of protection from, and resistance to, racism and class exploitation. Hence, the family cannot be construed as the unequivocal institution of oppression as some feminists, including some socialist feminists, do construe it. We must recognize how structural constraints, then, differ markedly within the category "woman."

Another concrete example is offered by Rose Brewer, who demonstrates how an emphasis on female-headed households misses the truth about black women's poverty: "black women are also poor in households with male heads. With or without a male present, there is a strong likelihood that black women and children will be living in poverty in America today."[1]

While it is very difficult for many women to find and keep jobs even in the female work ghettos of service and clerical work, it is *exponentially* harder for Native women.[2] For a Native woman, even the training for secretarial work is already circumscribed by the historically-rooted legacy of racism and state colonization. Jessie Littlehawk signifies how the struggle for work demands exponential courage.

> I remember the first day I went to secretarial school. I was very scared. I didn't have front teeth and I was wearing my only skirt. When I first walked in there I didn't know how I was going to last. When I look at all these white women who seemed to be smartly dressed, the thought of quitting entered my mind. I wanted to go back to the reserve where I knew everybody. The thing that kept me going was that at the end of the week I was supposed to get a fifty dollar clothing allowance. After that the *Neheyaw* (Cree) in me got the fighting spirit.[3]

Littlehawk tells of the stigma of having brown skin and black hair in a white culture; she also contends that "one of the worst forms of racism and sexism is that of omission. We as Native women are not there [in

---

[1] Brewer, "Black Women in Poverty," 334.

[2] I am indebted to Janet Silman for her insights about the interconnections of race, class, and gender, especially for naming and respecting differences between Native and white women. Silman articulates well how the combination of racism and sexism is not simply doubly oppressive but exponentially so; see her "Indian Rights for Indian Women," in *Justice as Mission*, eds. Brown and Lind, 162-70.

[3] "Up Against the Odds: Jessie Littlehawk," in *Hard Earned Wages*, ed. Penney, 29.

the history books]."[1] In Canada, Native people are the most disadvantaged, and among them women rank among the most severely oppressed. Figures for Native labour force participation indicate that one fourth of Native people have no regular wage-labour employment, and that if they are employed--and it is usually the men who are--they are in low status, low paying, and seasonal work.[2]

Asoka Bandarage has observed that "the profitability of the world capitalist economy is based to a very great extent on the unpaid labour of women; that is, women's poverty." She stresses, nevertheless, that poverty is different in female-headed households across cultures and social classes.

> At least one third of all households around the world today are headed by women. In the United States, this situation has created a greater dependence of women on the welfare state. A very great proportion of the women heading households and living below the poverty line in the U.S. are women of color. In 1981, 27% of the households headed by white women were in poverty compared to 53% of those headed by Black and Latina women; Black female-headed family income was 60% of white female-headed household income at the time.[3]

Bandarage's assessment of the different priorities of women points out the immediate irrelevance of many goals of the dominant, liberal, middle class women's movement for poor women, especially women of colour, who do not even have access to the resources of education or employment.

---

[1]Ibid., 36.

[2]James S. Frideres, "Native Peoples," in *Racial Oppression in Canada*, eds. B. Singh Bolaria and Peter S. Li (Toronto: Garamond Press, 1985), 42. For over a century, the Indian Act has defined who is an Indian, and thus entitled to certain rights and benefits, primarily membership in a band and residency on a reserve. This system of rule is readily defined as a white patriarchal colonial model based on capitalist economics. See Janet Silman, *Enough is Enough*, on the recent struggle of Indian women for their rights under white rule and Native sexism; and Howard Adams, "The Metis," in *Racial Oppression in Canada*, eds. Bolaria and Li, 61-80.

[3]Asoka Bandarage, "Women of Color: Towards a Celebration of Power" *Woman of Power* 4 (Fall 1986), 11.

Criteria for Theoretical Adequacy and Implications
for Priorities and Strategies

The most useful theoretical accounts for opening up women's work experience have been materialist approaches from theorists scattered across various disciplines, often allied under the broad wing of socialist-feminism.[1] Feminist economic analysis, however, must achieve greater clarity regarding the complexity of the roots of oppression. Without this focus, the economic lives of marginalized women, especially women of colour, will remain obscured and distorted.

If feminist theory is to challenge mainstream assumptions about women's proper place, and the invisibility of what women actually do, it must "restore conflict, ambiguity and tragedy to the centre of the historical process; to explore the variety and unequal terms upon which genders, classes, and races participate in the forging of a common destiny."[2] The current crisis has affected people in different ways within the general picture of the erosion of women's ground. For example, differences may increase between those women who have jobs and those who do not; between those who have full-time work and those who have only part-time work; between those who work, with or without pay in the home and those who go out every day to work; between

---

[1]In feminist theory several constructs are now commonly identified. For a succinct discussion of how different economic paradigms (for example, neo-classical, institutional, and marxian) explain women's poverty with varying degrees of adequacy, see Elaine Donovan and Mary Huff Stevenson, "Shortchanged: The Political Economy of Women's Poverty" in *For Crying Out Loud*, eds. Lefkowitz and Withorn, 47-69. Various feminist positions identify, for example, universal female subordination, the economic system of capitalism, or the sex-gender system of compulsory heterosexuality as the root causes of female oppression. For clear, succinct overviews of these discussions see Robb, "A Framework for Feminist Ethics," in *Journal of Religious Ethics* 9 (Spring 1981), 48-68; and Ellen Dubois, Gail Paradise Kelly, Elizabeth Lapovsky Kennedy, Carolyn W. Korsmeyer, and Lillian S. Robinson, "Women's Oppression: Understanding the Dimensions," in *Feminist Scholarship: Kindling in the Groves of Academe* (Urbana and Chicago: University of Illinois Press, 1987), 86-101. My purpose here is not to elaborate these various approaches or to contend with their strengths and weaknesses, although this is important metatheoretical work; rather, I will attempt to be accountable to the critiques from racial/ethnic feminists of the materialist analyses appropriated thus far, and to present alternative conceptualizations of the grounds for social transformation that are available in mainstream politics.

[2]Elizabeth Fox-Genovese, "Placing Women's History in History," 29.

those who must intensify their domestic labour and those who do not; between those who have employed spouses and those who have unemployed ones or none at all.[1]

Mainstream feminist political economists must face the charge that their analyses regularly float into universalizations about women's economic experience. They have all too often assumed that the experience and perspectives of white, heterosexual, Western European and North American middle-class women can be generalized to account for all women. An alternate approach must include the validation of difference as essential to feminism's intellectual and political task. Our task is to empower all women to speak for themselves.[2] If we are to build general theories which genuinely account for women's oppression, *difference* must, therefore, be a pivotal category in socialist feminist theory. Difference is a gift to be celebrated when communities struggling for shared power and resources recognize it not merely as a material indication of uneven power relations, but as a challenge to the hierarchy of a "hit parade of oppressions."[3]

Another important contribution difference makes as a construct for understanding women's economic reality is to push the discussion beyond class reductionism. To reiterate a key point in my argument: it is imperative that relations of power inherent in race, sexual orientation, class, and gender be assessed in terms of their dynamic interaction, i.e., the ways in which they intertwine, reinforce, and contradict each other. Hence, the standpoint I subscribe to here is one that "deconstructs the category of women [and], recognizes the centrality of difference, both in its oppressive and potentially liberatory forms."[4] While the structures of race, class, culture, and gender have distinctive historical manifestations and combinations, the point is to construe their relevance for the best possible strategies of social change, and not to be dogmatic about assigning timeless priority to one or another. For ex-

---

[1] Armstrong, *Labour Pains*, 176.

[2] Maroney and Luxton, "Editors' Introduction," in *Feminism and Political Economy*, 3.

[3] Letty Russell develops this term in *Household of Freedom: Authority in Feminist Theology* (Philadelphia: Westminster Press, 1987).

[4] I am indebted to Linda Briskin's lucid framing of this crucial conjuncture in her "Socialist Feminism," 23.

ample, the well-used term "capitalist patriarchy" tries to name the inter-linking structures responsible for women's oppression and exploitation. The problem with such language is how to identify and theorize the ways social relations based on racism and heterosexism are present *at the same time* in women's different class situations.

To confront our current social formation, Dionne Brand contends that "a feminist theory must root out the borrowed, unchallenged categories which have informed a mode of discourse used to repress the identity and claims of Black women. If not for the knowledge of Black women, the world, as felt by them and stolen from them, is lost."[1] Therefore, in order to recognize differences among women as marginalized groups, we must listen to the voices of those who experience different constraints on their moral and political agency.

Delores Williams, for example, compares typical agendas of Black and white women. She clarifies how black women's identity and survival are linked to the family's liberation, beginning with white-male/white-female systems of hegemonic control. The priority for change from this standpoint is the redistribution of goods and services. She compares this agenda with white women's emphasis on liberation from male control, and their placement of economic authority at the center of priorities for which to fight. The point is not to deny that equal pay and shared domestic work are common goods; rather, she makes clear that race, class, and gender take different tolls on different women, and thus demand different strategies for transformation.[2]

Criteria and Strategies for Women's Economic Well-Being

In order to take seriously significant differences in women's economic life, moral deliberation must occur in relation to several criteria which are assessed in terms of one basic question: Does this theory/practice transform political economy such that the sphere of private life

---

[1]Dionne Brand, "Black Women and Work: The Impact of Racially Constructed Gender Roles on the Sexual Division of Labour," *Fireweed* Issue 25 (Fall 1987), 29.

[2]Williams, "The Color of Feminism," passim.

and reproduction is brought into the public and political world?[1] I will now summarize the most significant criteria, recognized in various ways throughout the literature, which function to envision a vital range of powerful, yet flexible, intertwining elements.[2]

First, economic self-determination for women is a basic criterion. If women are to become moral agents--subjects of their own lives--and thus contribute fully to the wider community, they need to share responsibility for domestic labour with men. Critical related questions are "Do social services (e.g., child care, job training, and housing subsidies) reinforce gender segregation in the labour force simply by subsidizing low-waged work?" and "Do these programmes reinforce the familistic ideology which has conceptualized women as economically dependent on men?"

Second, the equalization of men's and women's share of paid and unpaid labour, and a radical alteration of who does the caretaking and nurturing in society are required. White, male, heterosexual, and class privilege will have to be transformed if the dualisms of head and hand, rural and urban, domestic and waged labour are to be overcome. Steps in this direction should be based on a shorter working day that would allow men and women time for household and caring labour, and the integration of men into female job ghettos, as well as women into male preserves and decision making bodies. The family must also be recognized as an institution with both positive and negative functions, given the different relationships women have to "family."

Third, sensitivity to differences of class, race, sexual preference, physical ability, and age among women is a criterion that must operate throughout our practice and theoretical activity. "Perhaps the key starting place is for feminists to accept that most black and poor women [and lesbians] never forget their blackness or their class [or their sexual

---

[1]Angela Miles uses this criterion to develop an "integrative feminist materialism." See "Ideological Hegemony in Political Discourse," in *Feminism in Canada: From Pressure to Politics*, eds. Geraldine Finn and Angela Miles (Montreal: Black Rose Books, 1982), 213-27.

[2]I am indebted to the useful organization and discussion of key criteria by Wendy Sarvasy and Judith Van Allen, "Fighting the Feminization of Poverty: Socialist Feminist Analysis and Strategy," *Review of Radical Political Economics* 16 (1984), 98-110. See also Ann Withorn and Rochelle Lefkowitz, "Talking Across the Table," in *For Crying Out Loud*, eds. Lefkowitz and Withorn, 339-56.

orientation] in discussions about their gender."[1] Policies must be developed that do not result in passing some women's domestic labour on to other women who are poorer or women of colour. Racial hierarchies everywhere must be eliminated, such as those in which whites are doctors and nurses while racial-ethnic minorities are assistants and orderlies. In addition, the wages, benefits, and hours of all women providing services must be improved.

Fourth, if women are to become economically viable, they must be involved in democratic planning and management of social programs. While women have been extensively employed by the state, often for tasks formerly performed voluntarily in the home and providing many of the front-line services, they have not had power to determine the policies for or the form of the services. In short, "they care for the clients of the welfare state but they have little influence on the direction of the welfare state."[2] Therefore, women continue to struggle for an adequate share of power to shape and run the programmes that effect so many women. Experience from battered women's shelters, rape crisis centres, and poor and disabled women's organizations can be instrumental in such designs. Further, "black women can often take the lead, since they are used to the tricks involved when whites try to make people ashamed of a condition that has been imposed upon them."[3] The list of mutual demands from women of diverse backgrounds would include full medical coverage, publicly funded day care, better housing, higher wages, and the reduction of domestic violence by expanding services to battered women.

The final criterion Sarvasy and Van Allen identify is the expansion of the conception of social responsibility. This goal represents "a vision of society in which people share responsibility for each other, both directly and through the socialization of many forms of labor that must now be performed or paid for by private individuals and families."[4] There are rich implications of this feminist materialist framework for Christian economic ethics.

---

[1]Withorn and Lefkowitz, "Talking Across the Table," 348.

[2]Andrew, "Women and the Welfare State," 678.

[3]Withorn and Lefkowitz, "Talking Across the Table," 347.

[4]Sarvasy and Van Allen, "Fighting the Feminization of Poverty," 100.

Evaluation of Radical Christian
Teaching on the Economy

How does the Radical Christian tradition in Canada fare in these terms? Its agenda for a new theological ethic based on economic democracy is to be lauded as a consistent and primary feature from the 1930s to the present. Its trenchant critique of reigning policies, especially of how state and business interests collude at the expense of the common good, goes a long way toward demonstrating the increasing injustices of class, and it places Canada's policies in the broader global economic context. Recognition of the conflict between classes and the suffering of unemployed persons, as well as acknowledgment of the vast numbers of other victims of the capitalist world system, are the concern in the literature explored.

We recall that in Radical Christian ethics, women's experience, economic and otherwise, was invisible. It assumed that the economic reality of class existed as an undifferentiated mass, such that economic reality was the same for women as for men and that the norms for economic justice would affect both genders in the same manner.[1] It assumed that when the cause of oppression--industrial capitalism--is eliminated, and replaced with a social democratic economic structure, exploitation and oppression will essentially disappear.

In the ecclesial statements of the 1980s, women are mentioned among those most vulnerable to economic hardship and recognized as the majority of "the poor." There is an enormous gap, however, between, on the one hand, their twin notions of the class-based "preferential option for the poor" and "solidarity with the victims," and, on the other, attention to the realities of the majority of the poor, that is, women. While the United Church of Canada's 1984 statement cites women as suffering doubly in periods of economic restraint, and especially affected among the growing numbers of the poor,[2] the earlier

---

[1]This point has been made most effectively in the work of Pamela Brubaker, "Rendering the Invisible Visible: Women's Global Economic Reality and Christian Social Ethics" (Ph. D. dissertation, Union Theological Seminary, New York, 1989); see also O'Donovan, "On Human Work: A Feminist Critique of LABOREM EXERCENS."

[2]UCC 1984, 5 and 11.

FCSO position assumed all workers were male and the Canadian Conference of Catholic Bishops' statement does not indicate any real attention even to issues specific to the lives of women who also work for a
wage. The everyday lives of women are absent from the ecclesial de-
liberations on the economic crisis. The causes of their oppression and
suffering are not explored adequately, and the strategies proposed are
consequently limited.

A clear example of the lack of attention to women's economic
lives can be discerned in the common definition of economic malaise as
unemployment: the "real" victims are assumed to be wage workers.
In practical terms, as we have seen, this approach advocates for worker
control of production and participation in determining the priorities of
allocating resources. The key focus is upon power and how it functions, particularly within the state in favour of the economic interests of
capital. If work is only understood as wage labour, and workers only
as men, however, then the social analysis of power in evidence
throughout these documents distorts and devalues the work women actually do every day. Their policy recommendations advocating full
employment strategies would *not* affect women's lives as they might
men's; that is, without addressing issues of injustice in the relationship
between domestic and waged work, or the patriarchal and racist dynamics under capitalism, equal access and equal pay will still perpetuate the
"double day" for women.

In short, according to the framework outlined for a feminist economic ethics, the radical faith-and-justice tradition in Canada has met
only the fourth criterion, namely, democratic planning and control of
social programmes. On the rest, it has fallen short: economic self-determination for women; equalization of men's and women's share of
paid and unpaid labour, and a radical alteration of who does the caretaking and nurturing in society; an expanded notion of social responsibility; and sensitivity to class and racial-ethnic differences among
women.

The failure of the Radical Christian tradition in relation to this
last criterion can be attributed largely to its exclusive reliance on social
theory predicated on class as *the* fundamental social contradiction.
Even the section on women and poverty in the 1984 United Church
document fails to integrate into its analysis the constraints on *women's*
economic participation and the unpaid shadow work they do. Its stra-

tegy statements move in the right direction, but do not sufficiently address the fundamental structural transformations needed for women's economic well-being. Attempts at defining women's situations exclusively through class analysis

> continually fall foul of the fact that women's familial location and responsibilities signify a completely different material position in the structure of society to that of men. Thus, any efforts to incorporate the majority of the population into a class system perceived in male terms cannot expect to include women in anything other than a marginal way. [Similarly] if blacks are more exploited than whites and women more exploited than men, this additional exploitation cannot be simply reduced to the operation of class relationships and capital.[1]

Precisely because the Christian principles of mutuality and justice are at the heart of the Radical Christian tradition, the near invisibility of women's lives in the existing documents is a deep moral problem. If we are to build a tradition more nearly inclusive of *all* people in its horizon of liberation from exploitation and oppression, the resources distinctive to different women's experiences must be identified and appropriated in this construction.[2] On the basis of the norms for economic justice, i.e., preference for the dispossessed and the dignity of labour, women must be placed central to our analysis since they *are* the most oppressed and least able to have their dignity shaped by the communal work advocated as necessary for "full humanity."

---

[1]Brittan and Maynard, *Sexism, Racism and Oppression*, 56. They state further that "[t]here is a difference between arguing that a woman's life is affected by economic conditions, and the claim that these necessarily determine and structure her position in society, to the extent that it can be analyzed and categorized only with reference to a form of conceptualization defined from a male point of view (i.e., class)." Ibid., 60.

[2]See Sandra Harding and Merrill B. Hintikka on the distortion of all bodies of knowledge when relying only on partial human experience, namely masculine experience understood by men. They also describe a dialectical method proper to feminist appropriation of existing tradition: having "deconstructed" the documents, I have also woven a "reconstructive" thread throughout this chapter. See their "Introduction," *Discovering Reality: Feminist Perspectives on Epistemology, Metaphysics, Methodology, and Philosophy of Science* (Boston: D. Reidel Publishing, 1983).

Towards Integrated Justice: Some Implications for Christian Feminist Economic Ethics

In conclusion, if women's economic well-being is to operate centrally in the faith-and-justice tradition, certain principles can be fruitfully employed to reflect theologically on the particularities of women's economic reality.[1] First, the affirmation of women's experience as structured by the reproductive and productive spheres is the appropriate starting point for an adequate feminist economic ethics. The premise undergirding this starting point can be identified as the value placed on the reproductive sphere, understood as

> a system of embodied values predicated on our mature self-directing capacity as culture creators to care for and value each other. . . . It is through the reproductive system that we come to grasp what life is about, who our people are, and what life and death mean in our community. The reproductive system, then, is the basic and initial transmitter of cultural values.[2]

Second, as for a feminist political economy, a feminist economic ethics attempts to understand the structures of women's oppression and to develop a strategy for liberation. I have sided with those who believe that gender divisions are as fundamental as class and race division for comprehending women's varied but linked lives. A multi-dimensional hermeneutic permits the analysis of women's experience as both dynamically structured and unique. Attention to power relationships is critical for a radical feminist agenda of transformation to be politically constructed with accountability to race and class. The particularities of women's lives are thus honoured as vital theological data, especially those of the women most burdened by unjust economic relations. We must test strategies for economic justice from the perspective of poor women. When the factors inhibiting those women's equality and full participation are addressed, then the strategies can be judged adequate.

---

[1] I have reached some conclusions similar to those of Theresa O'Donovan and am grateful for her lucid and constructive analysis of these issues; see "Towards a Feminist Theology of Work," in "On Human Work: A Feminist Critique of LABOREM EXERCENS," Chapter 3.

[2] Harrison, "The Older Person's Worth in the Eyes of Society," in *Making the Connections*, 156.

Third, the whole notion of "work" must be transformed on the basis of women's unpaid domestic labour as well as their waged labour. If a feminist economic ethics is to take seriously women's everyday lives as the fundamental theological resource, then it cannot accept the dominant assumption that women's economic realities are best kept private, invisible, and undervalued. To avoid the problem of theoretical dualism, the reproductive sphere of procreation, sexuality, and socialization must be kept analytically distinct from the productive sphere of the waged labour system, while recognizing that in actual material terms, of course, the public and private spheres are in a dynamic relation of domination and subordination.

To reconceptualize work as the activity fundamental to our development as human persons is to struggle against all dualisms which keep us alienated and without community.[1] To grasp fully what Beverly Harrison calls "the very real historical power of women to be architects of what is most authentically human" is to expand our conception of work to include love as a mode of action and human work as the basic activity of building human dignity and community.[2] A feminist ethic of work embraces this *telos*: justice, as the power of right relatedness, in all our activities of producing and reproducing life.

Finally, the norm of women's empowerment stands as the key for a feminist economic ethics. In keeping with the criterion of an expanded conception of social responsibility, and with a liberationist standpoint of the moral agency of women, those who bear the worst hardships of economic dependence will be the ones to shape and advocate for their own lives to be fulfilled as partners in work that is both loving and just.

---

[1]Dorothee Sölle and Shirley Cloyes have written a powerful critique of the nature of work under capitalism in the process of constructing a theological paradigm that places work and love as its central themes and activities; see *To Work and To Love: A Theology of Creation*. I have also found Nancy Hartsock's work helpful on the topic of estranged work and its non-alienated sister, creative work. The vision of work whereby we express ourselves, and do not oppress nor are oppressed by others, is a joyous one indeed. In the course of her discussion, and of relevance here, Hartsock articulates the now commonly accepted feminist notion of power as an interdependent, shared energy, strength, and effectiveness. See "Staying Alive," *Quest* 3 (1976-77), 3-14.

[2]Harrison, "The Power of Anger in the Work of Love," in *Making the Connections*, 11.

CHAPTER FOUR

TOWARDS A FEMINIST ETHICAL
APPROACH TO CULTURE

Introduction

Between the facts of our Canadian society and theological reflection on them, we need the mediating images of poets and artists, the revealing stories of writers, to give us a decisive insight into our reality here.[1]

[F]eminism defines itself as a political instance, not merely a sexual politics but *a politics of experience, of everyday life*, which later in turn enters the public sphere of expression and creative practice, displacing aesthetic hierarchies and generic categories, and which thus establishes the semiotic ground for a different production to reference and meaning.[2]

A revolution capable of healing our wounds. If we're the ones who can imagine it, if we're the ones who need it most, then no one else can do it.[3]

My central thesis is that critical attention must be given to the cultural practices of everyday life if women's voices are to be heard

---

[1]Mary Jo Leddy, "Exercising Theology in the Canadian Context," in *The Faith That Transforms: Essays in Honor of Gregory Baum*, eds. Mary Ann Hinsdale and Mary Jo Leddy (Mahwah, N.J.: Paulist Press, 1987), 129.

[2]Teresa De Lauretis, "Feminist Studies/Critical Studies: Issues, Terms, and Contexts," in *Feminist Studies/ Critical Studies*, ed. Teresa De Lauretis (Bloomington: Indiana University Press, 1986), 10; emphasis added.

[3]Aurora Levins Morales, ". . . And Even Fidel Can't Change That," in *This Bridge Called My Back*, eds. Moraga and Anzaldua, 56.

both in their diversity and in their concrete social contexts. The cultural activities of women are generated within quite particular contexts of responsibility, choice, and agency. We have examined the broad contours of the material conditions which variously shape women's lives in Canada. Having investigated the methodological criteria for a contextual analysis that includes these dynamics, I will now explain the additional methodological resources needed for the developing work of a Canadian feminist liberation ethics--namely, clarification of a method to integrate the cultural dimension theologically and ethically. The task at hand is to engage the cultural dimension wherein women's identities and the meaning of life and death are developed, contested, renewed, and transformed.

The focus here is on how we "read" our experience as embedded within particular cultural dynamics. Critical appropriation of cultural codes is an ongoing and pressing concern for feminist and womanist theologies trying to articulate concretely women's suffering, struggles, and sources of hope for embodied wholeness.[1] Without the stories, imaginings, and intimacies of the struggles to embrace our lives authentically, the theological task of encouraging people to yearn and work for institutional and interpersonal justice cannot root or bear fruit in the soil of our backyards. Indeed, without a normative engagement of the cultural milieu of everyday life, we often neglect the powerful connections between us and God.[2] We need these resources of body-affirming, evil-naming, hope-inspiring ordinariness, because, in the words of Dorothee Sölle,

---

[1] Alice Walker defines womanist as, among other things: "Responsible. In charge. *Serious*. . . . A woman who loves other women, sexually and/or non-sexually. . . . Committed to survival and wholeness of entire people, male *and* female." See *In Search of Our Mothers' Gardens* (New York: Harcourt Brace Jovanovich, 1983), xi.

[2] In reformulating the role of literature in culture and theology I have been inspired by the work of Katie Geneva Cannon, "Moral Wisdom in the Black Women's Literary Tradition," in *Weaving the Visions: New Patterns in Feminist Spirituality*, eds. Judith Plaskow and Carol P. Christ (San Francisco: Harper & Row, 1989), 281-92; and Delores Williams, "Women's Oppression and Lifeline Politics in Black Women's Religious Narratives," *Journal of Feminist Studies in Religion* 1 & 2 (Fall 1985), 59-71.

... it is up to us
what our earth becomes
a vale of tears starvation and tyranny
or a city of god
I believe in a just peace
that can be achieved
in the possibility of a meaningful life
for all people. . . .[1]

We can re-create the world so that all are welcome only by knowing *who and where we are*, that is, by assessing and creating cultures of resistance against all that thwarts our lives. To become co-creators with God is our moral vocation. Our theology is above all shaped by culture. It seeks to identify, create, and sustain traditions, values, and ways of life that shape and reshape our communities.

If we are to make common cause across barriers that divide women, then it is incumbent upon those of us with some power to listen to and learn from the cultures of women's lives--their struggles for identity and for a very different liberation from what we might imagine. If we are not going to use culture as an excuse for side-stepping the painful work of coalitional solidarity, then we must engage culture critically in struggles for justice. Wherever women experience themselves as participants in building community, authorizing their own lives and celebrating this resistance, we will meet the Presence of God. How then do we "read" such forms of cultural agency and celebration? Because we need not only to render women's experience visible but also to assess its complexities and contradictions, those approaches to culture which present tools most useful for this task are those which take seriously daily lived realities--the culture of everyday life wherein most women have been inscribed--as political sites of struggle.

This chapter, then, presents a theory of culture that grants access to the particularities of women's everyday lives. In the first section I will consider the contribution of Canadian Radical Christianity to cultural analysis and theology. In the second, I will address helpful constructs from contextual and liberation theological traditions that sharpen the cultural approach of Radical Christianity. In the third, my amplification of cultural analysis to include women's lives will draw upon the

---

[1]Sölle, "Credo" in *Revolutionary Patience*, trans. Rita and Robert Kimber (Maryknoll, N.Y.: Orbis Books, 1977), 23.

work of critical cultural theorists in the intellectual tradition of Antonio Gramsci and Raymond Williams. This critical theory of culture inquires primarily into consciously-lived life and attends to the dynamics of everyday life in the context of concrete social relations. Cultural analysis of women's experience, however, requires a theoretical consideration specifically focused on their lives. I therefore introduce, in the fourth section, resources from a cultural-political hermeneutic in feminist theory to enable a greater specificity reflecting accountability to the contradictions, similarities, and differences of women's lives. In the fifth section, I discuss the appropriation of culture in feminist theological ethics. In the final section, I develop an approach to narrative as a cultural resource in feminist ethics offering access to women's lives lived under varying conditions of moral agency.

In the next chapter I will encounter three Canadian narratives in novels that explore the moral ambiguities, conflicts, and wisdom of female characters in their struggles to come to terms with their ancestry and to author their own lives. In preparation for that encounter with marginated women's voices, I will now review the strengths and limitations of the Radical Christian tradition's approach to culture and indicate what is required for a more adequate method that includes women's experience and cultural distinctiveness.

Culture in the Radical Christian Tradition in Canada

As we have seen, the radical Christian tradition in Canada recognizes that cultural issues must be incorporated into theological reflection so that the Canadian context might be transformed to more nearly meet the demands of the gospel. Its impulse to transform culture came from its social analysis that perceived capitalism as the major dynamic of social sin. The mandate of Radical Christianity was to enable a Christian revolution, one that "seeks to end strife and injustice that are contrary to the will of God, and convert human society into a divine commonwealth of righteousness and love."[1]

---

[1]Line, "The Theological Principles," in *Towards the Christian Revolution*, eds. Scott and Vlastos, 50.

In service of this eschatological goal, cultural openness and diverse christologies and views of God were welcomed among religious radicals. Religious cultus, or worship, was ascribed special importance for the task of social reconstruction.

> If religion be defined as a way of living, determined by conviction and reverence towards the Ultimate Reality, worship is the reaffirming of that conviction and the deliberate expression of that reverence. It is in worship that the springs of life are fed. Religion is life, and life requires nourishment and periodic refreshment. . . . In its cultus as a whole a group of people expresses its common understanding of that which distinguishes it as a religious society and is the reason for its existence.[1]

Radical Christianity's conception of culture was based on embodying Christian reverence, affirmation, and vision in the society at large. The goal was to Christianize the social order,[2] to influence the culture of the nation by its radical agenda and way of life, especially through its worship practices.

Culture was defined as the whole complex of public activities and celebrations which create a distinctive pattern of life and thought.[3] Radical Christianity assumed that any authentic human culture was rooted in some type of religious conviction, because society was shaped by some ultimate conviction about the source and meaning of life, in other words, by religion. Participation in rituals and symbols involved and sustained people as members of particular communities, thereby reaffirming their ground of being. "It is the business of the cultus to preserve, transmit, and display that organic structure of vital ideas and beliefs by which the society orders its life. . . . It is their own, the society's articulation to itself of that which it holds precious."[4]

Genuine cultus, however, could not appear spontaneously or be made to order; rather, it was a response to the Word of Prophecy and

---

[1]Scott, "The Cultus of Community," in ibid., 191-92.

[2]This goal was elaborated by the United Church of Canada's Commission on Christianizing the Social Order in its report to the 1934 General Council.

[3]I base this overview of Radical Christianity's view of culture and society on Scott, "The Cultus of Community" in *Towards the Christian Revolution*, eds. Scott and Vlastos, 190-98.

[4]Scott, "The Cultus of Community," in ibid., 194.

the Evangel of the Kingdom present in the life of the worshiping community. The cultus embodied and exhibited the meaning of the Christian culture it was helping to shape. Culture, then, expressed the society's ultimate concern. But these ultimate values were not to be accepted uncritically in its entirety; rather, it was the task of Christian theology to discern the forces in culture which God was using to judge and take sides and "to gird the warriors on the eve of battle and sustain them through the long campaign."[1] Culture as understood in Radical Christianity embodied theological conviction. Its ethic prescribed conflict with the status quo in a struggle to permeate culture with the gospel of justice.

Today, others in the contemporary Canadian faith-and-justice tradition are calling for attention to the cultural sphere. Douglas John Hall, for instance, claims that culture is *the* neglected resource for enabling a Christian reading of "the spirit of the times" and a Christian awareness of one's own context. Cultural analysis is essential, he asserts, if we are to confront the truth about our world rather than deny the massive offenses we commit.[2]

Similarly, Gregory Baum has also stressed that the struggle for justice has a cultural, intellectual, and spiritual dimension, and that the ethico-political thrust of the gospel has "two distinct though interrelated dimensions, the cultural and the political." He warns that if the cultural dimension is neglected, people become activists, who remain uncritical of the dominant cultural presuppositions. As he understands it, the justice mandate of Christian religion first of all impacts people's consciousness and their cultural self-understanding. Since our present unjust society is legitimated by cultural symbols and values and maintained by the received common sense mediated by the cultural mainstream, Baum urges radical Christians to engage in a cultural mission, which provides a context for involvement in political action. Fundamentally Baum affirms that radical Christians' primary concern is "to decode the message of society, to resist the lies that pass for common

---

[1]Scott, "The Cultus of Community," in ibid., 193; cf. Line, "The Theological Principles," in ibid., 48.

[2]For a recent statement of his position, see Douglas John Hall, "The Future of Religion in Canada," The Ebbutt Lecture (Sackville, N.B.: Mount Allison University, 1988).

sense in a sinful world, and to look upon their own country from the alternative vision of society, more in keeping with divine promises." These counter-cultural strategies accompany struggle to transform the economy in keeping with ethical culture that enables people to live in harmony with the earth.[1]

Feminist theology shares the emphases of this faith-and-justice tradition on the importance of ritual and celebration, and the vital significance given to the cultural ethos as an aspect in theological formation. A feminist response affirms the development of a spirituality based on struggles to transform society. It is not clear, however, that the particular experiences of those suffering injustice were engaged in defining the earlier theological agenda of the church. Nor is it clear how the contemporary tradition attends to the positive resources in culture for empowering alternative communities to resist the destructive "signs of the times." Even when culture is a source for theology and ethics in the radical Christian tradition, it remains undeveloped as a source. Certainly no recognition is given women's role as shapers and bearers of culture. Therefore, just as women's experience must be privileged in social analysis, so it must be in interpreting culture theologically and ethically. Some preliminary attention must be given to insights that help sharpen this tradition's constructive direction regarding cultural analysis.

Culture as A Source for Theological Ethics: Resources from Contextual and Liberation Theologies

For women's experience to serve as the basis for theological reflection, we must have a more subtle and inclusive conceptualization of the relationship of culture and experience. In order to understand culture as a human construct limited by nonhuman constraints, as capable of oppressing as well as liberating, we must counteract prevailing definitions of culture as a means of domination of nature. To do so, we must carefully assess the relationship between culture/history and na-

---

[1]Gregory Baum, "Faith and Liberation: Development Since Vatican II," in *Theology and Society* (Mahwah, N.J.: Paulist Press, 1987), 27-28; and "The Impact of Marxism on John Paul II," in ibid., 63.

ture/creation.[1] For our task of clarifying how culture can serve as a theological source in keeping with a radical faith-and-justice tradition, let us consider Enrique Dussel's proposal. Dussel locates culture within the context of material relationships and suggests that the definition of culture include both material culture (the tools necessary to reproduce life) and the symbolic or spiritual expression of that production.[2] As a Marxist he maintains that human work is the substance and essence of culture, in the sense that culture is the actualization of the human being, the creation of human life. We sustain and reproduce life through our natural organs, such as our eyes, hands, or the body parts which allow us to move in space. We have learned to extend these organs by means of artificial, historical, cultural organs. This process is material culture--the interdependence with and transformation of nature. Dussel defines culture as human beings' way of working; therefore, culture as the symbolic ethos of a people always implies a relationship to the material culture of work, the fleshly dimensions of earthly existence. Feminist theoretical approaches to culture can appropriate Dussel's integration of culture and nature only if we expand the marxian notion of work, as we did in the previous chapter, to include aspects of women's culture that are not restricted to paid labour.

Joan Griscom also provides a useful criticism of the nature/history split in much feminist theory. She focuses her discussion on the four interlocking patriarchal systems of ecological destruction, sexism, racism, and classism, which accomplish their oppression not only by the domination of nature and women, but also by domination by race and class.[3] Griscom argues that the failure of much theory to integrate all of these analytical categories perpetuates the nature/history split.

---

[1] I am grateful to Larry Rasmussen for his insistence that the social construction of experience/reality be carefully set within the broader context of creation. I subscribe to the understanding that creation is more than culture and that history is constrained by creation in ways that impinge on human praxis, and thus the argument that a connection must be made between history and nature so that history, theologically speaking, does not simply become equated with creation.

[2] Enrique Dussel, *Ethics and Community* (Maryknoll, N.Y.: Orbis Books, 1988), 64, 199-200.

[3] Joan L. Griscom, "On Healing the Nature/History Split in Feminist Thought," in *Women's Consciousness, Women's Conscience*, eds. Andolsen et al., 85-100.

> Social feminists emphasize history and often disregard nature and biology; nature feminists emphasize nature and often disregard history and social structures. . . . In actuality, one can derive norms from history and still include nature, for our relation to nature is *part* of our history. And one can derive norms from nature and still include history, for human history is *part* of nature.[1]

We can rectify a dualism that views history as anything human and nature as anything other than human only if we connect our biology with our culture, nature with history, within a vision of liberated creation.

Feminists have long argued over women's relation to history and nature or creation. Sherry Ortner argues that women have been socially defined as occupying a bridge-like position of intermediary between nature/creation and culture/history: culture is equated with "the notion of human consciousness, or with the products of human consciousness (i.e., systems of thought and technology), by means of which humanity attempts to assert control over nature."[2] The definition of women's function as *mediators* between nature and culture, and the association of men with higher-order cultural production, results in the cultural marginalization of women on the periphery of culture's clearing in nature's forest. "Ultimately, it must be stressed again that the whole scheme is a construct of culture rather than a fact of nature."[3] Woman is not "in reality" any closer to or further from nature than man: both have consciousness, both have moral agency, exercised within the constraints of time, space, and cosmic process.

In a discussion of this nature-culture split, Ynestra King, a theorist of the ecofeminist movement, explains that "defining culture in opposition to nature has also resulted in defining culture in opposition to life, devaluing life-giving functions and life itself."[4] While women are not "more natural" than men, we are perceived as being closer to

---

[1] Ibid., 88-89.

[2] Sherry B. Ortner, "Is Female to Male as Nature is to Culture?" in *Woman, Culture and Society*, eds. Michele Zimbalist Rosaldo and Louise Lamphere (Stanford, Cal.: Stanford University Press, 1974), 72.

[3] Ibid., 85.

[4] Ynestra King, "Making the World Live: Feminism and the Domination of Nature," in *Women's Spirit Bonding*, eds. Janet Kalven and Mary I. Buckley (New York: The Pilgrim Press, 1984), 58.

nature and thus our cultural agency is also denuded of significance. Women's resistance to the domination of nature hinges on the recognition of the interconnectedness of all forms of life, including human life. While women cannot be confined within a statement such as "We are nature," neither must we forget that even our conceptions of nature are culturally constructed. Our social ethic must, therefore, acknowledge the interactive process between history/culture and nature/creation, and within this context, evaluate the interstructuring of injustices.

In light of the foregoing, then, culture, as a liberative theological source, must take its bearings from anthropological assumptions which interpret humanity as responsible for the tending and caring of all life. An ongoing dialectic of reciprocity with nature is presupposed. Indeed, "in the postmodern era, time and space are human projects, not just givens of nature."[1] It is increasingly clear that we do have the capacity to create in a way that destroys our wider environment. People are responsible for evil, that is, for the destructiveness of our action; so too we are responsible for shaping our environment for good in the world.[2]

From the politics of culture in relation to nature, we can move to the relation between culture and liberation, and draw on Roy Sano's argument for the role of cultural resources in liberation theology.[3] He articulates how a people's consciousness is created by stories, myths, plays, histories and biographies. Sano insists on the sociality and particularity of experience, and he asserts that culture can function both as critique of *and* the source of new paradigms. He analyses the interaction between what he calls "mythwriters" and their audiences. He finds that some only *reflect* people's experiences, or alternatively, some may *shape* the consciousness of the people. The first task in an analysis is *descriptive*: poets, dramatists, novelists, historians, musicians, and painters make visible the stories by which a culture lives. He distin-

---

[1]Elizabeth Bettenhausen, "Blizzard: Pluralism and Ethics," Lecture delivered at St. Andrew's College, Saskatoon, Saskatchewan, February 12, 1990.

[2]For a helpful critique of the effects of an overemphasis on human freedom and agency, see William C. French, "Ecological Concern and The Anti-Foundationalist Debates: James Gustafson and Biospheric Constraints," in *Annual of the Society of Christian Ethics* (1989), 113-30.

[3]Roy Sano, "Ethnic Liberation Theology: Neo-Orthodoxy Reshaped or Replaced?," in *Liberation Theologies: Mission Trends #4*, eds. G. Anderson and T. Stransky (Grand Rapids, Mich.: Eerdmans, 1979), 247-60.

guishes this moment from what I take to be the more critical moment of myth-making: the *prescriptive* task of creating new stories involving visions that function to move a society towards a different future.[1]

In Sano's schema, both kinds of culture, descriptive and prescriptive, are necessary for social consciousness, dignity and respect. Sano demonstrates how the reciprocal relationship between the telling of a people's story and participation in the struggle of that people for liberation makes personal identity possible. From this perspective, the history of a people is mirrored in the life-story of each community member, and persons know themselves through a common culture and society. Sano's position is consistent with Tom Driver's interpretation of a theology *of* culture: culture is the subject, while theology is the mode of analysis. A theology of culture, therefore, will explore the descriptive and prescriptive contents of culture in order to elaborate a critical theology of culture which addresses the needs, desires, and contradictions experienced by particular peoples.[2]

In theological terms, for example, sin on the level of culture is the domination of one culture by another.[3]   Here we can see two im-

---

[1]See for example Cornel West's important collection of essays on politics, theology and culture, *Prophetic Fragments* (Grand Rapids, Mich. and Trenton, N.J.: William B. Eerdmans and Africa World Press, 1988), 114.

[2]Tom Driver, Lecture, Union Theological Seminary, September 27, 1984. Elsewhere he states that "if Christians be not of their culture they cannot truly evaluate it, and if theology is not of culture it becomes authoritarian instead of revolutionary." See "Theology of Culture," Paper written for the Study Commission on Theology, Education and the Electronic Media, (New York: National Council of Churches of Christ, 1985), 10-11. Given the norm of revolution, this position must be distinguished from a liberal theological interpretation designated as the Christ of Culture position in the 19th and into the 20th centuries and which said an unqualified "Yes" to the Enlightenment project. See for example, H. Richard Niebuhr, *Christ and Culture*, (New York, Harper and Row: 1975, originally published 1951), 91-115; Daniel Day Williams, *What Present Day Theologians are Saying*, (New York: Harper and Brothers, 1952); Dorothee Sölle, "The Dialectics of Enlightenment," in *Doing Theology in a Divided World*, eds. Fabella and Torres, 79-84; Kenneth Aman, "Christianity and Social Change in a Postmodern Age," in *Border Regions of Faith*, 515-521. Rebecca Chopp, *Praxis of Suffering*, 118-133, suggests another stance, similar to that of the Canadian Radical Christian tradition, as "Christ Liberating Culture."

[3]For a third world perspective on the sin of cultural imperialism, see the African theologian Engelbert Mveng, "A Cultural Perspective," in *Doing Theology in a Divided World*, eds. Fabella and Torres, 72-75.

plications for a critical theology of culture. First, that since cultural mediation is a common human task, *not* a uniquely Christian one, we must reformulate *our* understanding of the relationship of Christ and culture: Christians must face the reality that many people have also experienced Christ as Oppressor, not necessarily as Liberator. Second, while the transnational culture sponsored by ruling elites is dominated by a manipulative technology which risks annihilating both human and ecological existence, culture does not exist only in this dominant mode. Alternative cultural sources critical of dominant values and lifestyles are always present and must be identified and celebrated.[1]

I locate this project of cultural theological analysis, then, in the primary strategy of Radical Christianity: the generation of alternative cultures in resistance to the dehumanization of dominating power. The radical faith-and-justice tradition in Canada encourages people to claim responsibility for shaping culture in the interests of justice for all, beginning with the victims of society.[2]

I will discuss further how the connection between social analysis and cultural criticism can function as a resource for theology and ethics. There is still, however, a need of greater specificity in cultural criticism. The cultural and political dimensions must take account of personal, everyday relations within societies. Cultural analysis must, therefore, be amplified if culture is not to be subsumed under social analysis *or* regarded as an abstract or universal theological source which continues to ignore and exclude the specifics of women's experience. We will begin by investigating a preliminary theoretical framework which may illuminate the use of cultural analysis as a resource for a feminist theological ethics.

---

[1]Raymond Whitehead writes that "Whenever we use Christ to support male, white, Euroamerican bourgeois thought forms, we are involved in oppression and are unfaithful to Christ's spirit"; see "Christ and Cultural Imperialism," in *Justice as Mission*, eds. Brown and Lind, 28, 33. See also Tom F. Driver, *Christ in a Changing World*, (New York: Crossroads, 1981) and Carter Heyward, *Speaking of Christ: A Lesbian Feminist Voice* (New York: Pilgrim Press, 1989).

[2]On culture as an ambiguous source for theology in a global context, cf. Charles West, "Culture, Power and Ideology in Third World Theologies," *Missiology: An International Review* 12, no. 4, (October 1984), 405-20.

Critical Cultural Theories[1]

Culture has no single definition. In social theory, it has been used to indicate the knowledge, beliefs, and customs peculiar to particular communities.[2] Some idealist social theorists treat it primarily as the sum of thoughts, moods, feelings, beliefs, and values of subjects. They do not address what people actually do, or on the institutions they construct, including the physical exchanges of money and power. This approach is flawed because it perpetuates the dualism which divides the human world between objective social structures, on the one hand, and subjective thoughts and perceptions, on the other. Culture is, then, reduced to a vague concept dependent on individuals' ascriptions of meaning and disconnected from the conditions, patterns, and rules of use which render symbols meaningful. Another approach to be avoided swings to the other end of the bifurcation between individual and social experience and interprets culture only as a function of the social structure. Some overly deterministic marxian theories rely on this approach when they relegate culture to a position within the superstructure. Both of these theories reduce culture to a one-sided, non-dynamic sphere of human consciousness. Neither definition is consistent with the theological norm of liberation and the understanding of human moral agency as substantively culture-creating, and as co-creating with God.[3]

Between these two extremes lies another theory which defines culture as interwoven with the social fabric, neither isolated from an attitudinal realm nor totally determined by the social structure. In this view, "cultural analysis is the examination of the symbolic-expressive aspect of behaviour."[4] Culture is, therefore, an inherent dimension of

---

[1]For an excellent study of critical cultural theory, see Richard Johnson, "What is Cultural Studies Anyway?," *Social Text* 16 (Winter 1986-87), 38-80.

[2]See Caroline Ramazanoglu's cogent discussion of culture in *Feminism and the Contradictions of Oppression* (New York: Routledge, 1989), 138-170.

[3]Robert Wuthnow, James Davison Hunter, Albert Bergesen, and Edith Kurzweil, *Cultural Analysis: The Work of Peter L. Berger, Mary Douglas, Michel Foucault and Jurgen Habermas* (Boston and London: Routledge and Kegan Paul, 1984); see also Robert Wuthnow, *Meaning and Moral Order: Explorations in Cultural Analysis* (Berkeley and Los Angeles: University of California Press, 1987).

[4]Wuthnow et al., *Cultural Analysis*, 255.

all social life. One can hardly disagree with this statement, but a critical edge is decidedly missing.

This definition of culture must be amplified on at least two points. First, we must locate culture and its institutions, values, and habits not in the past, but in ongoing forming and formative processes. Second, the assumption that people's cultural behaviour defines and expresses their whole lives must be qualified by greater attention to the realities of power. Any society has differences in power which cause significant inequalities in people's participation in symbolic-expressive cultural processes. Without attention to such inequalities, cultural power will continue to reside unproblematically in the dominant ethos.

If culture is neither determined by social structure nor a conflation of individual meanings, how shall we characterize it? The revival of Marxist thought, particularly in the 1970s, enabled the development of more critical conceptions of culture and a differentiation of culture and ideology. Seeking to counteract approaches which he identifies as reducing culture to fixed forms, Raymond Williams, social theorist and literary critic, established key terms and relationships for a critical approach to culture. Williams argues that culture should be studied as "a mediation of society": it can be identified as a constitutive social process which creates meanings and values inscribed in different and specific "ways of life" by which people generate, not necessarily intentionally or self-reflectively, their identities and interpretations of others in directly personal relationships, their understanding of the natural world and themselves in it, and their use of physical and material resources for what capitalist societies specialize to "leisure" and "entertainment" and "art."[1] Cultural studies in this mode, then, treats the historical forms of consciousness or subjectivities by which we live; these involve a consciousness of self and an active mental and moral self-production. This way of conceiving culture encourages us, then, to approach culture as a generative source of change in social life.[2]

---

[1]Williams, *Marxism and Literature* (Oxford: Oxford University Press, 1977), 100, 111-19.

[2]In Williams' *Marxism and Literature* and *Politics and Letters: Interviews with New Left Review* (London: New Left Books, 1979) he indicates the importance of culture in the commitment to justice and brilliantly reformulates the reductionist tendency in Marxism in his cultural and literary method.

Within this method of cultural analysis, we need a conception of ideology to enable us to locate the power of ideas and consciousness within specific cultures. Ideology is perhaps an even more problematic term than culture. For our purposes, it is "a particular set of ideas which shape the way in which most people make sense of their social world."[1] It is pervasive in the context in which culture is produced and reproduced. As we have noted, a dialectical approach places our consciousness and culture in reciprocal relationship with material conditions. Consciousness is not something passive which, like beeswax, could receive any imprint put into it. Consciousness is active in its own self-creation. It is also interactive with dominant ideologies about race, gender, class, and sexuality.[2]

Dominant ideologies are constantly being formed in response to contending values.[3] Hence, this reciprocal relationship of consciousness and culture implies that

> ideologies are not a set of deliberate distortions imposed from above, but a complex, and contradictory system of representations (discourse, images, myths) through which we experience ourselves in relation to each other and to the social structures in which we live. . . . [Ideology] is a structure of perception that helps maintain a particular set of social and economic relations at a particular juncture in history that affects the way all of us . . . construct our own subjectivities.[4]

---

[1] Ramazanoglu, *Feminism*, 148.

[2] For a brief and useful introduction to the origins of the concept of ideology in Marxist and non-Marxist traditions, see David McLellan, *Ideology* (Minneapolis: University of Minnesota Press, 1986); for a systematic and analytic treatment of ideology, see Jorge Larrain, *The Concept of Ideology* (London: Hutchinson and Co., 1979); on the connection of cultural studies and ideology, see the collection of essays in Centre for Contemporary Cultural Studies, *On Ideology* (London: Hutchinson and Co., 1978; originally published by the Centre for Contemporary Cultural Studies, University of Birmingham 1977); on the study of religion, ideology and popular culture, see Kenneth Thompson, *Beliefs and Ideology* (Sussex and London: Ellis Horwood and Tavistock Publications, 1986).

[3] Bruce Grelle discusses the reliance of Jose Miguez Bonino and Cornel West on this notion of culture: culture understood in the critical terms of ideology is the arena of struggle for hegemony--a struggle precisely to establish values such as democracy, justice, and the rights of the poor; see his "Christian Political Ethics and Western Marxism," *Journal of Religious Ethics* 15, no. 2 (Fall 1987), 173-98.

[4] Newton and Rosenfelt, "Introduction: Toward a Feminist-Materialist Criticism," in *Feminist Criticism and Social Change*, xix, xxi.

The connections between culture, ideology and power so crucial to our task of "reading" experience are usefully elaborated in radical social theory through the concept of hegemony.[1] The work of Italian cultural theorist Antonio Gramsci is crucial here. In Gramsci's view, culture is hegemonic if the intellectual and moral leadership is objectified ideologically through the institutions of "civil society": the ensemble of education, religious, and associational institutions. Gramsci assumed that a state or society could not be sustained by force alone, but by the exercise of ideological power to inspire attitudes and provide orientation for action so as to win and shape assent to its rule. Hence, ideology in hegemonic cultural terms is not only a system of ideas. It is also a whole dynamic social process aimed at securing acceptance of the status quo. As Cornel West points out,

> This legitimation takes place in the cultural and religious spheres, in the arenas where the immediacy of everyday life is felt, outlooks formed and self-images adopted. . . . Hegemony is a set of formal ideas and beliefs and informal modes of behaviour, habits, manners, sensibilities and outlooks that support and sanction the existing order.[2]

Hegemony thus refers to the organization of popular consent to the ideology of the dominant group. For hegemony to be secured, everyone must accept at some level of common sense the view of the dominant group.[3] According to Gramsci, the concept of hegemony clarifies the multiple ways in which a dominant culture works to define and

---

[1]The concept of hegemony is the way in which Gramsci reconceptualized the Marxian notion of ideology; see his "The Intellectuals" and "The Philosophy of Praxis," in *Selections from the Prison Notebooks* (New York: International Publishers, 1971; reprint ed., 1983), 3-23, 321-425; page references are to reprint edition. Raymond Williams provides a succinct statement of the meaning of hegemony as "a 'culture' but a culture which has also to be seen as the lived dominance and subordination of particular classes"; see *Marxism and Literature*, 110. Jorge Lorrain provides a useful overview of hegemony and its relationship to other views of ideology; see "Ideology," in *The Dictionary of Marxist Thought*, ed. Tom Bottomore (Cambridge, Mass.: Harvard University Press, 1983).

[2]Cornel West, *Prophesy Deliverance! An Afro-American Revolutionary Christianity* (Philadelphia: Westminster Press, 1982), 119.

[3]Gramsci distinguishes *common* sense, which is thought that has been unreflectively received from one's social and cultural environment and thus contains a hodgepodge of superstitions, folk wisdom, uncoordinated information, etc., from *good* sense, which is critical knowing; see *Selections*, 321-23.

shape all areas of human life, so that the legitimation of the dominant classes appears not only spontaneous but natural and normal. Ideological hegemony conceals social conflicts and disparity and creates illusions of harmony. It is always an active process with a more or less adequate organization and interconnection of otherwise separated and even contradictory meanings, values and practices, all of which it carefully incorporates in a significant culture and an effective social order.

Raymond Williams identifies various structural aspects of the cultural process which account for the determining power of culture.[1] He outlines four aspects of the incorporation of culture under the rubrics of tradition, institutions, formations, and structures of feeling.

First, "tradition" is "an intentionally selective version of a shaping past and a pre-shaped present, which is then powerfully operative in the process of social and cultural definition and identification."[2] For example, white male history in Canada is hegemonic to the neglect, exclusion, and distortion of indigenous people's and most women's involvement in Canadian tradition. The effective establishment of a selective tradition depends on a second structural aspect of social life: "institutions." In keeping with Gramsci, he identifies these as "civil society" institutions, including family, education, church, and major communication systems which incorporate a selected range of meanings, values, and practices. Williams reminds us, however, that culture cannot be reduced to its formal institutions. A third aspect of cultural life is "formations"--"those effective movements and tendencies, in intellectual and artistic life, which have significant and sometimes decisive influence on the active development of a culture, and which have a variable and often oblique relation to formal institutions."[3] According to Williams, in complex societies these formations play an

---

[1]For a fascinating treatment of the interplay of culture and power, including attention to Marxism and radical feminism, see Joan Cocks, *The Oppositional Imagination: Feminism, Critique and Political Theory* (London and New York: Routledge, 1989).

[2]Williams, *Marxism and Literature*, 115.

[3]Williams, ibid., 117. He specifies formations that are "residual," for example, rural communities which are in the process of adjusting to dominant culture's meanings; "emergent" formations move beyond attempts of practical incorporation into the select cultural tradition. The main sources of the emergent formation are the growing strength of a class and the excluded human area; see 121-126.

increasingly crucial role in resisting any simple reduction of culture to some generalized hegemonic function.

Finally, Williams introduces a fourth specification in the examination of any cultural process: "structures of feeling." This term denotes his concept of the cultural margins. By this term he means "a kind of feeling and thinking which is indeed social and material, but in an embryonic phase before it can become fully articulate and defined exchange."[1] For example, the movement known as Rock Against Racism and the phenomenon of black women's literature can be studied as structures of feeling: cultural processes which combine such elements as impulse, tone, and affective elements of consciousness. Structures of feeling can therefore be defined as social experiences "in solution" which expose and contradict dominant ideologies. Williams usefully distinguishes between cultural aspects which are more static and formal (i. e., "traditions" and "institutions") and those which are more resistant and informal (i. e., "formations" and "structures of feelings"). Hence, while the regulating "tradition" which operates to secure selected cultural definition is powerful, hegemony, as "effective *self-identification* with the hegemonic forms," can be resisted.[2]

In the critical cultural theories of Gramsci and Williams, hegemonic authority over civil society is most dramatically experienced in the realm of everyday life, where our identities as persons are most intimately shaped and expressed. A feminist praxis of justice has affinity with this critical-political approach to culture; in common are attending to the "private" sphere of everyday life and privileging the cultural practices as valid and hopeful activities of resistance and struggle.[3]

---

[1]Williams, ibid., 132-133.

[2]Williams, ibid., 112, 118.

[3]See Michele Barrett on this clarification of "relative autonomy" and for her lucid treatment of ideology and cultural production in a feminist voice; see *Women's Oppression Today* (London: Verso, 1980), 121 and passim.

Towards a Critical Feminist Method of Cultural Analysis

For the range of women's experience to come into focus a further conceptualization of culture and experience is necessary. The concept of hegemony offers insight into those processes which shape the subjective side of social relations: consciousness, motives, emotionality, memories and images that are organized to form one's identity, sense of self and others, and of our purpose and vocation. Feminism is a critical form of consciousness. "It enables us to make sense of existing social arrangements as patriarchal. Feminism, therefore, is critical of existing ideas, beliefs, customs, and practices, including scientific and religious knowledge."[1]

Feminist theorists have consistently emphasized the importance of ideas, language, and culture to women's oppression and liberation in the search for transformative responses and initiatives: How is it that women discover themselves to be complicit in their own undermining? Why do women thwart a genuine solidarity when we *know* what would be most life-giving? Can we name often enough women's gifts and love, and how often they are denied and abused? To answer these questions, we need the concept of ideology to explain how women are complicit in their own oppression and how women do not necessarily perceive whether or not they have interests in common with other women.

While ideology mystifies people's understandings of their social worlds, feminists use ideological critique to produce knowledge which reveals the social, political, religious, and economic structures and relationships constitutive of societies. Feminist analysis of patriarchal ideologies, for example, enables us to identify how men throughout much of human history have achieved and maintained domination over women. Furthermore, without some conception of ideology, the problems of the cultural diversity of women's experience would be seen only as problems of cultural differences, when in reality women can share common interests as women only in relation to some form of

---

[1]Ramazanoglu, *Feminism*, 140. Teresa De Lauretis explores the issues, terms, and contexts of the relation of experience to feminist discourse; see *Feminist Studies/ Critical Studies*, 5 and passim.

subordination of women by men, or to social structures and processes in which men's interests are dominant. Caroline Ramazanoglu writes:

> Patriarchal ideologies will necessarily present women's subordination to men as natural, desirable, and legitimate. It will also emphasize the divisions between women. But women's consciousness of the differences which separate them from other women are not simply false if women do . . . have different essential interests. Both marxist and feminist forms of knowledge seem . . . to be needed if we are to have a full understanding of the ideologies we live with.[1]

Ideologies, therefore, are interconnected with the organization of productive systems, with the operation of male dominated sex/gender systems, and with racial/ethnic cultural hegemony. Certainly the concept of patriarchal ideology, along with an understanding of its interaction with women's divergent and often conflicting material conditions, is necessary if feminists are to specify the connections between ideas and the exercise of power. What is most difficult to assess in any given society is *how* the ruling ideas of the dominant class, race, and gender affect women's lives.

Women are cross-culturally considered to be the bearers of culture. What this means in practice depends upon the cultural context. For example, for a black woman in a white racist culture to give her child self-esteem and value as a black person, it is necessary that she teach the child to be honest but not necessarily open to others in dominant culture. If the child is a daughter, then she must impart further wisdom for coping as a girl in a male-dominated community. This illustrates the multiple, contradictory strategy necessary for the child's survival. In everyday life, then, people create concrete cultural codes that are variously shaped by complex power dynamics.

Ideologies are strewn throughout women's histories and lives: familial, racial, religious, and sexual, to name but a few. A feminist amplification of cultural criticism will attend to these, discovering the

---

[1]Ramazanoglu, *Feminism*, 143; she elaborates this point to demonstrate how disclosing patriarchal ideology enables us to see where the power is located in specific societies. She also states that the concept of ideology has a limited use, however, since women cannot be treated as a class. By this I take it she means that we must always specify the conditions and effects of patriarchal or other ideologies as they function in specific historical contexts because the shifting process of culture is never identical from one social order to another.

wide diversity of contradictions of culture, ideology, and sexuality experienced by women. Women also, however share forms of oppression. This theological analysis from a recent Asian women's consultation probes the dynamics that sustain ideology and underscores the way in which hegemony develops:

> Oppression of and violence against women has, very definitely, a cultural, psychological, material and sociological base. . . . The suppressed group to some extent internalizes the dominant ideology, which shapes its own socialization, and so becomes filled with fear and ambiguity about its own humanity. Passive acceptance of this sinful and oppressive situation on the part of women themselves has helped to stabilize the situation. Thus we see two interconnected but distinguishable aspects to the ideology of the "other" as of lesser value: projection and exploitation. Projection externalizes the sense of inadequacy and negativity from the dominant group, making the other the cultural "carrier" of those rejected qualities. The dominant group can then rationalize exploitation as the right to reduce the other to a servile condition, abuse and even kill them.[1]

Ideology, therefore, is part of the cultural fabric of everyday life within which women weave a consciousness of themselves and their world. When this consciousness becomes common sense, hegemony has been secured in such a way that the members of the ruling elite perpetuate their position of dominance by the popularization of their own culture and morality.

The feminist insight that the personal is political captures the insight that there is indeed a direct relation, however complexly mediated, between the social order and subjectivity, between language and consciousness, between institutions and individuals. For the personal to be political involves placing personhood and peoplehood at the center of our ethics, valuing the human in relations informed by self-responsibility and love, and resisting all that concretely negates people. Hence, a feminist cultural theory continually sifts the praxis of everyday life and seeks to formulate multiple strategies to transform our lived realities into arenas for moral self-definition.

In sum, a critical feminist approach to cultural analysis focuses on the formation of subjectivities, that is, the way in which meaning is

---

[1]Asian Women's Consultation, "Women's Oppression: A Sinful Situation, Composite Paper," in *Proceedings, Asian Women's Consultation*, coordinator, Sun Ai Park (Manila: November, 1985), 88.

produced, challenged, and transformed under specific conditions of male-domination. Feminists develop critical knowledge of the connections between the private and the public in order to understand and transform the interstructured dynamics of oppressions. We deepen our consciousness and claim our lives in relation to each other and to social structures, in which contradictory representations, discourses, images, and myths shape our lives. This particular approach to culture is one of the central contributions of the global liberation movement of women. A liberationist perspective will pursue this understanding of the cultural dimension as a resource for resisting oppression as well as for making alternative cultures. Therefore, I have appropriated a method of cultural analysis which defines culture in relation to ideologies and power to give teeth to formulations of culture as "symbolic-expressive dimensions of social life." This formulation of culture is currently fueling the work of feminist theological ethics.

Appropriation of Culture in Feminist Theological Ethics

Women's experience is no less socially constructed than the word of God, and hence feminist justice like the righteousness of God is practised and understood within the boundaries of a given culture and society. Yet, human beings can never be reduced to the sum of social variables which configure their experience. There is *a surplus of experience*, not independent nor separable from the social construction of reality, but not contained entirely within its limits. To move into this surplus of experience is to enter the realm of ambiguity, where the ethical guides of one's society may lose their prescriptive force but not their capacity to torment conscience.[1]

Our analysis of women's experience as an authoritative source for feminist theology must include "the core of women's personhood, the relationship of women's selves to female social roles and most importantly feminist praxis as a means of change for women's lives in their personal and political dimensions, the private and public spheres, and beyond these divisions."[2] A feminist liberation ethics seeks, then, to identify the specificity of women's experience which gives rise to all

---

[1]Sheila Briggs, "Sexual Justice and the 'Righteousness of God,'" in *Sex and God*, ed. Hurcombe, 274; emphasis added.

[2]Ibid., 271.

theological reflection, searching critically for ways in which power is abused or shared. In order to disclose women's experience with its multiplicity and contradictions, its differences and commonalities, I will investigate the importance of narrative as a cultural resource which can serve as a bridge between cultures and women's private experience, and between the public realm and human subjectivities.

Although we cannot separate doing theology from culture, neither can we assume that culture does not have some "surplus of experience" that can shape society *and* theology in the direction of freedom for women. That is, a cultural-political approach must not be taken to imply that all experience is so ideologically restricted that human agency is denied; or, conversely, that cultural autonomy implies no limits to moral agency. Instead, the critical cultural method developed here presumes that the social construction of reality, including culture, is not based on individualist interpretations which deny the function of conflicts of power in shaping culture. Meaning and truth, including moral meaning and truth, are an intricate and relational venture situated in an historical and environmental context.

We can relate Sheila Briggs' notion of a "surplus of experience" to the task of women creating themselves as moral subjects. Consciousness of ourselves as subjects is an ongoing process in which women participate as a *political* venture: wherever women are bent on rooting out our consent to hegemonic cultural practices, we are involved in creating new meaning, truths, and communities within specific historical and ecological limits. We have to define our identities ever afresh because of constant challenges to female authority, dignity and self-definition. For women, the negotiation of hegemony is central to our lives, to the very constitution of female integrity. Identity or subjectivity, however, is not just a feminist ethical end but a means to effectual agency. We focus on ways to be centered, embodied selves who may be alive in the power of mutual relation.

The doing of theology and ethics is inseparable from culture. Culture, however, also has its own "surplus of experience" which can shape society and theology in the interests of freedom for women. This category, within the dialectical method of cultural analysis discussed above, enables us to focus on women's experience as agents of culture. For a simple illustration, let us consider a ritual from the everyday lives of a network of feminists of faith. Their regular gathering opens with the sharing of a home-made feast to which each has contributed. Food is piled high for all to enjoy, including casseroles and cakes. Some are made from recipes from the kitchens of friends, mothers, and grandmothers, and include soup and bread, preserves and pickles from summer gardens, and wine in sealer jars fermented from fruit gathered from hours of picking crab apples, chokecherries, and saskatoon berries. From the standpoint of culture as integral to daily life, this communal feast draws together and celebrates the hard labour of long days, recalls women's hardships and joys, and offers in ritual shared goals and tasks associated with struggles for justice. All of this provides food for the soul, heart, and body. The women gather mindful of the need for beauty, nourishment, and celebration as they affirm their work towards making a world where all women will be well. This common ritual marks the presence of an alternative culture dedicated to a society where justice means life. Thus, cultural analysis that attends to everyday life holds up women's selves in relationship to others and to ordinary symbols, rituals, objects, and activities, all of which depict their participation in the construction of social life. Within such analysis, a religious ritual can be seen as an attempt to transform our sufferings and share the hope amidst the struggle.

While the experience of everyday life is, doubtless, ambiguous terrain for revolutionary projects, how we shape the meaning of our daily acts of resistance and creation shapes our understanding of our moral agency in specific contexts. Recognizing that experience is embedded in culture and shaped by particular dynamics of power, all social practices can be resources for a critical cultural analysis of the hard work of creating ourselves as human subjects. Such an analysis can ask: How do women *live*, become subjects, sustain themselves? To answer this question, we must investigate the cultural forms we inhabit subjectively: language, ideologies, discourses, myths.[1]

For *women* to become *subjects* as culture makers and not just "conduits for the identities of others"[2] feminist ethicists must employ normative strategies which consistently seek to clarify the conditions of

---

[1]Johnson, "What is Cultural Studies Anyway?"

[2]Jill Vickers, "At His Mother's Knee: Sex/Gender and the Construction of National Identities," in *Women and Men: Interdisciplinary Reading on Gender*, ed. Greta Hoffman Nemiroff (Toronto: Fitzhenry and Whiteside, 1987), 478-92.

female responsibility in order to enable authentic moral freedom. More generally, feminist ethics raises the problem of how people can live together without oppressing one another. Because women do not have the same interests but often have contradictory ones, how women experience power can and must be explored in terms of historical, systemic forces other than gender. Unless we learn to identify the location of power in class, race and culture as well as sex/gender in the routines of everyday life, we will circumvent tackling the problem of the nature of power and the ways in which it is held by some rather than others. In addition, from a praxis of justice, revelation can then be understood as experiences of redemption and emancipation which emerge from women's experience in their struggle for well-being in personal and public spheres. Therefore, addressing our everyday issues of power, we can also find positive resources within lived experience, because it is *here* that we are renewed and inspirited to stand our ground, to voice resistance, and to create alternative ways of seeing, being and doing. Given these assumptions, we can move to a consideration of women's cultural work of becoming moral subjects.

Practices of Self-Invention as Cultural Criticism and Theological Activity[1]

Feminism ought to function as a political critique of culture both because of its marginalized standpoint, and because, at the same time,

> the practice of self-consciousness--of reading, speaking, and listening to one another--is the best way we have precisely to resist horizontal violence without acquiescing to institutional recuperation, the best way we know to analyze our differences and contradictions.[2]

Discursive investigations are necessary, but feminist ethics also gives central importance to the *quality* of our stories and the mutual decoding and conceptual transformations that enable us to discern together what

---

[1] I base this title on Delores Williams' term "anatomy of self-invention," in "Women as Makers of Literature," in *Women's Spirit Bonding*, eds. Kalven and Buckley, 141.

[2] De Lauretis, "Issues, Terms, and Contexts," in *Feminist Studies/Critical Studies*, 8.

that means in our struggle to go beyond dehumanizing gender and sexual criteria and relations. If feminist theory is to function as a critique
of ideology, which organizes experience on its own terms in isolation
from embodied experience, then "we must continue to test thinking
against experience, making sure that it remains rooted in the real lives
of women."[1] A feminist understanding of culture is related, therefore,
to the lived experience of female self-creation.

Womanist theologian Delores Williams has a provocative way of
describing women's struggles to become the agents of their own lives
in terms of the "anatomy of self-invention":

> When women realize the inadequacies of the "selves" designed for them by
> patriarchal social, political, religious, and educational institutions (inadequa-
> cies they often passively accept), they can begin to shape themselves. But
> this is not easy. The process of self-invention often involves an encounter
> with an abyss, when the old forms of identity no longer get women beyond
> the hurt, the pain, and the feelings of nothingness oppression creates.[2]

If we are to focus on women's acts of self-invention as *varied positions
of outsiderhood*,[3] we thereby count as morally valuable activity that
which has long been considered unimportant for shaping human ethics:
at the cultural level, the "private" social relations for which women
have long been accorded responsibility and which incorporate moral
reason foreign to the dominant instrumental reason. To privilege ways
women sustain life through everyday relations of work enables us to
see traditions of resistance to the powers of domination. That women
possess skills necessary for our survival and hope that have not been
examined as a source of moral insight means that the more we learn
about the structures and fabric of everyday life, the greater our hope.

---

[1]Nannerl O. Keohane and Barbara C. Gelpi discuss this notion of feminism as a critique of ideology; see their "Foreword" to *Feminist Theory: A Critique of Ideology*, (Sussex, Great Britain: Harvester Press, 1982), ix.

[2]Williams, "Women as Makers of Literature," in *Women's Spirit Bonding*, eds. Kalven and Buckley, 141.

[3]This term is from Cherrie Moraga, *Loving in the War Years* (Boston:
South End Press, 1983). An excellent resource for exploring this process is Elly
Bulkin, Minnie Bruce Pratt, and Barbara Smith, *Yours in Struggle: Three Femi-
nist Perspectives on Anti-Semitism and Racism* (Brooklyn, N.Y.: Long Haul
Press, 1984).

The moral wisdom generated there may also offer fresh resources for moral theory.

Because narrative is an available and valuable cultural resource for investigating women's ways of inventing themselves, my research has led me to extend my awareness of the lived-world value of marginated Canadian women through a critical reading of selected novels.

Narrative in Feminist Theological Ethics

The late Margaret Laurence declared that literature is able both to describe our predicaments and to enable us to resist effectively the despair of our lives. "Fiction binds us to and frees us from our ancestors; it acknowledges our dilemmas; it mourns and rages at our inhumanity to one another; and sometimes it expresses our faith in growth and change, and honours our children and our trust in them."[1] Narrative is, therefore, an excellent medium for exploring the rich and ambiguous terrains of women's struggles for personhood and peoplehood.

The hermeneutical framework I develop to interpret narrative coheres with the feminist conviction that "to become a moral subject is itself a moral task, if not the central moral task."[2] To engage this task intentionally requires the tending of relationships, for to do so deepens personhood and is itself what creates community. To acknowledge this form of women's power demands that we also recognize our radical freedom to destroy one another through radical acts of lovelessness. An ethical and theological reading of women's narratives, then, requires that the texts be addressed with a key question foregrounded: under what conditions do female characters experience their dignity and power as human agents or warp it? Above all, we will approach culture as an arena in which the demystification of power is possible. Therefore, deconstruction of power relations must be at the heart of cultural analysis if women's liberation is to be served.

I approach narrative with a view to identifying the theological "surplus of experience" at the margins. Tom Driver theologically con-

---

[1]Margaret Laurence, in *Canadian Novelists and The Novel*, eds. Douglas Daymond and Leslie Monkman, (Ottawa: Borealis, 1981), 252.

[2]Ruth Smith, "Feminism and the Moral Subject," in *Women's Consciousness, Women's Conscience*," eds. Andolsen et al., 245-49.

nects human experience and narrative in terms of *patterns of grace*. Through experience, he explains, we come to know ourselves as co-creators in a lifelong process of *making a life* out of countless experiences. Through this process we praise and enjoy our Creator. Driver embraces human experience as revelation, as Word of God, because it is through this co-creative process that we participate in transcendence.

Driver focuses on certain themes project which provide an open-ended affirmation of human experience as both the occasion and source of revelation: the ground of a pattern to each and all life; the relationality of all experience, or co-creation to form the meaningful patterns of our existence; change as a constant unevenness in our experience out of which we must extract or discern a pattern; action or "the initiative, motive and authoring of one's experiences"; and the "awareness," or unjudging acceptance of what is going on which signals our entry upon holy ground and moves us to praise.[1] Driver's theological approach is important because, like feminist liberation theology, he makes action central to what makes experience *experience*. "There is only one question: are we willing to form, and be responsible for, our own experiences in the world?"[2] Responsibility is central for theological knowledge. How we shape our life's story, then, is determined by our encounter with transcendence in our experience.

> Transcendence is existential. It has to do with freedom, intentionality, and choice. It is as finite as it is infinite. It is preeminently felt in . . . "the good heart" moving courageously into the tension between the finite and the infinite. A moment of transcendence is a moment of courageous freedom and creativity, and from this its ethical and theological importance comes. . . . *To transcend is to choose.* But a choice cannot be made unless one is *in* a situation. Therefore, transcendence requires immanence, with which it is . . . identical.[3]

From the perspective of feminist liberation ethics, there are deep affinities between Driver's emphasis upon human experience as the authorizing moment of theological discourse, and the centrality given to the

---

[1]Tom F. Driver, *Patterns of Grace: Human Experience as Word of God*, (San Francisco: Harper & Row, 1977), 119, 143 and passim.

[2]Ibid., 143.

[3]Ibid., 162-63; emphasis added.

responsible construction of human subjectivity as agency. If we are to heed the very diverse conditions under which women invent themselves, we must, however, hear our narratives not only as existential quests but also as social and historical acts of struggle.

Particular readings of women's narratives in literature help us to reconstruct the deeper moral ethos in which differing women live. In fiction we can learn about cultural dynamics of power and clarify women's diverse experiences of moral agency and moral vision. Hence, narrative enables us to focus due attention on women's "private" experience as something related to, but distinct from, the "public" realm, because narrative, as many theorists claim, has always been

> a way of saying, not so much, "There *is* another world" as, "Another world can be imagined." When we turn from the political statements about power to the literary works that may bear upon them, we turn from the abstract to the imagined specific, and not just to specific characters in specific circumstances, but to the deeper specification of meanings through language, imagery and structure. . . . This is feminist criticism. It picks up the discord between vitality of existence and the rigidity of social myth [about women].[1]

We listen to and feel how some female characters are trying to exercise their own will and options not vicariously, but directly as moral agents.

Envisioning narrative as opening up the life-blood of a "surplus experience" that has theological and moral meaning also encourages us to look more closely at the deep ambiguities of experience within which women might move more creatively into their own experiences of power, that is, power defined as ability, competence, energy, and endurance. Jean Bethke Elshtain compellingly reminds us that the "powerful and resonant themes we associate with intimate life, themes conjured up by ordinary understanding of what it means to have a 'private life' or an 'intimate relation' lose their emotional resonance when one attempts to incorporate them into aggregate, collective nouns [such as 'class']."[2] Although stories or narratives are essential and basic to life,

---

[1]Barbara Bellow Watson, "On Power and the Literary Text," *Signs* 1, no. 1 (Autumn 1975), 112. I am indebted to her nuanced consideration of women's power in terms of literature; her discussion has enhanced my explorations of women's moral agency/power in this section.

[2]Jean Bethke Elshtain, "Feminist Discourse and Its Discontents: Language, Power and Meaning," in *Feminist Theory*, eds. Keohane and Gelpi, 138.

they are not the whole of life.[1] Fiction is an excellent medium for exploring the multiplicity of women's struggles for personhood. While I do not wish to privilege reflection on literature over other aspects of work in theological ethics, and while I recognize that literature is no substitute for forging more adequate strategies of solidarity, narrative can help us to define and clarify the commitments, obligations, and loyalties we have begun to identify. I therefore contend that by applying a critical interpretive method to narrative we gain access to culture as a source of religious ethical insight .

Criteria for a Feminist
Reading of Narrative

Adrienne Rich speaks of a feminist critique of literature which looks at narrative first of all as a clue to how we live, how we have been living, how we have been led to imagine ourselves, and how we can begin to see and name, and therefore live, afresh. "Re-vision--the act of looking back, of seeing with fresh eyes, of entering an old text from a new critical direction--is for women more than a chapter in cultural history: it is an act of survival.[2] Feminist research into a female literary heritage has uncovered an astonishing collection of material that was formerly silenced or ignored. For the most part, however, these "traditions" have been discovered and developed by white women in academic settings which have posited white, privileged female experience as universal. These presuppositions and definitions have been challenged by women outside this dominant ethos.[3]

From this marginated view, hermeneutical and aesthetic criteria cannot be understood as universal; the value of any text is not simply

---

[1]See Driver, *Patterns of Grace*, 143. For a helpful discussion of mainstream relationships between theology and narrative, see Michael Goldberg, *Theology and Narrative: A Critical Introduction* (Nashville: Abingdon Press, 1981).

[2]Rich, "When We Dead Awaken," in *On Lies, Secrets and Silences: Selected Prose, 1966-1978* (New York: W. W. Norton and Co., 1979), 35.

[3]Notable exceptions have been Tillie Olsen, Meridel Le Sueur, and Lillian Robinson; see respectively *Silences*, (New York: Delacorte Press, 1978); *Ripening: Selected Work, 1927-1980*, ed. and with an introduction by Elaine Hedges (Old Westbury, N.Y.: The Feminist Press, 1982); and *Sex, Class and Culture* (Bloomington: Indiana University Press, 1978).

there, to be swept out like snow from a porch. Literary criteria are, rather, "culturally and historically specific, produced in the act of reading."[1] Hence, my approach to literature acknowledges that race, age, sexual orientation, and class are among the important constituents of writing as well as interpretation,[2] and recognizes difference as a critical resource for discerning the meaning and value of texts. The narratives I have selected as resources for feminist theological ethics each relate the struggle of the protagonist to become a whole person.[3] Personhood is employed as a category in an ethical reading of fiction. Achievement of full personhood requires that we reflect intelligently on our obligations to others, our values, and our decisions. I have chosen narratives with female characters who are portrayed as engaged in the process of "inventing themselves." Delores Williams argues that a variety of experiences will represent this activity; for example,

> In some women's literature this process of self-invention begins when the protagonist realizes her understanding of herself has been determined by social customs, myths, and gender-role expectations designed and assigned her by males dominating the culture in which the woman participates.[4]

In the search for personhood, or processes of self-invention, women must also learn to identify power as the ambiguous root of both our agency and our oppression. For example, any definitions of women's experience must realistically portray situations in which women are oppressors, for example, white women in racist social structures.[5] Renditions of the realities of power, then, are at the heart of women's narratives. Approaching narrative as a resource for exploring the female

---

[1]Mary Eagleton, *Feminist Literary Theory: A Reader* (New York: Basil Blackwell, 1986), 4.

[2]I recommend Maggie Humm's *Feminist Criticism: Women as Contemporary Critics* (New York: St. Martin's Press, 1986) for an overview of feminist critical approaches.

[3]I describe the process of selection of the narratives in the next chapter.

[4]Williams, "Women as Makers of Literature," in *Women's Spirit Bonding*, eds. Kalven and Buckley, 139-40.

[5]Williams demonstrates how the concept of racial history in feminist theology encourages theologians to expand their definitions of women's experience; see "Black Women's Literature and The Task of Feminist Theology," 102.

experiences of both alienated and transformative power enables us to ask: What have some crucial experiences of power been like? Where have events of resistance and accommodation occurred?

Teresa De Lauretis argues that we cannot know ourselves without a broad based frame of reference in our present world. To the extent that we can see beyond and through history, by knowing women's power under very different conditions from our own, we will be able to go beyond our own personal experiences of cultural, geographic, social, and sexual displacements and be challenged and empowered by the connections we discover.[1] Importantly, the view from the margins will do most to undermine the cultural hegemony of dominant morality:

> Marginal people have their own culture, including their own moral expression, that challenges the monolithic presence of the hegemonic dominant culture. This alternative is expressed in actions that have no significance from the perspective of the center, and, as a consequence have no status as moral action. . . . The power of this view is in its recognition of subjectivity and creativity that, though unrecognized by the dominant culture, nonetheless mark the limits of that domination.[2]

In my reading of selected narratives, I will also employ the hermeneutical criteria applied by Barbara Smith to black women's literature.[3] She affirms three guidelines that have special relevance to feminist theological and ethical interpretation: a focus on relationships between girls and women; a critical stance towards compulsory heterosexuality; and attention to women's struggle to create themselves. I endorse these guidelines for the selection and criticism of narrative because they treat narratives that deal with female experience as autonomous sources of knowledge, relevance, and imagination. Above all, Smith's criteria sharpen the focus on women's marginated experience.

In interpreting narratives of women's experience, we can discern the dynamics of power most clearly in the shape that women's anger

---

[1]De Lauretis, "Feminist Studies/Critical Studies," in *Feminist Studies/Critical Studies*, 18.

[2]Smith and Valenze, "Mutuality and Marginality," 296.

[3]Barbara Smith, "Towards Black Feminist Criticism," in *All the Women are White, All the Men are Black, But Some of Us are Brave: Black Women's Studies*, eds. Gloria T. Hull, Patricia Bell Scott, and Barbara Smith (Old Westbury, New York: The Feminist Press, 1982), 157-75.

and rage takes. The militant or courageous woman not only protests her own objectification but also claims her own capacity for power as an appropriate share of available social resources; the way she breaks this ground teaches us not only about the realities of being victimized by other's power, but also instructs as to the future shifts necessary in the world's realities, if *different* women are to be empowered. Feminist criticism suggests how to forge strength in relationship. As Greta Hoffman Nemiroff states:

> Our source of power should be a generative rather than a reactive one. . . . There are sources other than raw "power over" available to those women who wish to change our conditions and to develop a collective ideology and set of short- and long-term objectives. The concept of empowerment defines us as drawing power in the form of energy from within ourselves as individuals and through our mutual and collective support as a group.[1]

The interpretive schema I have developed for the reading of narratives stresses the sources of power resisted, as well as those which are learned and shared by the female characters.

If women's consciousness is approached as a legitimate and valued source of knowledge, then expressions of female rage in narrative can signify those places where something deep is at stake in women's experience: for example, their acts to remove the crushing burdens of deadening relationships, their opposition to fragmentation, and their ability to stand up and demand conditions that offer life, not death. Anger is understood, then, as a resource for discovering what is rightfully ours and as a spark for moral agency, grounding the move to define self, and to begin the search for ethical and material criteria for social organization that will be appropriate to women's well-being. Women's rage opens the way to forms of knowledge hidden in dominant discourse, especially the means of fashioning a strong sense of self in defiance of processes which seek to objectify us, of creating and nurturing relationships and communities, and enabling women to "make do" under nearly impossible life conditions.

The importance of rage in decoding women's moral agency in literature lies also in its visceral nature: when expressed openly, anger

---

[1]Nemiroff, "On Power and Empowerment," in *Women and Men*, ed. Nemiroff, 538.

has the embodied strength to enable us to move beyond acquiescence and internalized inferiority. It belies the mind-body split and roots us in the integrity of our embodied personhood; without anger there can be no justice among us. Julia Lesage, film maker and cultural critic, articulates the necessity of understanding the different structures behind women's rage:

> Black women rage against poverty and racism at the same time that they rage against sexism. Lesbians rage against heterosexual privilege, including the denial of their civil rights. Nicaraguan women rage against invasions and the aggressive intentions of the United States. If, in our political work, we know this anger and the structures that generate it, we can more genuinely encounter each other and more extensively acknowledge each others' needs, class position, and specific form of oppression. If we do not understand the unique social conditions shaping our sisters' rage, we run the risk of divisiveness, of fragmenting our potential solidarity. Such mutual understanding of the different structures behind different women's anger is the precondition of our finding a way to work together toward common goals.[1]

Conclusion

What narrative offers is a representation of the world from the varied standpoints in which women engage the moral possibilities of becoming subjects of their particular lives. The critical cultural method that I will apply to selected narratives can be used ethically and theologically within the dialogue between our own experiences and those of more marginated women whose voices must be heard to test the moral and religious depth of our own. We need this knowledge to strengthen our critique of dominant cultural hegemony, as well as to form alternative visions and create strategies aimed at viable alternatives to them. From the process of reading fiction we glimpse authentic female personhood: women who in the end may stand alone but strong and spiritually sustained; women who are on their feet and not on their knees; women who are pleased with themselves and trust what they know because a broader purpose guides them; women who are not despairing but look forward with hope in the future; women who see life as a

---

[1]Julia Lesage, "Women's Rage," in *Marxism and the Interpretation of Culture*, eds. Cary Nelson and L. Grossberg (Urbana and Chicago: University of Illinois Press, 1988), 420.

meaningful whole based on a vision of love, in spite of pain, obstacles and defeats, and therefore affirm a life where female suffering can be transformed and experiences of contentment and wholeness enjoyed.[1] In three Canadian novels we will meet women's varied struggles for moral agency. The next chapter belongs to them.

---

[1]I am indebted to Geraldine Finn's excellent summary of a normative stance for women's well-being; see "Feminism and Fiction: In Praise of *Praxis*, Beyond *Bodily Harm*," in *Socialist Studies: A Canadian Annual* (1983), 51-77.

CHAPTER FIVE

ELIDED VOICES IN CANADIAN WOMEN'S FICTION: HEARING WOMEN'S COMMITMENTS TO AUTHENTIC LIFE

Introduction

This chapter represents my own effort to live into the question: How do white women of certain privilege learn from and respect *difference* among women, so that making justice is a *common* vision and shared task? In the next chapter I will examine a related question: How is this task theologically significant?

My selection of women's voices in literature from or related to the Canadian prairies is rooted in the context where I do theological ethics. I have also chosen the three narratives to portray a spectrum of women's struggles to become subjects of their own lives. These novels are selected, following the criteria for a feminist materialist approach to culture, because they bring to life marginalized women's suffering and hope, and depict strategies of survival and sustenance for their well-being. The struggles of the female protagonists I focus on here vary because of their diverse life circumstances affected by racial, ethnic and class histories. Nevertheless, the narratives share some common ground: they touch the heart, compel the intellect, stir the imagination and suggest more fruitful ways of life for women. In attending to these stories I will exemplify a method for a cultural resource base necessary for a multi-dimensional theological ethic that is grounded in women's varied experiences of claiming their own lives as moral agents.

Selection of Texts

I have already made clear the basic criteria of a feminist liberation position that led me to select texts for a literary portrayal of varied
positions of outsiderhood. My search for Canadian cultural resources
uncovered a large number of such literary works. I began my research
by tracing a literary tradition of Canadian women writers starting with
Frances Brooke's novel, *The History of Emily Montague*, set in Quebec
City in 1796. Once I established the general contours of women's writing in Canada, I read those novels and short story collections that
promised to depict female characters questing after their own lives,
struggling to break out of their suffering and silence. In this process I
discovered a growing body of women's literature that expresses both an
authentically Canadian imagination and an authoritatively female perspective.[1] I discovered the truth of Margaret Laurence's contention
that a firmly Canadian fiction was not produced until many generations
after the country gained its nationhood in 1867:

> Canadian writers, like African writers, have had to find our own voices and
> write out of what is truly ours, in the face of overwhelming cultural imperial-
> ism . . . [Although in] Canada our dilemma was . . . more subtle . . . we
> remained colonial for many years. In literary terms, our models remained
> those of the British and more recently of America.[2]

Because a decidedly Canadian consciousness emerged only in the second half of this century, I decided to concentrate on women's fiction
after World War II.

Following the lead of feminist criticism I have adopted an approach that willingly expands the recognized literary canon; that is, I
do not look upon literary tradition as a continuum of "classics." Instead I have been involved in a search for alternatives to mainstream

---

[1]For example, I recommend the work of these Canadian authors: Edna
Alford, Margaret Atwood, Joan Barfoot, Marie-Claire Blais, Sandra Birdsell,
Sharon Butala, Anne Cameron, Beatrice Culleton, Marion Engel, Betty Lambert,
Alice Munro, Helen Potrebenko, Gabrielle Roy, Jane Rule, Lois Simmie, Donna
Smyth, Gertrude Story, Audrey Thomas, Ethel Wilson, Christine Van der Mark,
Aritha Van Hirk, Adele Wiseman.

[2]Laurence, in *Canadian Novelists and the Novel*, eds. Daymond and
Monkman, 253-54.

texts, for ones which foreground the critical questions, experiences, and visions arising from marginated voices. The value of any text, therefore, is created in terms of its ability to open up possible lives beyond what Carolyn Heilbrun has called "the blunted female destiny."[1] I have discussed how my criteria of difference, diversity, and self-invention would render some fiction more relevant than others for a liberative feminist social ethic. From a group of some thirty authors I narrowed my selection to three narratives. Beatrice Culleton, Joy Kogawa, and Margaret Laurence all depict female characters who were formed in what Audre Lorde calls "the crucible of *difference*," those women who stand outside the circle of society's definition of acceptable women, those who are poor, who are lesbian, who are Black, who are indigenous, who are older.[2] Since Canadian history is rife with examples of exploitation and subjugation of native peoples and working class immigrant groups by dominant classes, it should not be surprising that I have found only a handful of published sources from the most marginalized women.[3] There is, however, a strong body of literature from the perspective of white impoverished, often rural, women who present alternative and resistant interpretations of the dominant ethos. Among them, Margaret Laurence is exemplary.

In order not only to dwell on narratives from the margins but also to imagine a conversation among them about common ground women might share as moral agents, I have selected these three diverse voices: Beatrice Culleton's *In Search of April Raintree*, Joy Kogawa's

---

[1]Carolyn Heilbrun, *Writing A Woman's Life* (New York: W. W. Norton and Co., 1988), 51.

[2]Lorde, "The Master's Tools will Never Dismantle the Master's House," in *Sister Outsider*, 112. In Canada, indigenous women are the most invisible and oppressed.

[3] Besides Joy Kogawa's *Obasan* and Beatrice Culleton's *In Search of April Raintree*, I know of no novel-length works. Maria Campbell's *Halfbreed* (Toronto: McLelland and Stewart, 1973; reprint ed., Halifax: Goodread Biographies, 1983) is her Metis autobiography, and Jeanette Armstrong's *Slash* (Penticton, B. C.: Theytus Books, 1985) is written for adolescents. Short stories by indigenous or minority women can be found in journals such as *Fireweed* or in collections such as The Fictive Collective, ed., *Baker's Dozen: Stories by Women* (Toronto: The Women's Press, 1984); Rosemary Sullivan, ed., *Stories by Canadian Women* (Toronto: Oxford University Press, 1984); and Lorris Elliott, ed., *Other Voices: Writings by Blacks in Canada* (Toronto: Williams Wallace, 1985).

Obasan, and Margaret Laurence's *The Diviners*.[1] All three works emerge from the prairies. This limited scope enabled me to use resources set in my present work situation at a prairie theological college. This geographical frame of reference makes it possible for me to test the dictum guiding a liberationist hermeneutic, that we best approach the universal by way of the particular. The method of rooting ourselves in our own particularities and struggles towards solidarity is thus embedded in the design of this chapter even as it aims to hear women's voices in their specificity.

The dictum to start with the particular also functions to remind me of the different levels at which I enter this task of reading women's literature. In terms of Canadian culture I subscribe to the view, well-articulated by Malcolm Ross, that "a national identity which demands cultural uniformity is the opposite of authentic unity. . . . Nationalism as a substitute for religion is worse than empty. It is a blasphemy." Ross also points out that the imaginative sense of the Canadian artist responds to the uniqueness of regions and localities--and this is the key issue here--which "serve to illuminate the larger sense we begin to have of ourselves in all our diversity. . . . [E]ach region as it grows in social and cultural and racial complexity, incarnates in varying degrees a Canadian-ness, at once precarious and propitious, which is born of the tensions that interplay and interact in the national life."[2] In short, the best avenue for articulating and addressing "difference" as a constructive element in Canadian consciousness can be explored by way of regional identity and diversity, in this case, the prairies. Happily, even with this *regional* focus, the cross-cultural dimension of Canadian experience is illuminated in the narratives chosen, which reflect the indigenous Metis, the white pioneer settler, and the more recent Japanese minority-immigrant identities.

Historically the prairies have demanded that women be self-reliant and inter-dependent, as aboriginal women or immigrant pioneers,

---

[1]Beatrice Culleton, *In Search of April Raintree* (Winnipeg: Pemmican Publication 1983); Joy Kogawa, *Obasan* (Toronto: Lester and Orpen Denys, 1981; reprint ed., Markha Penguin, 1982); and Margaret Laurence, *The Diviners* (Toronto: McLelland and Stewart, 1974; reprint ed., New York: Bantam Windstone, 1982).

[2]Malcolm Ross, "The Imaginative Sense and the Canadian Question," *Mosaic* 9, no. 1 (Fall 1977), 1-13.

evacuees or migrants, in rural areas or small towns.[1] The politics of this region have shaped and sustained a hope for socialist vision throughout Canada in which, as I noted in chapters two and three, women are key actors in church and state. For example, the first woman officially recognized as a minister of Word and Sacrament in the only indigenous church, the United Church of Canada, was Lydia Gruchy, a prairie woman who was ordained in Moose Jaw, Saskatchewan in 1936. These historical features of the prairie blend well as context and sub-text for exploring marginalized women's voices in a region that is itself marginalized within the Canada.

Nevertheless, a wealth of fiction written by women from the prairies did not fit my criteria as well as those that I chose.[2] Each of the works of fiction selected establishes a distinct female voice from the margins of Canadian life and focuses sharply on issues of moral agency specific to the protagonist's cultural history. I did not select Beatrice Culleton's *In Search of April Raintree* for its literary quality. Its style is not distinguished by traditional standards, its characters are not complex or finely developed, and its plot is perhaps too simple. I selected this novel, nevertheless, because it gives us a clearly rendered Metis woman's point of view. Its monumental value lies in Culleton's "breaking silence" to tell a story that has not been told before. Her protagonist represents those women of indigenous heritage who have been exponentially oppressed in Canada. Joy Kogawa is a powerful Japanese-Canadian literary voice. Her novel has received accolades for its fine design. It is a brilliant testimony by a poet and lay theologian to her people's spirit and effort to survive with dignity. Margaret

---

[1]Linda Rasmussen, Lorna Rasmussen, Candace Savage, and Anne Wheeler, eds., *A Harvest Yet to Reap: A History of Prairie Women* (Toronto: The Women's Press, 1976); Dolores and Irene Poelzer, *In Our Own Words: Northern Saskatchewan Metis Women Speak Out* (Saskatoon: Lindenblatt and Hamonic Publishing Inc., 1986).

[2]In preparing my selection I discovered 15 to 20 creative writers, many still active in the region. Some of these artists do not write novels, preferring to create plays or short stories. Barbara Sapergia and Sandra Birdsell are examples. From the fiction explored I could have chosen at least five other authors or over 12 works. On the prolific development of creative writing in this region, see Birk Sproxton, ed., *Trace: Prairie Writers on Writing* (Winnipeg: Turnstone Press, 1986), and E. F. Dyck, ed., *Essays on Saskatchewan Writing* (Regina: The Saskatchewan Writers Guild, 1986).

Laurence's *The Diviners* is the last of her Manawaka series about prairie women's struggles to create themselves. This novel is a skillful construction from within rural white culture depicted from a doubly marginated voice, that of a poor woman and an artist.

Obviously not all women's experience is represented in my selection, but taken together these three voices provide a valuable prism of marginalized female experience. The authors of the three novels also have feminist backbones. Each tells a story of a woman who strives for a life beyond those structures that demoralize and crush girls and women. It is my hope that my reading of these narratives coheres with the basic stance of each novel. In the words of Nancy Miller, I aim "to articulate a self-consciousness about women's identity both as inherited cultural fact and as process of social construction"[1] and to hold up women's lives in fiction that protest the failures of cultures and societies to make women visible in their struggles to author their own lives.

The protagonists defy the dominant cultural conventions, learn to risk all for the sake of their own souls, and forge lives of meaning and purpose even if it means standing alone. At each story's close they stand on their own terms. They are not male-defined, auxiliary, or helpless. These protagonists protest the limits of female existence lived under various constraints of racism, ethnocentrism, class elitism, and misogyny.[2] A tenacious energy and insight characterize these fictional creations; they are not nice or sweet or without negative personal features. Rather they are seriously human and struggle to know and live fully into the possibilities of their own particular lives as creative participants in shaping their own destinies. These narratives develop critical standpoints outside the dominant culture from Metis, Japanese-Canadian, poor, rural, and older female perspectives. All three treat a common theme--how women come to terms with their roots, ancestors, and life on the prairies--and in the process discover spiritual empowerment and a sense of social belonging.

---

[1]Quoted by Carolyn Heilbrun to define *feminist* in *Writing a Woman's Life*, 18.

[2] In my search for resources by or from marginalized women's perspectives, I found few fictional voices from lesbian women and no lesbian authors from the Canadian prairies. Attention in fiction to homophobia and heterosexism as cripplers of all women's lives is thus woefully absent in this study. For Canadian lesbian voices, see Jane Rule and Marie-Claire Blais.

Especially in my reading of the two novels by racial-ethnic women, I have followed Delores Williams' method in her engagement of Black women's religious narratives, and attended to their work of "inventing themselves."[1] Combining Culleton's and Kogawa's main themes with Williams's interpretive framework, we find that three actions are involved in the process of self-invention: assessment of the past, lamentation, and affirmation of faith and hope. These three actions are indeed portrayed in the characters of April Raintree and Naomi Nakane. The authors render these actions as necessary for the development of both main characters. Williams also names three areas of the multidimensional assault on Black women: upon their reproductive and nurturing functions; upon their self-esteem; and upon women's right to choose and maintain positive, fulfilling and productive relationships. In varying degrees these experiences are also narrated by Culleton and Kogawa.[2]

My exposition will also explore the varied representations of the sufferings and sources of hope that the characters experience. I will conclude the chapter with key learnings--the metaphors and images discovered in these readings--for use in constructive theological formulations that are accountable to the varied positions of female outsiderhood. The narratives may judge or nudge, enliven or rebuke, but they also offer a "purposive sense of vocation" and can give us clues for prioritizing our own norms and values, and for identifying concrete goals in the forging of a common life. I will return to these matters in the final chapter.

---

[1]On this process, see Williams, "Women's Oppression and Lifeline Politics in Black Women's Religious Narratives," 59-71; "Black Women's Literature and the Task of Feminist Theology" in *Immaculate and Powerful*, eds. Atkinson et al., 88-110; "Women as Makers of Literature," in *Women's Spirit Bonding*, eds. Kalven and Buckley, 139-45.

[2]Williams, "Women as Makers of Literature," in *Women's Spirit Bonding*, eds. Kalven and Buckley, 142; also "Women's Oppression and Lifeline Politics," 62 ff.

Themes of Suffering and Empowerment: The Prairie, [Dis]placement, and Ancestors

The literary portrayal of these varied lives of outsiderhood weave the stories of suffering with a common struggle to come to terms with the land and the place of the characters' heritage. While not a concern peculiar to Canadian fiction, this search for a living tradition, a felt presence, is a central struggle in the creation of voices that have been silenced or trivialized within national or group identities. Moreover, "the land" is a cultural code in most discussions about tribal, national, and regional sovereignty. Whether the land is blessing or curse, it has thoroughly structured the Canadian imagination and context. For example, while the indigenous peoples and early *coureurs de bois* inhabited the vast Canadian landscape pursuing natural resources of fur and fish, the first generation of pioneers had to conquer themselves, often with Calvinist repression, in order to conquer the land. Contemporary fiction writers, including those I am discussing, are involved from different cultural vantage points in reexamining their ancestors' attempts to make themselves at home on the land and in society.[1]

The search for a past where women and children matter, despite all historical evidence to the contrary, is a dominant motif throughout the chosen narratives. These writers dig deep into their particular plots of prairie soil to discover the roots of female presence. Their re-search is urgent. Without this knowledge the characters cannot know and claim their own contemporary value or significance. Their fictionalized identity quests are metaphors for their larger groups' survival and empowerment.

Each author explores the context of the prairie and the sense of horizon, destiny and community that needs to be both confronted for its oppressive elements and embraced for its liberative events. As the characters redeem what is possible from their heritage, they also participate in their own salvation: authorizing themselves and a different vision of the world.

---

[1]For a discussion of contemporary fiction from the prairies, see Dick Harrison, "Re-Naming the Past," in *Unnamed Country: The Struggle for a Canadian Prairie Fiction* (Edmonton: University of Alberta Press, 1977), 183-213.

To Say Different: Beatrice Culleton's
In Search of April Raintree[1]

Beatrice Culleton is an indigenous Canadian voice who writes
from her experience in the Metis community, people of mixed ancestry, "a little of this and a whole lot of Indian." *In Search of April
Raintree* is a metaphor of the near genocidal experience of the Metis of
the prairies. Even the fact of its publication attests a concerted effort
of the Metis to survive: it saw the light of day in 1983 only when published by a Manitoba press dedicated to Metis work. On the book's
cover Margaret Laurence confirms, "one cannot read this moving account of two Metis sisters without feeling terrible anguish, bewilder-
ment and anger as they try in their different ways to live in a society
that frequently rejects and abuses them, as it has rejected and abused
their parents and ancestors," thus preparing the reader for a story that
is "a tragic one, yet [signaling that] its final outcome is one of affirmation and bitterly won resolve."

Another back-cover endorsement cites Gertrude Stein's advice:
"All you have to do is write one true sentence. Write the truest sentence that you know." The critic advises us that *In Search of April
Raintree* has been written with exactly that sort of unflinching honesty
in a prose and attitude Stein would admire. Even though I sometimes
found the style artless, the novel defies literary categories of high culture by the more urgent need to break silence about the lived consequences and the real distortions and dehumanization resulting from the
intersection of race, gender, class, and cultural oppression.

The theme of struggle saturates the book's 230 pages, as the account unfolds of the lives of two sisters, Cheryl and April Raintree, and
of a people nearly destroyed by alcohol and drug dependency, rejection, and all manner of abuse. Related in April's first person narrative
voice, the story focuses on the immediacy of the two main characters'
struggles to discover and create themselves. The novel recounts the
lives of the two sisters beginning with their removal, while still under
the age of five, from their alcoholic parents. They were made wards of

---

[1]"I just stood there meekly, too scared to say different." Beatrice Culleton, *In Search of April Raintree* (Winnipeg: Pemmican Publications, 1983), 43; all
references from this edition and subsequently indicated in parentheses in text.

the state by the Winnipeg Children's Aid Society. Cheryl is initially well-placed, first with a Metis foster mother with whom she can be a happy child who learns to be proud of her Indian heritage, and then in a middle class home. Armed with a sense of security and well-versed in middle-class mores, she later wins a scholarship to university, studies social work, and fights for her people's dignity and rights.

April is also placed briefly in a kind and loving foster home but is later moved to a cruel and uncomprehending one. As she realizes that her misery is caused largely by reactions to her race, she determines to hide her native ancestry and blend into white society. She diligently pursues her education and becomes a legal secretary, marries a wealthy Toronto business man, and, after the marriage breaks down, returns to Winnipeg to make a new life with her sister. April discovers that Cheryl, the student of social work and Metis advocate, has made contact with their father who had long ago disappeared; he is without self-respect and lives on skid row. Cheryl has also started to drink and now supports herself by prostitution. After a series of revelations about their parents' destinies and the horrific event of April's rape, the novel closes with April, sobered but strong, holding in her arms Cheryl's child, her nephew, a symbol of hope for the future. Hence in the end April stands, strengthened by her ordeals. She has confronted and faced the ugly truth of her family's demise and she has found a core of self-respect that integrates the liberative elements of Metis history and culture.

Underscoring the origins of the Metis, the audience for the narrative is culturally mixed. At times only the dominant group is addressed--"white Man, to you my voice is like the unheard call in the wilderness. It is there, though you do not hear. But, this once, take time to listen to what I have to say" (168). While the Metis are recognized as one of Canada's Native peoples, their historical and moral significance needs to be explicated. "In a sense [the Metis] are the epitome of Canadian history, a mingling of the blood and traditions of Europe with the aboriginal people of this continent. Their search for the undiscovered conscience of their race, therefore, is an important one."[1] It is unsurprising that April's search for identity is largely directed to coming to terms with the Metis people and their struggle

---

[1]Paul Wilson, "First Novels," *Books in Canada* (February 1984), 30.

against obliteration, but neither can she avoid the white culture. We hear her lament:

> It would be better to be a full-blooded Indian or a full-blooded Caucasian. But being a half-breed, well, there's nothing there. You can admire Indian people for what they once were. They had a distinct heritage or is it culture? Anyway, you can see how much was taken away from them. And white people, well, they've convinced each other they are the superior race and you can see they are responsible for the progress today. Cheryl once said, "The meek shall inherit the Earth. Big deal, because who's going to want it once the whites are through with it?" So the progress is questionable. . . . But what have the Metis people got? Being a half-breed, you only feel the short-comings of both sides. You feel you're a part of the drunken Indians you see on Main Street. And if you inherit brown skin like Cheryl did, you identify with the Indian people more. . . . And when people say off-handedly, "Oh, you shouldn't be ashamed of being a Metis," well, generally they haven't a clue what it's like being a native person (156-57).

The external constraints on Metis people and their dilemmas of identity clearly unfold through the relationship of April and Cheryl and the different choices each makes to survive. April's lighter skin influences her decision to deny her background and seek security in a quiet, private, non-conflictual existence. Her earliest self-conscious strategy for survival was to remain silent and wait until she was released into adult responsibility at age eighteen:

> When I grew up I wouldn't be poor. I'd be rich. Being a half-breed meant being poor and dirty. It meant being weak and having to drink. It meant being ugly and stupid. It meant living off white people. And giving your children to white people to look after. It meant to take all the crap white people gave. Well I wasn't going to be a half-breed. When I got free of this place, when I got free of being a foster child, then I would live just like a real white person (49).

In the hope of realizing this dream, April marries a wealthy white businessman and moves with him to Toronto--only to learn that she was a pawn in his unresolved family problems. This false hope in freedom granted by someone other than herself continues to deceive April until she comes to grips with her own need to embrace the truth of her Metis heritage and, in full recognition of this fact, forge her own life.

Unlike April, her younger sister, Cheryl, with her father's Ojibway features and dark skin, cannot try to ignore her roots. When placed in a Metis foster home Cheryl is given a foothold into reclaiming her own life through learning with pride of her people's history, especially the freedom fighter Louis Riel. While April explains to her sister that "I can't accept being a Metis . . . being Metis means I'm one of the have-nots, and I want so much . . . what white society can give me" (111), Cheryl responds with an alternative vision of survival: "And I decided that I was going to do what I could to turn the native image around so that one day you could be proud of being Metis" (111). Cheryl represents "the stalk in the field of grain which never bent to authority. At the same time, that stalk could bend to the gentle breezes of compassion" (121). We are stunned, therefore, by the tragic irony of the novel when this sister, Cheryl, who constantly finds hope in being "aware of who we are, what we are, and what's been happening to us" (120) is dead at the end of the narrative.

Throughout the novel one is reminded of the twenty-four year old narrator's opening lines:

> Memories. Some memories are elusive, fleeting, like a butterfly that touches down and is free until it is caught. Others are haunting. You'd rather forget them but they won't be forgotten. And some are always there. No matter where you are, they are there, too. I always felt most of my memories were better avoided but now I think it's best to go back in my life before I go forward (9).

At the outset Culleton establishes the theme of the protagonist coming to terms with her heritage through an act of critical remembrance, and consistently relates April's initial denial and search alongside of her sister Cheryl's choices. In short, the stories of April and Cheryl Raintree represent two coping strategies. They are not only victims; they are also resisters.[1] Each sister creates a vision of survival in the process of resisting many emotional and physical assaults, and each takes active steps to create and sustain community.

The reader is told little about their mother, Alice Raintree. She worked as a housekeeper for the priest in her home town before mov-

---

[1] Margaret Clarke, in "Revisioning April Raintree," *Prairie Fire* 7, no. 3 (Autumn 1986), 136, 138-42, stresses victimization in her reading of this text. While I agree with her that violence against women is at the book's core, I do not conclude that women are simply victims. I also contend that Culleton's characters serve as prototypes, representing different forms of victim and agent. Thus I interpret each character in terms of her options for resisting victimization, such that April and Cheryl are sometimes pro-active for their own and others' well-being.

ing to Winnipeg. She and her husband Henry are loving parents, but alcoholism leads to the breakup of the family when the state the intervenes. Her powerlessness to alter her fate or her children's, and the erosion of the father's self-respect and loss of his traditional trapper's role in an urban environment, are both placed in sharp contrast with the power of the Children's Aid institution. The damage done to the girls' mother is disclosed only near the end of the book: "She jumped off the Louise Bridge. . . . Committed suicide. You know why she stopped seeing us? Because she couldn't bear the pain" (198).

One shudders as April and Cheryl are taken from their birth parents and forced to live in foster homes, some of them utterly dehumanizing. The sisters' lives represent generations of Metis, "because we don't have very many choices" (171). For example, at the orphanage April's long hair is cut off, symbolizing the attempt to destroy the power of her ancestral connection and to impose the standards of white culture. This child's early years typify the historical conditions that silence the Metis. April, like her people, survives by consciously adopting a position of silence, remaining quiet and doing well in her work at the Catholic school.

> Eventually, I figured out what the different nuns wanted and avoided many scoldings. My parents had never strapped us and I never had to think about whether I was bad or good. I feared being ridiculed in front of the other children, I feared getting the strap, I feared even getting a harsh word. When I was quietly playing with some toy, and somebody else wanted it, I simply handed it over. I longed to go over to Cheryl and talk and play with her but I never dared cross that invisible boundary (19).

It is through her childhood recollections that one senses, except for her first foster home, a young girl's overwhelming burden of isolation and vulnerability, of loneliness and passivity because she is stranded in a chain of hostile environments over which she has no power.

Another of April's placements, in the loving home of the Dion family, inspires some hope for her life; she has a totally different experience with this family because she is warmly included and accepted. Her deep fear of life, caused by abandonment and cruel treatment, begins to subside. All too abruptly, however, the love and security ends--the foster mother is diagnosed with a terminal illness. This scene closes to signal the hand of fate brutally ending all possibility of appropriate care for a small Metis child.

April is sent next to the DeRosier farm, where the domineering foster mother pours out all the rage she has felt as a rural woman onto April, the obvious scapegoat. April remains docile in order to survive the cruelty. For many years, she functions as a servant before and after school. Ordered to cook, clean, do farm chores, sleep in a miserable back room, she is ridiculed with names like "Gramma Squaw" and taunted about her clothes, intelligence, hair and heritage by foster family and schoolmates alike. The narrative of April's physical coercion and humiliation creates a mood of unrelieved gloom, establishing the instances and weight of victimization she experiences.

The reader cannot help but wonder how this child survives the lies, hate and loneliness she endures. April prays, which includes expressing anger at her circumstances to God. While saying the Lord's prayer for comfort one night she decides that she has done nothing so wrong as to deserve the brutal treatment she receives at home and school alike; rather, *she* is being tested and ought to think of herself as "saintly" (42). Such inner spunk helps her to endure. She also fantasizes reunions with her family. But one day the DeRosier children accurately caricature her parents as drunkards; April charges across the grain fields in a rage of denial. The incident functions, however, as a revelation in her ten year old imagination. No longer could she believe her parents would recover from their sickness and reunite their family. Immediately following her apprehension of this truth, we discover one source of the hope that sustains April's tormented life. That source is her relation to nature:

> I got up and started walking back to the house because I still had floors to wash. I stopped and thought, "No. Why should I? They can beat me if they want to. . . ." I turned back into the woods and made my way through the heavy underbrush. I don't know how far I walked before I came upon a small clearing which bordered the Red River. The sunlight filtered through the towering trees, warming even the shady spots. The area was alive with the sounds of birds, squirrels and bugs. But I felt at peace . . . (48).

April is able to visit with Cheryl infrequently. She envies Cheryl's foster situation with a Metis family. The relationship between the sisters is central to the narrative. Often it is April's faith in Cheryl that keeps her going. When the sisters are reunited in an exploitative foster home, it is Cheryl who takes courage and lets her anger surface in successful rebellion. April, too, temporarily abandons her state of self-control. "From the day she arrived, I changed. I was more alert and openly defiant towards the DeRosiers, sending them silent warnings to leave my sister alone" (55). While they collude in protecting one another from the truth--April never acknowledges their parents' alcoholism to her innocent sister, the racist accusations of stealing, or the rumors of Cheryl's sexual promiscuity at school--their bond above all is the key source of strength and courage to continue through the nearly hopeless times.

In the context of being oppressed as a Native child, April decides she would rather be white:

> I felt torn in different directions and often changed my mind regarding my parents. . . . So what if we were poor and lived in slums. Being together would be a million times better that living on this horrible farm. Other times, I would remind myself that my parents were weak alcoholics who had made their choice. And then I would loathe them. Or I would think of the Dions and all their religious teachings. What was the sense of praying to a God who didn't care about me either? Oh Cheryl, it was still the question of how I was going to live as a white person with her around. . . . Seven years [at the DeRosiers] of not having control of my own life (52).

Culleton underscores this confusion of values in her young protagonist by juxtaposing April's insecurity with Cheryl's confidence. Cheryl is the sister who learned through a liberal education to be proud of her ancestry and outspoken against injustice done to her people. On one birthday visit she enthusiastically gives April a book about Louis Riel.[1] April's disgusted reaction is one of an internalized white racism: she thinks of Riel as a rebel hanged for treason, a savage who had no bearing on her life at all. "Worse, he had been a crazy half-breed" (44).

Cheryl's foster mother encourages her to learn about Metis history. She translates this subversive knowledge into a solid pride in her difference. She slaps children who insult her and fights back in the classroom when the teacher expresses the views April had internalized:

---

[1] Louis Riel was the political and religious leader of the Metis in two rebellions in what was then the Northwest Territories. The first, in 1871, resulted in the foundation of the province of Manitoba. The second, in 1885 in what is now Saskatchewan, resulted in the conquest and "diaspora" of the Metis and the confinement of Indians on reserves. For a creative study of Riel, see Douglas Daniels, "Louis Riel and Liberation Theology," in *The Ecumenist* 25, no. 3 (March-April 1987), 33-36.

> If this is history, how come so many Indian tribes were wiped out? How come they haven't got their land anymore? How come their food supplies were wiped out? Lies! lies! lies! Your history books don't say how the white people destroyed the Indian way of life. That's all you white people can do is teach a bunch of lies to cover your own tracks! (57).

While April is trying to fit into white culture, Cheryl is learning all she can about the history of her people and drawing strength from her discoveries. Cheryl's honest thinking stands in sharp contrast to the mind set of one of the girls' white social worker, Mrs. Semple. Regularly shunted as faceless cases through bureaucratic channels, the girls at one point are placed in the hands of this destructive social worker who verbally abuses them with a speech about the "native girl syndrome":

> . . . you girls are headed in that direction. It starts with the fighting, the running away, the lies. Next come the accusations that everyone in the world is against you. There are the sullen uncooperative silences, the feeling sorry for yourselves. And when you go on your own, you get pregnant right away or can't find or keep jobs. So you'll start with alcohol and drugs. From there, you get into shoplifting and prostitution and in and out of jails. You'll live with men who abuse you. And on it goes. You'll end up like your parents, living off society (67).

This threat implanted fear in April. It would continue to haunt her and later to chip away at Cheryl's pride and hope for change. In response to the debasing stereotype with which Mrs. Semple verbally whips them, April resolutely tells Cheryl: "This won't last forever. When we're old enough, we'll be free. We'll live together. We're going to make it. . . . We are not going to become what they expect of us" (68-69). April even tries to sustain this spirit by reading Cheryl's essay on Louis Riel and the Red River Insurrection, but it only reinforces her belief that if she could assimilate into white society, she would be free.

The contradictions of race within her intensify as she considers her future options. "I bet those girls who ended up on skid row just wanted freedom and peace in the first place. Just like me" (86). Her statement foreshadows the theme of the odds against remaking history, a theme that is later presented in a university paper of Cheryl's: "The Metis were an independent breed. Freedom lovers--but we don't have that kind of life . . . because we don't have very many choices" (171).

April secures some measure of independence by completing high school and, typically for her class upbringing and female conditioning, sets her sights to work as a legal secretary. One senses the determination and will necessary to accomplish on her own what other young Metis women rarely did. She is successful, moves into her own apartment, and begins searching the streets of Winnipeg for her parents. In a few months April turns her back on the dream of family relatedness because the reality of Metis life she discovers disgusts her. She quits the search. From then on she decides to erase her family and, one supposes above all, her Metis origins from her past.

April's next decision moves her toward this goal. When she receives a proposal of marriage from Bob Radcliff, a visiting businessman she met at work, she accepts and moves with him to Toronto. By this strategy April achieves a new identity, complete with financial security, an upper middle class life, and volunteer work in charitable organizations. The contradictions of race, class, and gender deepen, however, as her relationship with her mother-in-law, Barbara Radcliff, symbolizes an ongoing saga of being ordered about, obeying and feeling empty, alone, restless, and useless. Her dream of establishing her own nuclear family is also dashed.

When Cheryl visits April, it becomes apparent that while April was comfortable, surrounded by socially prominent people, she did not belong. Cheryl's presence awakens in April a yearning to "live by her own approval, not that of others. Just like Cheryl. . . . She had a reason for being. She was her own person" (122-24). The formerly ignored racism of April's new white home and community surfaces. Two incidents bring her exclusion to completion. Once her native ancestry becomes clear as a result of Cheryl's visit, her mother-in-law expresses fear that she might have "brown-skinned babies." In addition, April learns of her husband's affair with a woman of whom his mother had formerly disapproved, but now condones. Thus, April's capacity to assimilate into white culture is dealt a further harsh blow. She has been used by the three persons she had trusted--by Bob, who married her to avenge his mother's rejection of the woman he wanted to marry; by his white ruling class mother, who saw April only as an extension of herself and then, in complicity with her son, as someone to be discarded; and also by a woman she had considered a friend, who wanted merely to get close to her husband. Anger spurs her into action: "With my face burning hotly and my heart thumping like a war drum, I headed downstairs to confront them. They were both surprised and off-balance when I stepped out on the terrace to face them" (126).

April recovers her spirit and sues for an ample divorce settlement. Gaining her ground, though, required her to rely on Cheryl
again. An encounter during their Toronto reunion clarifies the different values and terms of behaviour operating in both sisters' lives:

> [April confesses] "I am ashamed. . . . I can't accept being a Metis. That's
> the hardest thing I've ever said to you, Cheryl. And I'm glad you don't feel
> the same way I do. I'm so proud of what you're trying to do. But to me,
> being Metis means I'm one of the have-nots. And I want so much. . . . I
> want what white society can give me." [Cheryl responds] "And I decided
> that I was going to do what I could to turn the native image around so that
> one day you could be proud of being Metis" (110-11).

The sisters thus confront the truth of their lives. It clarifies the strategy
each has adopted in order to claim agency over their futures.

Although April successfully sues her husband for a sizable divorce settlement, she gains control of her life and a sense of herself by
returning to secretarial work. April and Cheryl have kept in touch by
mail, Cheryl sporadically relaying news of her work towards a social
work degree. Communication is cut off, however, when April's letters
are returned, addressee unknown. The mystery continues for some
months until April receives a call from a Winnipeg hospital announcing
that Cheryl had been admitted, quite drunk and badly beaten.

April leaves Toronto to be with her sister. One shares her shock
when she learns that Cheryl had many months ago quit school and let
her connection with the Friendship Centre lapse; in fact, Cheryl had
been living with an abusive man and had no life of her own left. What
had severed this strong and passionate woman's hold on life? Cheryl
explains to April her demise in terms of shattered hope: Cheryl had
finally located their father and, instead of meeting the warrior she had
always imagined, discovered a worn-out alcoholic. Cheryl feels
ashamed, defeated, her ideals crushed; she gives up on her dream of a
self-respecting and self-reliant Metis people.

After a period of convalescence in the home April bought for the
sisters to share, Cheryl identifies how their different truths have con-
verged: "I was right about it not working out for you in Toronto and
you were right when you said the native people have to be willing to
help themselves. It's like trying to swim against a strong current. It's
impossible" (136). After the shock of Cheryl's destitution, April now
moves deeper into facing the chasm inside herself created by her twin

ancestry. She begins to resist the strong current of denial of who she really is. Critical consciousness for her begins when she identifies with her heritage and what that means to her:

> I'm a Metis. . . . It would be better to be a full-blooded Indian or a full-blooded Caucasian. But being a half-breed, well, there's just nothing there. . . . In today's society, there isn't anything positive about them that I've seen (156-57).

This tragic assessment comes only after April has returned to Winnipeg and confronted Cheryl's dissolution. April, however, still has the full extent of Cheryl's victimization to learn, and it will come at perilous cost to herself.

Horribly, the relationship between the sisters damns them both before it is fully restored. But critical consciousness of her history was not a sufficiently deep reorientation for April to live her own life. The depth of violence perpetrated against native women is depicted by her brutal gang rape. The denouement of the novel occurs when a group of white men, looking for Cheryl who was known to them as a prostitute, mistake April for her sister and savagely attack her. A white woman, the former girlfriend of the man Cheryl lives with, had told the gang to punish Cheryl for taking her boyfriend away. April was on her way to visit Cheryl when this gang mistakenly identified her as the woman against whom they had the vendetta. The rape scene renders the total violation of April *as a native woman* at the hands of white men. The violence meted out on April represents the forces of white men and women colluding against the sexualized Other. Culleton's use of this metaphor also reveals that the evil of the act against a Metis woman is the same as the damage done by the near genocide of her people. The rapists' language indicates the inseparability of April as Metis and woman: during the rape, the men call her "bitch," "cunt," "a real fighting squaw," and "little savage" (139-45).

The rape scene's power and terror may have no peer in Canadian literature.[1] It echoes the rupture of all people's dignity when judged on terms identified by women themselves. The entire novel is formed around the rape scene, as symbolic of the great odds against which the

---

[1] I am indebted to Margaret Clarke's presentation of the power of the rape scene; see "Revisioning April Raintree," 140-41.

main characters fight. There are no details spared as Culleton narrates unthinkable male violence, describing the facts of gut-churning horror that characterize the three stages of rape: victimization by forced genital vaginal penetration, forced anal penetration, and forced fellatio. In order that the degradation which April feels for months after is thoroughly assimilated by the reader, Culleton culminates the rape scene by having the lead rapist urinate into April's mouth.

While one would sympathize with strategies of either madness or quiet survival, April, in keeping with her growing inner strength and self-knowledge, refuses to remain a victim. Her resistance to this brutality begins when she vomits at the rape's conclusion, and goes to the nearest farm house to call the police to press charges. Culleton portrays April's defiance when her resolve shifts into a courageous stance of struggle: April decides to take her assailants to court. She faces the possibly deranging costs when she goes to identify the criminal:

> Not being able to control myself scared me. I really feared the possibility of losing my mind. Going crazy. In that way, rape was a double assault. Rapists abused their victims both physically and mentally. Some victims' minds really did snap after brutal sexual assault. Maybe it had something to do with what I had tried during the assault. Separate my mind from my body (160).

April's fortitude is all the more astonishing in light of the exponential savagery she, as a native woman, confronts in the white legal system.

April quite deliberately defines a strategy to make justice--with her rapists, with her body, and with her sister, who was inadvertently at the heart of the tragedy. She proceeds, through a court battle, to win a five year sentence; she takes ritual baths to exorcise the evil done to her; and she encourages Cheryl to attend a Pow Wow with her. At this point in the novel, the sisters' roles begin to reverse, with April more active, nurturing, and protective, and Cheryl more passive, dependent, and lethargic. The trauma of the rape and the events of Cheryl's street life also rupture April's internalization of white standards. She realizes that Cheryl's drinking and prostitution were rooted in factors larger than her own individual life. Thus, while April would like to blame her, she is able to see Cheryl's life in a broader perspective.

Attending a Pow Wow as part of rebuilding their relationship, both April and Cheryl *relax*. The experience evokes a strong sense of belonging, of healing, and of the beginnings of reconciliation.

That night, we sat, Indian style, around a bonfire, listening to the chanting and tales of Indian singers. Cheryl told me that was probably how it had felt on those long-ago buffalo hunts. I was impressed by all the sights and sounds. It went deeper than just seeing and hearing. I felt good. I felt alive. There were stirrings of pride, regret, and even inner peace. For the first time in my life, I felt as if all of that was part of me, as if I was a part of it (166).

In the passage above we find the central norms and values of right relationship: a bodily fullness of spirit, presence to oneself and others, and a spiritual belonging to all things that are alive and good. Here, during the Pow Wow, April tastes acceptance and transcendence, the crossing-over she has longed for--with her sister, between the separated parts of her life, and with all created things.

At the Pow Wow, Cheryl also describes her understanding of the uneven terrain that a friend named Nancy has tread towards empowerment. Nancy is depicted as a woman to be respected and admired, a character who figures briefly in the latter part of the novel as a symbol of agency in the face of overwhelming odds. We thus have an example of the struggle for an Indian "lifeline politics":[1]

I see all the possibilities that we have. Nancy, for instance. . . . Well, she does drink and does other things that you would never dream of doing. But she also holds a steady job and she's been at the minimum wage for a long time. They use her and she knows it. And she gets depressed about it. But with her education and the way things are, she knows she doesn't have many choices. She helps support her mother and her sister and a brother. The reason why she left home in the first place was her father. He was an alcoholic who beat her mother up and raped Nancy. Okay, so she doesn't have much, maybe, she never will have much but what she's got she shares with her family. And she's not an exception (167).

Cheryl cites her friend's life as witness to the incredible fact that her people have survived at all. Because April, however, has understood

---

[1] Delores Williams has created this term to articulate the political strategies of Black women; see "Black Women's Literature and the Task of Feminist Theology" in *Immaculate and Powerful*, eds. Atkinson et al., 88-110. Lifeline politics include defiant attitudes and developing physical strength; strong bonds with women and men to increase self-esteem and possibilities of mutual relationships; economic independence; distancing themselves from sources of their oppression; and reexamination and change of consciousness about the accepted norms and values of their community. There are parallels between these strategies and those of Culleton's characters.

survival as escaping Metis identity, this survival strategy of affirming that identity is news to her.

Her views about the roots of shame and self-blame are also significantly moved by the one Old Woman figure who functions as shaman to her reclaiming her own soul. Cheryl takes April to visit the Native Friendship Centre where she had been volunteering during her student days. When she meets the Thunderbird Woman, the shaman figure in the novel, April comes face to face with her heritage and finally, rather than running away, stands her ground:

> Her gaze held mine for I saw in her eyes that deep simple wisdom. . . . And I no longer found her touch distasteful. Without speaking a word to me, the woman imparted her message with her eyes. She had seen something in me that was special, something that was deserving of her respect (174).

The possibility of self-love offered by her elder transforms her. April's vision is clearing, slowly focusing on the good in herself and thus on the possibilities of her Metis people. The process detailed is not a gradual or assumed one; it is rough and uneven and often presented as a mine field through white male territory where "shame doesn't dissolve overnight" (168). April remains horrified at the legacy she confronts through her own family's story.

Cheryl had always understood alcoholism as a disease brought by Whites--the way of dying without enjoying life (170). In the end, Cheryl's hope for her people is resurrected in the promise of her child, Henry Liberty Raintree. In one sense, she died for her people, her story living on to empower her sister and her people to learn to love and enjoy themselves, their neighbours, and the "wet, good-smelling Earth." Her suicide near the end of the novel might be seen as an act of struggle for self-respect: she could no longer live as she knew she was entitled to, and so she chose to die. She jumped off the same bridge that her mother had years before, torn between her ideal for her people and the reality of her own pain.

The lives of April and Cheryl represent a reversal of the "tragic victim" and "catalyst and moral agent" models of female experience.[1]

---

[1]These are Williams's models that open up Black women's lived experience, "Black Women's Literature and the Task of Feminist Theology," in *Immaculate and Powerful*, eds. Atkinson et al., 88 ff.

Nevertheless, the two sisters act as touchstones for one another and as guides to the possibility of wholeness. Both characters explored their inheritance and participated in shaping the terms by which they were able to live it. For April, the birds do not begin to sing their morning praises to their Creator (226) until she moves beyond denial of her ancestry. In undergoing the spiritual struggle of shedding her false consciousness about the value of "being white," April stands economically secure and able to forge a life with her nephew, thankful for the wisdom Cheryl bequeathed to her: "Cheryl was that stalk in the field of grain which never bent to the mighty winds of authority. At the same time, that stalk could bend to the gentle breezes of compassion" (121).

Since April has taken on Cheryl's commitment to her people, the image stands as a beacon for April's newly forged identity. In addition, it can represent her courage to withstand the violence done to her already and that which will be meted out every day in the lives of Native people. Culleton has crafted a story where hope comes from a struggle "to accept those Main Street people" (175), that is, to look her people's suffering in the eye because it is hers as well. The sisters' relationship does not end when Cheryl commits suicide. The novel closes with April's vision:

> I remember that during the night I had used the words "MY PEOPLE, OUR PEOPLE" and meant them. The denial had been lifted from my spirit. It was tragic that it had taken Cheryl's death to bring me to accept my identity. But no, Cheryl had once said, "all life dies to give new life." Cheryl had died. But for Henry Lee and me, there would be a tomorrow. And it would be better. I would strive for it. For my sister and her son, for my parents, for my people (228).

Flowing Both Ways: Margaret Laurence's
The Diviners[1]

Like Culleton's *April Raintree*, the central theme of Margaret Laurence's *The Diviners* is the discernment and recovery of one's heritage by returning to and accepting that past--and expressing its suffer-

---

[1]Margaret Laurence, *The Diviners* (Toronto: McLelland and Stewart, 1974; reprint ed., New York: Bantam Windstone, 1982); all references from reprint ed. and subsequently indicated in parentheses in text.

ings and riches. Both authors are in quest of meaning and the possibility of communication between human beings; each recognizes the mystery at the core of life. Both protagonists face the future as a task and ultimately as a gift. From their different cultural contexts, both learn not to succumb but to shape actively their own lives. But here the similarity ends. Laurence's 450 page novel is rooted in the prairie where the protagonist's poor white Scottish ancestry provides her initial intersections with the rest of her small town world. Unlike Culleton's almost flat prose and simple characterizations, Laurence develops an earthy style, and intricate structure, and complex characters.

The Diviners takes its shape by depicting the barriers to and empowerment of a variety of characters from the margins of prairie life: the artist, the Metis, the single mother, the garbage collector. The Diviners is above all about a woman who tells us "I WAS born bloody-minded. It's cost me. I've paid through the nose. As they say. Also, one might add, through the head, heart and cunt" (13). It is the story of Morag Gunn, a Canadian writer in middle age. One may get lost in the complexities with which Laurence handles time. The story line shifts between Morag's life by a southern Ontario river in the present--which is most often written in the past tense--and her childhood during the Depression years and early 1940s in the small prairie town of Manawaka--which is explored using a series of "Memorybank movies," "Snapshots," "Innerfilms," and "Tales and Songs" written mostly in the present tense. Two narrative voices, a first-person and a third-person, are used to underline the fact that this is not Morag's story exclusively; the reader discovers the protagonist's inner intimacies while also being invited into a broader cultural story: "The conflict in the The Diviners is between an intense desire to belong to a rejecting and constricting society, and a desire for a life of one's own."[1] No Canadian is immune to this struggle.

One requires some orientation to the book's complicated structure. Fortunately the first page announces the five parts: River of Now and Then; the Nuisance Grounds; Halls of Sion; Rites of Passage; and The Diviners. These sections are unified by the opening theme:

---

[1] Marian Engel, "Steps to the Mythic: The Diviners and Bird in the House," in Margaret Laurence: An Appreciation, ed. Christl Verduyn (Peterborough, Ontario: Broadview Press, 1988), 160.

"The river flowed both ways." The past is alive in the present, as Laurence skillfully portrays through Morag's tribal roots in Manawaka, just as the future horizon awaits shaping by the inheritors of the past.

As the book opens, Morag is a middle-aged writer living beside a river in southern Ontario and worrying about her teenage daughter:

> The river flowed both ways. The current moved from north to south, but the wind usually came from the south, rippling the bronze-green water in the opposite direction. This apparently impossible contradiction, made apparent and possible, still fascinated Morag, even after years of river watching (3).

The river represents grace (170), a moving presence that "never lost its ancient power for her, and it never ceased to be new" (285).

The Diviners is the climactic work of Laurence's Manawaka series, a group of novels whose protagonists struggle for their own way to escape the fictional town, but finally come to terms with it. In this novel Laurence "crosses the tracks" to write from the perspective of a poor white woman who is raised by the town's garbage collector and his obese, donut-eating wife. To meet Morag as a child raised in poverty and derision, and as an adult artist, a writer, is to become aware that her life and work are that of an outsider. First as an impoverished child, and later as a self-sustaining novelist, her continually marginalized status leads her to join others who reflect, revision, and assess their own lives at the edges of the dominant culture. In conjunction with different marginalized traditions and experiences--Metis, rural, youth--she "divines," along with a few other characters, the mysteries hidden beneath the surface of life's soil.

Morag's development as an artist provides the continuity of the book. It is about her struggle for self-acceptance and freedom. The third person narrating voice, however, underlines the fact that this is not exclusively Morag Gunn's story but the story of many peoples, of a country, of a past that needs telling and revising for the future to have a horizon.[1] As a Canadian prairie woman the protagonist is involved in a search for her cultural and national place of belonging as well.

"The method of presentation also stresses the ways in which past and present, fact and fiction, history and myth, ever penetrate each

---

[1] Marian Engel, "Steps to the Mythic: *The Diviners*, and *A Bird in the House*," in *Margaret Laurence: An Appreciation*, ed. Verduyn, 167.

other and, in so doing, reconstitute reality."[1] A central theme of Morag's story is how "private and fictional words" (453) are indeed of public import: "A popular misconception is that we can't change the past--everyone is constantly changing their own past, recalling it, revising it" (60). Morag realizes that we live in a world of contending truths. It is this profound involvement in negotiating her loyalties and commitments that undergirds and charts her moral development. She lives by faith born of bleakest doubt. She searches and confronts, adopts myths and sheds skins of false conventions. Ultimately she lives "on the boundary" of different margins of life. In short, Morag's story embodies a politics and ethics of choice, based on the twin criteria of self-determination and mutuality, like the river that flows both ways.

We are drawn into the ambiguities and trials of moral agency by the portrait of Morag's own struggles to divine both her mistaken judgments and necessary further actions. As Phyllis Webb advises, the connection between the novel's structure and the protagonist's participation in her own salvation is well designed:

> . . . this complex novel is more than a retrospective quest for self-discovery. Through its portrait of Morag, the artist, it explores the power of the creative imagination to redeem the apparent chaos of human experience. . . . Laurence underlines Morag's role as shaper of experience by giving titles to individual episodes from past and by interjecting into her memories her admissions of distortion and invention.[2]

Thus Morag is set apart by her creative power, not by any special goodness or verve. Her strength and her salvation come from her discovery of the mysteries of life through forging her own destiny. This working out of salvation has a clearly rendered point of view: the outsider or dispossessed.[3] We meet Morag's girlfriend, next door neighbour Eva Winkler, battered and soul-destroyed for life; Morag's lover and father of her child, Jules Tonnerre, singer of the ballads of his

---

[1] A. Barry Cameron, "*The Diviners*," *Queen's Quarterly* 81 (1974), 639.

[2] Phyllis Bruce, "*The Diviners*," *The Canadian Forum* 54 (1974-75), 15.

[3] This is a significant departure from Laurence's other novels, which depict female protagonists from the small prairie town's middle class; see *The Stone Angel* (1964), *A Jest of God* (1966), *The Fire Dwellers* (1969), and *A Bird in the House* (1970).

Metis ancestors in beer parlours; Jules' sister Piquette, burned alive with her children in a tragic but not uncommon fire; the barely moving Prin, whose obese body outlives her mind; and Morag's step-father, Christie, the town scavenger.

Orphaned at age five when her parents die of polio, Morag is unofficially adopted by her father's army buddy, Christie Logan, and his feeble-minded, donut-devouring wife, Prin. (Morag wonders as a child: "She is so fat--Can she be a person?") Christie inhabits excluded space as Manawaka's garbage collector. He is ridiculed and taunted as scavenger but it is a job he proudly chose upon returning embittered from the war. Because Christie and Prin are social outcasts, Morag too is dispossessed. As a member of this household, she lives halfway up Hill Street:

> Hill Street was the Scots-English equivalent of The Other Side of The Tracks, the shacks and shanties at the north end of Manawaka, where the Ukrainian section hands on the CPR lived. Hill street was below the town; it was inhabited by those who had not and never would make good. Remittance men and their draggled families. Drunks. People perpetually on relief. Occasional labourers whose tired women supported the family by going out to clean the big brick houses on top of the hill on the streets shaded by sturdy maples, elms, lombardy poplars. Hill Street--dedicated to flops, washouts and general no-goods, at least in the view of the town's better off (28).

In this context, Morag's childhood is a shack-full of painful memories. Morag suffers because of this social location, like the Tonnerre family farther down the valley, who are also denied "a place to stand on."

We are introduced to the wealthy of Manawaka by what they discard, literally in their garbage and figuratively by their religious practices. One day while scavenging, Christie "divines" the garbage, giving young Morag her first lesson in the social relations of the town.

> I say unto you, Morag Gunn, lass, that by their bloody goddamn fucking garbage shall ye christly well know them. The ones who eat only out of tins. The ones who have to wrap the rye bottles in old newspapers to try to hide the fact that there are so goddamn many of them (39). . . . Garbage belongs to all. Communal property . . . the socialism of the junk heap. . . . Let the Connors and the McVities and the Camerons and Simon Pearl and all of them in their houses up there--let them look down on the likes of Christie Logan. . . . They don't touch me, Morag. For my kin and clan are as good as theirs any day of the week (47).

By such ranting and raving, Christie gives Morag a strong, if unorthodox, schooling in how much people have in common, despite appearances to the contrary.

Christie warns her not to believe everything told in history books: "We believe what we know" (83). And Christie *knows* the legacy of her Scots highland ancestors, Piper and Morag Gunn, leaders of the Sutherland immigration to Canada. He creates this truth in part through his tale-spinning rants which thrill Morag. Piper Gunn, "with the voice of drums and the heart of a child and the gall of a thousand and the strength of conviction" (49), led displaced Highland crofters on a long march out of bondage to a new land in the Red River Valley. The spirited rhetoric and identification with the heroine give her a story of which she is proud. As a child, Morag accepts this legacy as truth. She makes it her own by recreating her own version of Piper Gunn's woman, who was never afraid and who had "the power and the second sight and the good eye and the strength of conviction" (52).

One thrills to read Christie's fabrications just as one would a fairy tale and they give Morag a sense of belonging. Even though the community is bent on excluding the child, in her ugly oversize dresses cut down from Prin's, she survives. Like the tip of an iceberg, the cruelty, rigidity and ignorance of the upper crust is hinted at in the context of the United Church. As a fourteen year old, Morag wants to know: Which Side is God On?

> Morag stands beside Prin, the back row of the church, hating her own embarrassment but hugging it around her. . . . Prin still looks like a barrel of lard with legs. . . . [Her hat] is, well, a hat which Christie found at the Nuisance Grounds, and Morag is in agony, wondering if it once belonged to Mrs. Cameron or Mrs. Simon Pearl or somebody who's here today and will recognize it and laugh and tell everybody. . . . She loves Prin, but can no longer bear to be seen with her in public. . . . Morag is dressed nicely. Nobody could deny it. . . . But all this makes no difference. When church is over, and they're filing out, chattering, the Camerons and MacLeods and Duncans and Catses and McVities and Halperns and them, no one will say *Good Morning* to Morag and Prin. Not on your life. Might soil their precious mouths. . .
>
> > In Christ there is no East or West,
> > In Him no North or South--
> Oh yeh? Like fun there isn't (108-09).

One cringes with Morag as she suffers such humiliation. Her theological astuteness is remarkable!

Earlier in her life we are told, "Morag loves Jesus. And how. He is friendly and not stuck up, is why. . . . He was Okay to everybody, even sinners and hardup people and like that." Mirrored in the callousness and hypocrisy of the congregation is the theology Morag has learned: "Morag does not love God who is the one who decides which people have got to die and when" (77). She has put her finger on the duplicity of cherishing this kind of God. In comparison to the life-giving stories she has heard about Jesus, the God she encountered in church has no good news for her. She turns her back on this God to learn elsewhere about life.

Her earliest self-discovery is a gut-wrenching contradiction of having to learn the codes of school and church while at the same time resenting and resisting their pretensions, cruelty, and lies. With Jules "Skinner" Tonnerre, Morag shares the outsiders' life, albeit for different reasons. Morag lives out in her own life the memory that her ancestors were forced off their land during the Highland Clearances; Jules in his life lives out his Metis people's dispossession of their land and culture by western colonizers and white supremacy. Morag also learns about some other terms of exclusion during the singing of "The Maple Leaf Forever" in class. Here Laurence deftly signifies the illusion of Canadian multi-culturalism, where Morag *hears* the words for the first time because of her connection with Jules.

> The THISTLE SHAMROCK ROSE entwine
> The MAPLE LEAF FOREVER!
>
> Morag loves this song and sings with all her guts. She also knows what the emblems mean. Thistle is Scots, like her and Christie (others, of course, too, including the stuck-up kids, but *her* definitely, and they better not forget it). Shamrock is Irish like Connors and Reillys and them. Rose is English, like Prin, once of good family. Suddenly she looks over to see if Skinner Tonnerre is singing. He has the best voice in class, and he knows lots of cowboy songs, and dirty songs. . . . He is not singing now. He comes from nowhere. He isn't anybody (70).

The silence of her friend moves Morag to consider the classroom from a different perspective.

As Christie is a diviner for Morag through his tale-telling and "reading" the town's garbage, so too is Jules Tonnerre through sexual intimacy, as the father of her child, and as song writer and teller of Metis tales. On their first accidental meeting outside school, they swap tales of their ancestors. Jules informs her that his family has been around longer than hers and that he was named after his grandfather, who had fought with Louis Riel. This encounter occurs at the Nuisance Grounds, the garbage dump, signifying their similar position as social misfits. Their life-long friendship is one place where Morag learns that divining means figuring out things for herself. Morag learns what Adrienne Rich succinctly names "responsibility to yourself":

> refusing to let others do your thinking, talking, and naming for you; it means learning to respect and use your own brains and instincts; hence grappling with hard work. . . . It means insisting that those to whom you give your friendship and love are able to respect your mind.[1]

For example, Morag has to confront the fact that Christie's version of history might not be truthful. Such a rupture of awareness occurs, for example, when she recognizes with a shock that Christie is just what Jules depicts him as, another "goddamn *Anglais*" (145) set on disparaging the Metis in order to boost the (false) image of his Sutherland ancestors. She senses, in her own experience of betrayal by Christie and in Jules' pain, what some today designate as horizontal oppression.

Jules is also a diviner for Morag's sexual life. She moves fully and freely into her first experience and discovers the beauty and pleasure of her body and mutual love-making: "The pulsing between her legs spreads and suffuses all of her. The throbbing goes on and on, and she does not realize her voice has spoken until it stops, and then she does not know if she has spoken words or only cried out somewhere in someplace beyond language" (138).

Morag's humiliation and anger with the narrowness and cruelty in her life, however, make her determined to escape Manawaka. She works at the local newspaper to save money for her salvific step out to university. But in her desperation to leave she has closed off all appreciation for the circumstances into which she was born. Lachlan, Morag's editor, sharply observes a condescension at work in her:

> Those people know things it will take you the better part of your life to learn, if ever. They are not very verbal people, but if you ever in your life presume to look down on them because you have the knack of words and they do not, then you do so at your own eternal risk and peril (155).

---

[1]Rich, "Claiming an Education," in *On Lies, Secrets and Silences*, 233.

In her shame about Christie and Prin and in her rejection of them, Morag had unwittingly internalized the very values of exclusion and fear that she detests in the proper middle class of the town who had ostracized her as a little girl. It will take Morag a long struggle to comprehend this revelation, and to understand how she has created her life by a dialectical process of agency and denial. For instance, throughout the novel idiomatic and "incorrect" forms of grammatical language are used to capture the reality of the town's characters. At the outset, improper language use annoys the young Morag, yet she slowly learns to value the many ways in which those silenced by illiteracy, poverty, or culture express their own linguistic wisdom, in songs and stories especially, and finally she is humbled by it.[1]

Morag is shocked into adulthood by the tragic deaths of Piquette Tonnerre and her children. Covering the event for the newspaper, Morag reaches the ruins of the shack where three generations of Tonnerres have lived. She is told that the blaze started when Piquette had been home drinking while using a faulty stove.

> She can see only smokened metal and burnt wood, but there is something else in there as well. Burnt wood. *Bois-Brûles.* Lazarus [Jules and Piquette's father] shambles over to the two men. "I'm going in," he says. "They're mine, there, them." Dere mine, dere, dem (159).

The terror and connection she feels, because of her relationship with Jules and his family, are vomited out in shock. This horrifying event makes Morag more firmly convinced of her need to flee Manawaka.

Christie prophesies correctly: "it's a bloody good thing you've got away from this dump. . . . It'll all go along with you, too" (207). Morag denies it vigorously. She consciously adopts a position of exile in order to forget her past. But university and Winnipeg are not far enough away; she marries her English professor, Brooke Skelton, and moves not only to Toronto--Canada's supposed paradise--but for the first time into the established, respectable realms of social life. "She wouldn't go back to Manawaka for all the tea in China or Assam. And yet the town inhabits her, as she once inhabited it" (227).

---

[1]On Laurence's use of language, see Linda W. Wagner, "Margaret Laurence's *The Diviners,*" *University of Windsor Review* 16, no. 2 (Spring-Summer 1982), 10 ff.

Morag slowly loses herself in the designs her husband has for her. He is not interested in her past and tells her not to think of Manawaka. He loves her as he needs her to be: innocent and young. Morag is complicit in this arrangement, suppressing her contradictory knowledge. Brooke may insist on calling her "little one," but she silently recalls the cruelty she has witnessed in life:

> Vernon Winkler, as a small boy being beaten by Gus. Eva crying in the dancehall, and the night that followed, and Christie taking the small unformed corpse (could it be called that? . . .) and giving it burial. The valley, the snow and the fire [when Piquette and her children died] (198).

There is no escape from the pain of Manawaka because all that has moved her there is a part of her.

Because Morag tries to repress her formative years, she becomes totally isolated and feels increasingly separated from herself. This homesickness for herself[1] is brought to light through her fiction writing. The rupture with Brooke is epitomized in his response to her novel, when he wonders if her protagonist has expressed anything which has not been said before. Morag thinks to herself "No. She doesn't. But *she* says it. That is what is different (247)." But she overrides this inner voice and verbally agrees with Brooke's judgment. Morag accidentally meets Jules again and brings him home for a visit. Jules is the bridge back to living her life in her own skin.

> "Your past certainly is catching up with you," Brooke says. "I suppose he tracked you down and is here in the somewhat unlovely role of freeloader. . . . He seems to have gone through a fair portion of my scotch." "*Your* scotch!" "Yes, my scotch. Anyway, I thought it was supposed to be illegal to give liquor to Indians" (269).

Morag now clearly sees her marriage not from Brooke's point of view but from her own.

The contradiction between her life's work as a writer and her marriage is not resolved easily. Eventually, though, she takes action to start, quite literally, a new life. She leans on the support of her friendship with Jules and goes out with him for the night. The deep recipro-

---

[1] See Adrienne Rich's poem "Transcendental Etude" in *The Dream of a Common Language: Poems, 1974-1977* (New York: W. W. Norton and Co., 1978), 78.

cal connection renews her commitment to herself and enables her to act on her decision to leave her marriage. Morag's connection with her roots is doubly reestablished--that is, she recovers both her past and future--when she makes love with Jules and tells him she hopes to become pregnant: the past will indeed become present in the future. They agree, neither one expecting the other to share responsibility for the anticipated child.

> In her present state of mind, she doesn't expect to be aroused . . . as though this joining is being done for other reasons, some debt or answer to the past, some severing of inner chains which have kept her bound and separated from part of herself. . . . She linked her legs around his, and it is as though it is again that first time. Then they both reach the place they have been traveling towards, and she lies beside him, spent and renewed (271).

This scene expresses the mutual passion in Morag's relationship with Jules and beautifully alludes to the depth and healing of their intimacy.

Sex becomes another way of divining for Morag. It remains a hunger she will not deny and a source of deep communion. Jules asks her if he is a shaman to her. "I don't know," Morag replies, "I never thought of it like that. But I know that whatever I'm going to do next, or wherever I go, it'll have to be on my own" (273). This stance affirms a newly-dawning self-reliance in the midst of significant, life-giving relationships. Jules remains her ally over time and distance.

Her friendship since college with Ella Gerson is another source of divining. During her years at college Morag was deeply influenced by the Gersons, a household of Polish Jewish women. While still classmates, Morag discusses with Ella what it is like to be intelligent, well-read students. In a moment of luminous awareness Morag concludes that, despite discrimination against women's self-development, "All I want is everything" (182). Ella confirms that "I'm a survivor, just like you are" (331). In Mrs. Gerson, Morag discovers the intellectual and emotional mentor she needed. Mrs. Gerson stomps out evenings to left-wing meetings, raises her daughters not to pretend to be brainless, and encourages open expression of pain and joy as essential to a full life.

Morag's enormous courage to have a child alone has its roots in these life-affirming ties. She herself was raised in a non-traditional household, of course, and perhaps in her conscious decision to leave the security of marriage opted to continue the critique of this cultural norm. Christie and Prin had chosen her and had never parented her in a "normal" fashion nor ever desired to do so. In any event, the pregnancy gives her an embodied and "fixed centre" as she again returns to perilous and impoverished circumstances. She cannot, however, return home. She had left Manawaka because she refused to follow alienating social conventions. She had also learned how the "Halls of Sion" she yearned for in her marriage proved to be just another set of alienating cultural values from which she felt excluded. She understood that she could not keep Brooke's love on his terms alone. She stows up her renewed commitment to herself and leaves the empty shell of her lifeless marriage.

Morag heads west, from Toronto to Vancouver, for her new beginning. As she crosses the prairie she may not be ready to stop and visit, but it serves as a blessing on her journey of reclaiming herself.

> She looks out at the flat lands, which from the train window could not ever tell you anything about what they are. The grain elevators, like stark strange towers. The small bluffs of scrub oak and polar. . . . A gathering of trees, not the great hardwoods of Down East, of forests of the North, but thin tough-fibred trees that could survive on open grassland, that could live against the wind and the winter here. That was the kind of tree worth having; that was a determined kind of tree, all right. The crocuses used to grow out of the snow. You would find them in pastures, the black-pitted dying snow still there, and the crocuses already growing, their greengrey, feather stems, and the petals of pale grey mauve. People who'd never lived hereabouts always imagined it was dull, bleak, hundreds of miles of nothing. They didn't know. They didn't know the renewal that came out of the dead cold (282).

The prairie thenceforth becomes a metaphor of the hope planted in her decision to make changes in her life.

Morag's new life is amply created with her delivery of the daughter she had conceived with Jules. During the birth in a Vancouver hospital, she shouts at the nurse as if giving birth to herself: "You try holding back. You just try. I can't. I can't" (304). She names the child Piquette, after Jules' sister, to honour the father; but she can never bring herself to use the name in full. Pique inherits Morag's position on the fringes of society and a host of ancestors she would some day have to discover for herself. The pain of being an exile is manifest in Pique's deep ambivalence about who she is: "'Why did you have me?' cries Pique. 'I wanted you.'. . . 'You never thought of him, or of me'" (235). And to this accusation there could be no reply. Pique, like Morag's other creation, her novels, ". . . could be you and not you, at the same time" (377). Now Morag has additional responsibility and inescapable memories because of her living creation. She wrestles with old wounds from her past, assessing the price paid for her integrity in the face of Pique's teenage suffering and resentment: "You've never had somebody tell you your mother was crazy because she lived here alone and wrote dirty books and had kooky people coming out from the city to visit" (421).

It takes another move and some years in England, including a pilgrimage to Sutherland, her adopted ancestral land in Scotland, before Morag can accept her inheritance. Only after this sojourn does Morag feel able as well to bless Pique's quest for her own place of belonging. Scotland, Morag discovers, is not the land of her ancestors as she had always imagined it. Her true roots on the Canadian prairie finally become clear to her: "Christie's real country. Where I was born" (391). This realization is a revelation that returns her to childhood heritage. Finally she can authorize and possess herself and by so doing transcend herself: Instead of being crippled by her cultural heritage she is enriched, she is a diviner, divining not only her own past, but also the past of a collective cultural memory. She finds the water of inspiration--the "Strength of Conviction." Like the prairie trees, Morag's strength and determination enables her "to acknowledge the sacredness of her past and her deep loyalty to community and tradition."[1]

As characters displaced by dominant society, Christie, Morag, and Jules share a common survival strategy: the telling of tales. They invent themselves by mythologizing historical "facts." These become living traditions capable of mobilizing them into further self-authorizing acts. This strategy also provides income for Morag, as an author, and for Jules, as a song-writer and singer who travels "all over the place. All over the country" recalling and telling the tales of his ancestors. In "The Ballad of Jules Tonnerre," written for his grandfather who fought with Riel in 1885, Jules memorializes the struggle for his people's survival. In his song for his father, Lazarus, Jules captures the savagery of a community that rejects and despises a person for being "Other,"

---

[1]Sherrill Grace, "Portrait of the Artist as Laurence Hero," in *Margaret Laurence: An Appreciation*, ed. Verduyn, 173.

and laments his father's pain while honouring him as a trapper who
kept his family from starving.

> Lazarus, he was king of Nothing;
> Lazarus, he never had a dime.
> He was sometimes on Relief, he was permanent on grief,
> And nowhere was the place he spent his time.
>
> Lazarus was what they called a halfbreed;
> Half a man was what the Town would say.
> What made him walk so slow, well, they didn't care to know--
> It was easier to look away . . .
>
> Lazarus was not afraid of fighting;
> It was the only way he knew to win.
> But when the fight was o'er, he'd be in the clink once more;
> Those breeds must learn that anger is a sin . . .
>
> Lazarus, he had a bunch of children;
> He raised them in the Valley down below.
> So that they could eat he shot rabbits there for meat
> Where his ancestors had shot buffalo.
>
> Lazarus, he lost some of those children,
> Some to fire, some to the City's heart of stone.
> Maybe when they went, was the worst time that was sent,
> For then he really knew he was alone . . .
>
> Lazarus, rise up out of the Valley;
> Tell them what it really means to try.
> Go tell them in the Town, though they always put you down,
> Lazarus, oh man, you didn't die.
> > Lazarus, oh man, you didn't die.

Morag finally returns to visit her prairie home when Christie is
in hospital. She acknowledges "You've been my father to me." He
responds, "Well, I'm blessed" (396). The healing of broken bonds and
the new ability to rejoice in the sources of wisdom learned through
these bonds is also paralleled in Jules's visits with Morag and Pique.
He finally claims Pique as his child too and bequeaths her a heritage of
the songs and tales of his ancestors. The novel is brought to a close
with "a fair trade," imaging the river that flows both ways. Morag and
Jules exchange Lazarus Tonnerre's knife, given to Morag by Christie,
for the plaid pin Lazarus had given to Jules. This ritual is duly interpreted in Morag's final conversation with her neighbour Royland, the

diviner of water wells: Morag proclaims, "The necessary *doing* of the thing--that mattered" (452). Royland confirms that sharing divining power, learning to seek after life's mysteries, is not a matter for mourning. This ending signifies that *The Diviners* is dedicated to the transmission and transformation of life-affirming values from one generation to the next.

In the course of the novel we have witnessed Morag's deepening insights into who she is and who and what have contributed to her struggle to live her own life. Her deepened self-acceptance by the close of the story is manifested in her greater understanding and acceptance of her daughter. Pique, herself a song writer and singer like her father, is presented as a strong, positive character who, like her mother, will risk embracing and shaping that inheritance.

> I came to taste the dust out on a prairie road
> My childhood thoughts were heavy on me like a load
> But when I left behind my fear
> When I found those ghosts were near
> leadin' me back to that home I never knowed.
> Ah, my valley and my mountain, they're the same
> My living places, and they will never be tame
> When I think how I was born
> I can't help but be torn
> But the valley and the mountain hold my name
> ("Pique's Song," 467).

In this teenage voice one can hear the early signs of one who knows the need to explore and endure and come to terms with the inherited contradictions that shape one's identity.

The central characters have been "diviners," or seekers of the hidden wells of truth-making and right relation.[1] Through Morag's life, and those in her life who help her keep "divining," we find indications of the "rebellion and desire" of a female sensibility that enables breaking with dominant moral practices and creates allegiances for human well-being across various margins. This portrait of a Canadian artist is credible and significant because she is so human. In Phyllis Bruce's words, Morag

---

[1]On the "diviners" theme, see Eleanor Johnston, "The Quest of *The Diviners*," *Mosaic* 11, no. 3 (Spring 1978), 107-17.

> is not an exalted being, she is fallible, at times imperceptive. Yet she is set
> apart by her creative power. . . . It is in this knowledge [of the mysteries of
> life] that Morag finds her strength and her salvation. By the end of the novel
> she has reached an acceptance of her destiny not only to endure but to create,
> to "look ahead into the past, and back into the future, until the silence."[1]

And by the close of the novel, Morag's right to be herself, to demand
what she needs, and to share her wisdom is affirmed as forecast in the
symbol of the rare Great Blue Heron, whose soaring and measured
flight is certain, its sweeping wings masterful and serene, creating a
rush of wind; the wind of its wings is like an angel to her (357).

The Song of Mourning is Not a Lifelong Song:
Joy Kogawa's *Obasan*[2]

Joy Kogawa's *Obasan*, like Margaret Laurence's work, has received critical acclaim in Canada. Both authors were mature artists
when they wrote the novels under examination. Like Beatrice Culleton, Kogawa deals with the theme of survival of a minority group
against untold oppression. The title, *Obasan*, means "aunt," and it signifies concern with the dynamics of close relationships, including those
between families within the Canadian "family." The story, told in a
tight 250 pages, is technically and artistically compelling. While the
story is told in the first-person voice of the protagonist beginning in the
summer of 1972, it focuses on the period between 1941 and 1948 when
the civil rights of Japanese Canadians were revoked through the evac-
uation and relocation policies of the Canadian government. The poign-
ancy of *Obasan* is difficult to describe. Perhaps the simplest explana-
tion is the combination of a Japanese sensibility for a spare and direct
yet searching tone, and the power of Kogawa's language. (She wrote
poetry before turning to write prose fiction.) One is absorbed by the
haunting, horrific, and historically based story of the persecution of
Japanese Canadians during and after World War II. Kogawa produces
an exacting rendition of the evil of engineered suffering through the

---

[1]Phyllis Bruce, "The Diviners," *The Canadian Forum* 54 (1974-75), 15.

[2]Joy Kogawa, *Obasan* (Toronto: Lester and Orpen Denys, 1981; reprint
ed., Markham: Penguin, 1982), 246; all references from reprint ed. and subsequently indicated in parentheses in text.

story of Naomi Nakane's struggle to achieve wholeness in terms of her silenced past and to come alive in the present.

We are taken by the child Naomi's voice into the experience of a young girl being made into an outsider, an enemy, and an outcast in her homeland.[1] Through this narrative, Kogawa portrays what one can barely imagine--the internment and dispersion of the Japanese in western Canada. Kogawa creates the story of a people in exile in the voice of her narrator, Naomi Nakane, through her earliest memories, dreams and nightmares, to her discovery as an adult of the long-silenced sufferings of her family. Kogawa delicately and relentlessly follows Naomi's life and the Nakane-Kato clan, beginning on the west coast, traveling inland to the British Columbian interior, and remaining on the prairie of southern Alberta, where Naomi goes through public school, enters womanhood, and finally "speaks the silence" to contradict the lies that have kept her chained in the stone of a silenced past.

The novel opens on August 9, 1972 when Naomi Nakane, now in her thirties, goes to her childhood home in southern Alberta to bury her Uncle Isamu, who, with his wife Obasan Ayako, had raised Naomi and her brother Stephen when their immediate family dissolved during the days of internment. Naomi begins to unearth her hidden past when she starts to face the disturbing memories, childhood dreams, and nightmares that surface on this occasion of her uncle's funeral. For the past eighteen years, she has made an annual pilgrimage with her uncle to a special place on the prairie. The prairie setting undergirds and mirrors the spiritual struggle of the narrator-protagonist, Naomi Nakane.

> The coulee is so still right now that if a match were to be lit, the flame would not waver. The tall grasses stand without quivering. The tops flop this way and that. The whole dark sky is bright with stars and only the new moon moves (1).

In the first of the flashbacks woven throughout the story, Naomi thinks of their first visit in 1954 when her uncle, agitated by a reunion with her Aunt Emily, had brought Naomi to this place. His distress had abated as he walked through the waving grasses. On their last visit she

---

[1]For an excellent overview of this novel, see B. A. St. Andrews, "Reclaiming a Canadian Heritage: Kogawa's *Obasan*," *The International Fiction Review* 13, no. 1 (1986), 29-31.

asked in a whisper, "why do we come here?" "Uncle could be Chief
Sitting Bull squatting here" (2). And he had remained silent. The connection with the Native struggle for survival and Isamu's silence pose
the tension and mystery around which her life, and the novel, spiral.

    We are introduced to three generations of the Nakane-Kato clan
through Naomi's earliest memories of life with her Isei grandparents
(first generation), her Nisei musician father and mother (second generation), and her only sibling Stephen. Comfort is deep in a close family
life: "My parents, like two needles, knit the families carefully into one
blanket. Every event was a warm water wash, drawing us all closer till
the fibre of our lives became an impenetrable mesh" (20). When this
stability ends in 1942, one is unwillingly drawn into the confusion,
fear, and chaos as the family is interned and evacuated. The death of
Naomi's uncle represents the obliteration of the Isei generation and the
beginning of her realization that "the past is the future" (42).

    The structure of the novel is built around Naomi's attempt to
solve the mystery of her mother's disappearance during a return trip to
Japan when Naomi was a young child. The metaphor introduced in the
preface is "the word is stone." The narrator Naomi searches for "the
living word" out of "the silence that will not speak": "Unless the
stone burst with telling, unless the seed flowers with speech, there is in
my life no living word" (Preface). The themes of Kogawa's novel are
laid out in poetic lines on the first two pages--the connections between
the living and their ancestors, the tension between truth and facts, and
the tension between silence and telling. The biblical quote carries the
hope Kogawa brings to her own and her narrator's "telling":

> To [those] that overcometh
> will I give to eat
> of the hidden manna
> and will give [them]
> a white stone
> and in the stone
> a new name written . . .

In the quest for the truth, not just the facts, lies sustenance and the living word, the promise of full life.

    When the persecution of the Japanese Canadians begins in 1941,
when Naomi's father dies in a prison hospital, when her mother's absence is no longer a mystery, Obasan and Uncle remain silent. In the

face of Naomi's unresolved queries they utter this haunting refrain "Kodomo no tame--for the sake of the children--gaman shi masho--let us endure" (245). "Why did my mother not return?," Naomi beseeches. "I was consumed by the question. Devoured alive" (26). The search and longing provided in metaphor at the start of the book frames the scope of her quest: "If I could follow the stream down and down to the hidden voice, would I come at last to the freeing word?" (Preface).

The tension between the numb protection of silence and the need for truth is embodied in Naomi's aunts. This crucial contrast is composed early in the novel. On the one hand, there is Obasan Ayako's way of the Isei, the way of Japanese stoicism and restraint. On the other hand, there is the Nisei stance of Aunt Emily, the forthright, make-right approach. The battle between these two ethics--between the survival strategies of silence and of naming--threatens to tear Naomi apart, and so she must discover her own resolution. The Isei Obasan accepts what has happened to her through two attitudes: "Everything is forgetfulness" (26). And "Arigatai. Gratitude only" (42). Naomi portrays her as ancient wisdom, as

> every woman in every hamlet in the world . . . . Everywhere the old woman stands as the true and rightful owner of the earth. She is the bearer of keys to unknown doorways and to a network of astonishing tunnels. She is the possessor of life's infinite personal details (15).

With Obasan Ayako locking the doors and blocking the tunnels with her silence, Naomi is denied the facts of the Japanese-Canadian experience. Because "the language of her grief is silence" (14), Naomi finds Obasan's land impenetrable. But where her elderly aunt "lives in stone," her other *obasan*, her mother's sister Emily, is "a word warrior. She's a crusader, a little old grey-haired Mighty Mouse, a Bachelor of Advanced Activists and General Practitioner of Just Causes" (32). While the former accepts what has happened, the latter wants to make justice by having the perpetrators of the dispersal and relocation policies of the Canadian state see and accept what they had done.[1]

---

[1] "There are two poles in the Japanese way of thinking. One is a fatalistic attitude of acceptance, endurance and stoicism and the other is a sense of justice, honour and fair play. The former is manifested in the attitudes of Uncle and Obasan and the latter is presented by Aunt Emily." Michiko Lambertson, "*Obasan*," *Canadian Woman Studies* 4, no. 2 (Winter 1982), 94.

Because of their radically different responses to injustice, the aunts disagree about when tell Naomi the truth about her past. The younger Emily defers to her elder and maintains the stone of silence, but only insofar as the family history is concerned. Aunt Emily makes sense of "the randomness of experience" (5), with which Naomi is unwilling to live, by documenting the injustice and by political activism. She energetically proclaims, "We're gluing our tongues back on" (36). While answers to her questions remain stone with Obasan Ayako, Aunt Emily is the one with the vision who seeks justice.

> Write the vision and make it plain? For her, the vision is the truth as she lives. When she is called like Habbakuk to the witness stand, her testimony is to the light that shines in the lives of the Nisei, in their desperation to prove themselves Canadian, in their tough and gentle spirit (32).

Naomi, however, doubts that so much effort is yielding the nourishment for which she longs. When Aunt Emily asks the adult Naomi if she really wants to "know" everything, Naomi lies and says "Sure." For Naomi, the truth is more murky, shadowy and grey. "I can only see a dark field with Aunt Emily beaming her flashlight to where the rest of us crouch and hide, our eyes downcast as we seek the safety of invisibility" (32). Some fifteen years after the war, with constant prodding and cajoling by Aunt Emily, Naomi is reluctantly ready to open the parcel of Aunt Emily's papers, documents, newspaper clippings, and letters that represent her life's work and vision.

If it is Aunt Emily who functions as the archivist of the Nakane-Kato family and Japanese-Canadian history, Obasan Ayako bore the task of raising the two Nakane children. She maintained the family as a dignified community whenever possible, part of which included bearing up in silence the unspeakable horrors her loved ones endured. She puts special food in Naomi's lunch box. She teaches Naomi that interpersonal ethics rest on honouring the wishes of others before one's own. (If not, the sin of "wagamama" or selfishness would be committed and she would disgrace herself.) We can hear the collaboration of her Japanese and Christian traditions which in part account for her endurance over the years of brutal treatment and upheaval.

The safety of Naomi's relationship with her Obasan is illustrated by their ritual attendance at the public bathhouse built by the relocated Japanese community in Granton, Alberta.

The bath is a place of deep bone warmth and rest. It is always filled with a slow steamy chatter from women and girls and babies. It smells of wet cloth and wet wood and wet skin. We are one flesh, one family, washing each other or submerged in the hot water, half awake, half asleep (160).

This memory is one of the few that bring Naomi happiness as an adult. It fills her child's need for touch and physical presence in a world of heavy, haunting silence. Recognizing Naomi's upbringing in the home where Obasan has been her ever-present, if silent guide, we can better appreciate her difficulty with Aunt Emily's discursive, energetic, all-Canadian style. Next to the weariness and wordlessness of Obasan, Aunt Emily's tireless struggle to obtain justice for Canadians of Japanese origin contains its own disruptive agony for Naomi.

Naomi has been protected from the "facts," but she experiences nightmares from an early age. "We die again and again. In my dreams, we are never safe enough" (227). Obasan's long-suffering presence throughout Naomi's life keeps sealed the history Aunt Emily has worked with equal dedication to expose. She has documented the curfews, the removal from jobs, the searches without warrants, the seizures of property, the evacuations, forced labour camps, eventual relocation, and rescinded nationality.

When Aunt Emily learns the fate of her sister, Naomi's mother, she travels to tell Obasan and Uncle. (We realize that it was on this occasion that Naomi first accompanied her Uncle to the coulee.) They determine to keep this news from the children. After Naomi is an adult, Aunt Emily encourages her to stop keeping her memories inside.

"You have to remember," Aunt Emily said. "You are your history. If you cut any of it off you're an amputee. Don't deny the past. Remember everything. If you're bitter, be bitter. Cry it out! Scream! Denial is gangrene" (49-50).

Initially Naomi is too fearful and for protection adopts Obasan's position: "What is past recall is past pain" (45). It is not surprising that Naomi follows Obasan's path of "forgetfulness," given the many gaps in her knowledge, as well as the loyalty she must feel toward the woman who raised her as her own with such devotion since Naomi was five. While Naomi would never forget Obasan's selfless care or lose the appreciation of her Japanese customs and values, she could not help thinking that Obasan had known little happiness. For example, Naomi recalls the lack of touch between her uncle and aunt, that as a child she wondered if they were in love, but that when she asked her uncle he did not even understand the query (6).

Naomi compares herself with Aunt Emily, described early in the book as an "old maid." "Why indeed are there two of us unmarried in our small family? Must be something in the blood. A crone-prone syndrome" (8). Although she sees Emily only on her rare visits from Toronto, Naomi decides that she has no husband because her political organizing leaves no time for that kind of intimacy. Naomi has dated without pleasure a widower in her small prairie town. In the context of her family and the examples of her aunts, she understands herself to be a lonely, unhappy woman with a tense personality who is "bored to death with teaching and ready to retire" (7).

Then her uncle dies. She is 36 years old, miserable and in need of the healing waters of love and life. His death initiates Naomi's uneasy exploration and reassessment of her life. Naomi has been a victim of "the silence that will not speak" (Preface). Before the funeral, as she leafs through the documents, sent to her by Aunt Emily, concerning the silenced years of the internment and relocation, the alternative that she sees in Aunt Emily is both unfamiliar and threatening. "Like Cupid, she aimed for the heart. But the heart was not there" (40). While Aunt Emily urges her to remember, Naomi struggles to find the sustenance she longs for to give her courage.

In response to her own deepest longings, Naomi wrestles with the example of Aunt Emily's protest work. Aunt Emily uses the power of words like buckshot: "The government called them 'Interior Housing Projects'! With language like that you can disguise any crime" (34). Naomi is spurred on by demystifying the official story. Analysis and activities, however, do not overcome her emptiness:

> All of Aunt Emily's words, all her papers, the telegrams and petitions, are like scratchings in the barnyard, the evidence of much activity, scaly claws hard at work. But what good they do, I do not know. . . . They do not touch us where we are planted here in Alberta, our roots clawing the sudden prairie air. The words are not made flesh. Trains do not carry us home. Ships do not return again. All my prayers disappear into space (189).

Naomi's disillusionment seems only to harden in this Aunt's company.

Earlier Naomi had insisted that "It does not bear remembering. None of this bears remembering" (49), but she is also confused by the terrible conflict between silence and her living memory rooted in the never-explained absence of her mother. She lives into womanhood with the heaviness of this unsolved mystery pervading her waking and her sleeping.

> I am not certain whether it is a cluttered attic in which I sit, a waiting room, a tunnel, a train. There is no beginning and no end to the forest, or the dust storm, no edge from which to know where the clearing begins. Here, in this familiar density, beneath this cloak, within this carapace, is the longing within the darkness (111).

Naomi's confusion and pain register without signpost, as if in a wilderness. The prairie ghost town to which she, Uncle, Obasan and Stephen had been relocated held infinite misery for them. Part of her resentment of Aunt Emily's activism is the reminder of the overwhelming despair during their years working on a sugar-beet farm in southern Alberta. "The fact is I never got used to it and I cannot bear the memory. . . . There is a word for it. Hardship" (194).

There are also other memories that sever her from her mother. She remembers how quiet a child she was, not inside their Vancouver home, "[b]ut outside, even in the backyard, there is an infinitely unpredictable, unknown and often dangerous world. Speech hides within me, watchful and afraid" (58). It is unlikely that her mother causes such reticence, given the narrator's description of her calm efficiency and presence:

> Her eyes are steady and matter of fact--the eyes of Japanese motherhood. They do not invade and betray. They are eyes that protect, shielding what is hidden most deeply in the heart of the child. She makes safe the small stirrings underfoot and in the shadows. Physically, the sensation is not in the region of the heart, but in the belly. This that is in the belly is honoured when it is allowed to be, without fanfare, without reproach, without words (59).

This exquisite portrayal of the mother-daughter bond accents Naomi's childhood experience of being accepted for herself. The portrayal of this four year old's openness leads into the lies she has had to perpetuate about her experience of sexual abuse by the neighbour, Old Man Gower. This long repressed experience of shame and guilt had broken her spiritual link with her mother. Originally, she had felt like an offshoot of her mother, attached by right of flesh and blood.

> Where she is rooted, I am rooted. . . . But here in Mr. Gower's hands I
> became other--a parasite on her body, no longer of her mind. My arms are
> vines that strangle the limb to which I cling . . . . If I tell Mother about Mr.
> Gower, the alarm will send a tremor throughout our bodies and I will be torn
> away from her. . . . In the centre of my body is a rift (64-65).

The age-old violence of sexual abuse pulsates deeply in the heart of the
narrative. Violence is integral to maintaining this theme of silence.
Violence against innocent children and entire communities of people.

Naomi must dredge this burden up to conscious memory if she is
to find out what happened to her mother: Naomi feared she had caused
her mother's disappearance because it occurred shortly after Naomi, at
the age of five, had been sexually abused. Naomi had somehow felt
her Mother's absence was punishment for the horrible experience at
Mr. Gower's. Throughout the novel, Kogawa keeps personal events
closely entwined with revelations of the broader political scene. Her
plotting on these two grids achieves a remarkably subtle and believable
unfolding of the protagonist's life and spiritual struggles by integrating
brutal "public" facts with her own "personal" nightmares and longings.

In the face of Aunt Emily's insistence and perseverance, Naomi
reluctantly begins to poke through the box of "facts": Emily's diary,
addressed to Dearest Nesan, her elder sister, Naomi's mother; newspa-
pers clippings; letters from exiled Nisei and sympathetic missionaries;
copies of her extensive correspondence and other documents; headlines
from World War II on the domestic scene. "She finds this Pandora's
box filled with hatred and historical woes which offers, paradoxically,
her only hope. This inclusion of precise documents and speeches--from
Stanley Knowles' address opposing disenfranchisement of Japanese-
Canadians to details of the Japanese Repatriation Program--underscores
how completely the stone of silence had covered those victimized by
[the racist policies of the Canadian state]."[1]

Kogawa implies the need to revise history in light of different
"facts" by juxtaposing the official version of government propaganda
about the Japanese "threat" with the events of Naomi's experience. As
Naomi recognizes this contradiction, her strength to rely on the power
of memory over forgetfulness increases. Aunt Emily's tireless work is
based on her belief that "It matters to get the facts straight. . . . Rec-

---

[1]St. Andrews, "Reclaiming a Canadian Heritage," 31.

onciliation can't begin without mutual recognition of facts" (88). At end of World War II, the narrator recalls this admonition as she recounts their removal from the ghost-town of Slocan in the interior of British Columbia to a sugar beet farm in southern Alberta.

The relocation to Alberta meant "exile from the place of exile":

> "Grinning and happy" and all smiles standing around a pile of beets [as one newspaper had reported]? That is one telling. It's not how it was. . . . We have come to the moon. We have come to the edge of the world, to a place of angry air. Was it just a breath ago that we felt the green watery fingers of the mountain air? . . . Facts about evacuees in Alberta? The fact is I never got used to it and I cannot, I cannot bear the memory. . . . There is a word for it. Hardship (197; 194).

The unbelievable becomes real when considered next to lies. Naomi learns, however unwillingly, to bear this memory, to open up more of the information brought by Aunt Emily, and to confront it. "The orders given to Uncle and Father in 1945, reach me via Aunt Emily's package in 1972, twenty-seven years later. The delivery service is slow these days. Understanding is even slower" (172-73). "'Nothing but the lowest motives of greed, selfishness and hatred have been brought forward to defend these disgraceful Orders,' the Globe and Mail noted" (199). While restrictions on Japanese-Canadians may in 1945 no longer have been justifiable by national security, they were nonetheless perpetuated by the official rationale of giving white people a year to heal their hatred. Naomi laments:

> Which year should we choose for *our* healing? . . . I can cry for the flutes that have cracked in the dryness and cry for the people who no longer sing. I can cry for Obasan who has turned to stone. But what then? Uncle does not rise up and return to his boats. Dead bones do not take on flesh (198).

Naomi's longing for transformation is still suffocating under the "lies, secrets and silences"[1] surrounding her personal history. "The sadness and the absence are like a long winter storm, the snow falling in an unrelieved colourlessness that settles and freezes, burying me beneath a growing monochromatic weight. Something dead is happening. . ." (200). She aches for liberation:

---

[1] The term is from Adrienne Rich, *On Lies, Secrets and Silences*.

> I want to break loose from the heavy identity, the evidence of rejection, the
> unexpressed passion, the misunderstood politeness. I am tired of living bet-
> ween deaths and funerals, weighted with decorum, unable to shout or sing or
> dance, unable to scream or swear, unable to laugh, unable to breathe out loud
> (183).

The effect of the internment is visible in Naomi's psyche; there is an
internal imprisonment that must also be overcome.

One stirs painfully as the narrator moves into the transition between facts and hope: Naomi has to hear the tragic story of her family
in order to reclaim her place in her clan after the onslaught of the official, racist events. In order to learn to live with a thirty year history of
pain, silence and humiliation, Naomi must first of all take on "the burden of commitment," a step she finally makes before her Uncle's funeral. The facts of Aunt Emily's package do not heal her *until* she
starts to put them together with a rehearsal of her own personal memories from childhood and beyond.[1]

As a lonely school teacher in a small prairie town, she confronts
on the one hand, the demise of her familial past. "If we were knit into
a family once, it's become badly moth-eaten with time. We are now no
more that a few tangled skeins--the remains of what might once have
been a fisherman's net" (21). On the other hand, she grasps the salvific role the Japanese and other minority groups play in Canadian history. Their collective silence is portrayed as "undemanding as dew"
when a group of evacuees heads to Slocan in 1942:

> We are despised and rendered voiceless, stripped of car, radio, camera and
> every means of communication. . . . We are the man in the Gospel of John,
> born into the world for the sake of light. . . . We are sent to the sending,
> that we may bring sight (111-12).

The salvific purpose of these people is well indicated as they are sent
into the designed wilderness of enforced labour and reopened ghost
towns. This is also where Naomi meets Rough Lock Bill, an Indian
living on Slocan Lake, whose people have experienced similar destruction at the hands of white injustice. The Biblical significance of the
two social histories becomes clear when she recalls his story of the ori-

---

[1]Erika Gottlieb, "The Riddle of Concentric Worlds in *Obasan*," *Canadian
Literature* 109 (Summer 1986), 38.

gin of his people's name for the settlement: "Slo Can go"--because of their perseverance going through the mountains to reach it. Shortly after this conversation Bill saves her from drowning. The common theme is underscored: the Japanese Canadians, like the Native peoples before them, by their suffering, uphold life and "bring light" so that no other group should endure injustice. The relationship between Naomi and Rough Lock Bill is a fine testimony to the grace of solidarity.

The issue of injustice had been muted and hidden by both the dominant version of history and in part, despite their good intentions, by the memories buried by her family, by being "drowned in a whirl-pool of protective silence" (21). Naomi knows she will never find the "living word" to break the stone of her heavy identity until she finds out what happened to her mother. When her uncle dies, the justifica-tion for maintaining the mystery is broken, interestingly, with the in-tervention of the Nakane's life-long Christian minister.

The novel's resolution is created by Naomi's description of the ideographs for the word love. "The first contained the root words 'heart' and 'hand' and 'action'--love as hands and heart in action to-gether. The other ideograph, for 'passionate love' was formed of 'heart,' 'to tell,' and 'a long thread'" (228). Love, fully present in her life, is what she has struggled to find in her search for the truth about her mother's absence. Through her painful remembering, she has slowly and vaguely had intimations of trust in love's existence. When she finally determines to judge her dead mother for her absence no longer, Naomi's quest is answered: she can feel and receive her moth-er's undying love in the silence.

Nakayama-sensei, the minister, finally induces Obasan to tell Naomi and Stephen what happened, to speak about "their suffering and deep love." Evidence of her mother's silent love and of her martyrdom in Nagasaki is contained in a blue rice-paper letter from her Grand-mother found amongst Aunt Emily's papers.

> In the dark Slocan night, the bright light flares in my dreaming. I hear screams and feel the mountain breaking. Your long black hair falls and falls into the chasm. My legs are sawn in half. The skin on your face bubbles like lava and melts from your bones. Mother, I see your face. Do not turn aside (242).

Naomi's nightmares contain vivid reactions to the news of how her mother died and why she had never returned. In response to "their grief that is not fit for human habitation," the Sensei offers this insight: "That this world is brokenness. But within brokenness is the unbreakable name. How the whole earth groans til Love returns" (240).

Kogawa unfolds her theological stance at the novel's closure. She testifies that "the freeing word," the unbreakable name of Love, is found in breaking the stone of silence about her family and the lives of Japanese Canadians. In the end, we realize with the narrator that she and her mother "were lost together in our silences. Our wordlessness was our mutual destruction . . . the earth still stirs with dormant blooms. Love flows through our roots of the trees by our graves" (243). In naming the unspeakable pain Love heals us and blooms.

Naomi is now able to be reconciled to her mother and upon returning to "Uncle's spot" in the coulee, she goes to the very bottom of the prairie valley:

> Above the trees, the moon is a pure white stone. The reflection is rippling in the river--water and stone dancing. It's a quiet ballet, soundless as breath. . . . The perfume [of the wild roses and the tiny wildflowers that grow along the trickling stream] in the air is sweet and faint (247).

Like the biblical promises of manna and a new name, quoted as preface to the narrative, Naomi had overcome because the flow of love had overcome the power of death. When the prairie came alive to her senses we feel Naomi dropping her heavy cloak of despair and torment. We witness signs of Naomi's new life in her feeling at home on the prairie when formerly it meant a land of exile, and in her broader sense of connectedness in recognizing and affirming in her past the value of political protest--she has learned how "the government makes paper airplanes out of our lives and flies them out the windows" (242).

Naomi has also respectfully observed that Obasan "does not dance to the multi-cultural piper's tune or respond to the racist slur. She remains in a silent territory, defined by her serving hands" (226). In other words, silence for Obasan was the way to endure the truth. The novel ends with an excerpt from the 1946 memorandum of the Cooperative Committee on Japanese Canadians to the House and Senate of Canada, naming the Orders-in-Council as a crime against humanity. It is made indelibly clear that, if any authentic Canadian identity be achieved, this past public condemnation of crimes against humanity must stand in judgment over our future and call the state to account.

Aunt Emily's diagnosis--without accurate remembrance there can be no redemption--is affirmed. It takes the loss of Naomi's Uncle and the reunion of her remaining family to release Naomi from denial. While she finds neither aunt's model of moral agency appropriate for her own life, she recognizes that she can now live in gratitude and with responsibility to chosen aspects of both of their values. Naomi's journey has been rendered throughout the novel with a magnificent sober, poetic tone; it ends with an epiphany out on the prairie, under the vast sky that now beckons as an open horizon. She is making right relation with her internal, historical, and communal landscape.

Conclusion

All three narratives command our attention as social-spiritual journeys engaging fundamental questions: Can the female characters, victimized so often by impersonal, unyielding forces, social conventions, and lies, overcome the degrading humiliations and silences of personal pain? Is there meaning to the persecution of and racism against aboriginal and Japanese Canadians? Can the evil against women and children, as well as whole groups of human beings such as the poor, ever be rightly remembered in order to come to terms with that experience? These issues are tackled in distinct and courageous ways as the protagonists search for their authentic life-blood amidst the betrayals, lies and exclusionary devices of official societal ethics. They have all rejected their positions as victims and, at least to a degree, "claimed their own souls."[1]

As do Culleton and Laurence, Kogawa asserts that truth must be sought in memory: "The past is the future" (42). The novels by minority authors, Kogawa and Culleton, and by Laurence, a white woman, can be characterized as a search for and a claiming of their people's voice, for a usable past. There is certainly a large measure of difference. For example, Kogawa's has Aunt Emily states, "we're gluing our tongues back on" (36). This aunt plays a similar role to Culleton's Cheryl Raintree. "She's the one with the vision. She believes in the Nisei, seeing them as networks and streamers of light dotting the

---

[1]This term is from Carol Christ.

country. . . . Injustice enrages Aunt Emily. Any injustice" (31-34).
Naomi, on the other hand, is more like April Raintree: "I can only see
a dark field with Aunt Emily beaming her flashlight to where the rest
of us crouch and hide, our eyes downcast as we seek the safety of invisibility (32)." "She [Aunt Emily] asked me if I really wanted to 'know'
everything. . . . Sure, I lied" (43).

A similar dialogue might have taken place between April and
Cheryl, with Cheryl reciting the litany of persecution and oppression of
the Metis. And like Cheryl, Emily researches her people's history in
the hopes of attaining justice. Laurence's study of history revolves around the knowledge that everyone changes their version of the past, in
light of ongoing experience, to create new meaning: "A popular misconception is that we can't change the past--everyone is constantly
changing their own past, recalling it, revising it" (60). "But, there's no
one version. There just isn't" (350).

A common discovery for all three protagonists at some time in
their journey is that there is no safety in invisibility. "Denial is gangrene," Kogawa states through Aunt Emily. It is a hard battle to break
through the numbness of and collusion with the official history each has
heard. They eventually endorse an alternative vision because, once
they have told their pain--to themselves and significant others--they
recognize that it means life and the waters of new energy.

A central motif operative in the novels is the task of rewriting
history from the experiences of the women themselves. Each protagonist has to figure out ways to include herself in the larger picture, starting from her family's past. Accurate representations of a particular
past, from those rendered invisible and no longer willing to stay hidden, is the work of the main characters. Moreover, they indicate the
life-giving necessity of redoing history by figuring out who is here to
change the present.

> Where do any of us come from in this cold country? Oh, Canada, whether it
> is admitted or not, we come from you we come from you. From the same
> soil. . . . We come from the country that plucks its people out like weeds
> and flings them into the roadside. We grow in ditches and sloughs, untended
> and spindly. We erupt in the valleys and mountainsides, in small towns and
> back alleys, sprouting upside down on the prairies. . . . We grow where we
> are not seen, we flourish where we are not heard, the thick undergrowth of
> an unlikely planting. . . . We come from the cemeteries full of skeletons,
> with wild roses grinning in their teeth. We come from our untold tales that

wait for their telling. We come from Canada, this land that is like every land, filled with the wise, the fearful, the compassionate, the corrupt (*Obasan*, 226).

The theme of Canadian identity as "an unlikely planting" is constructed within each narrative through the metaphor of the landscape: the process of shaping communal and personal identities is depicted in terms of a struggle to live *with*, not at the mercy of or by conquering, the land and all who dwell in it.

The protagonists' relationship with the land represents their journeys towards authorizing their own lives: the more alive they are to their natural surroundings, the more centred they are in themselves. This metaphor relates to the whole character: her racial, ethnic, and national identities. These elements of identity are presented as inseparable and necessary to tend as fruitful ground for full life. And the vastness of the land seems to stand in the narratives for the ready possibility of welcoming the diversity of its inhabitants.

I read these narratives as invitations to re-search Canadian and personal narratives that give power to the margin. A new knowledge is being formed that asserts the way to a better world is through hearing and speaking the suffering, not cutting ourselves off from it. These narratives proclaim that suffering is not meaningless and that peace will be born out of breaking "the stone of silence" out of which springs "the living word." Further, Laurence is a significant voice for enabling white Canadians to recognize how some of our displaced ancestors became oppressors themselves. A critical representation of the social landscape is accomplished by portrayals of social relations as dynamic contradictory constructs. For example, while Morag struggles to write her own fictions as truth, at other times she realizes it is right to not speak. Conscious of her white privilege in the face of Piquette's tragic death, Morag has no right to say anything (*The Diviners*, 268).

The three narratives signify how "the person" is at once a social and unique individual: April, Morag, and Naomi achieve their self-definition and integrity *because* of their social connections, with friends, lovers, and family members. What Terrie Goldie has observed about Morag holds true for the others: "Her various shamans are living humans with whom she must function. The insights provided by Christie and Jules [and Cheryl and Aunt Emily], cannot be divided from the torment caused by their socially unacceptable lifestyles and difficult personalities."[1] Thus, while the novels have portrayed individual women's stories of coming into fuller self-affirmation and acceptance, it would be a gross misreading to conclude that these characters could be solitary or isolated. When they have indeed known remoteness, it signified an alienation not only from themselves but also from their roots and communities. In other words, without confronting their socio-historical conditions and critically appropriating them through a long and arduous interaction, these women would *not*, as they stand at the close of the novels, be centred in themselves while sustaining life in relationships. In short, we learn most from a story that is effected by "the facts."

These novels demystify and revise particular traditions by holding together personal experiences (i. e., the lives of their main characters) and the historical practices that have shaped them (i.e., Culleton's use of Cheryl's essays; Laurence's use of myths, songs and symbols; and Kogawa's use of historical documents). Empowerment happens: "there's energy, there's strength being transmitted from the storyteller to the listener."[2] A reclamation of suppressed heritages emerges through the process of self-invention, which is simultaneously a process of creating an empowering connection with the so-called public reality of Canada where Naomi, Morag, and April can "breathe out loud."

Laurence's image of the river flowing both ways symbolizes that mutuality is the means of grace. Mutuality contradicts the experience of outsiderhood, which is "like being offered a pair of crutches while . . . striding down the street" (*Obasan*, 225). These narratives reach beyond the suffering of their own protagonists' histories, of their own cultural, geographic, social, and sexual displacements, by knowing their sorrows and joys intimately. To that extent, they see beyond and through history.

In the protagonists' struggle to shape an animating past, we witness the attempt to break through barriers that block a moral ethos

---

[1]Terrie Goldie, "Folklore, Popular Culture, and Individuation in *Surfacing* and *The Diviners*," *Canadian Literature* 104 (Spring 1985), 106.

[2]Beth Cuthand, "Transmitting Our Identity as Indian Writers," in *In the Feminine: Women and Words*, eds. Ann Dybikowski, Victoria Freeman, Daphne Marlatt, Barbara Pulling, and Betsy Warland (Edmonton: Longspoon Press, 1985), 54.

more conducive to women's well-being. We feel how walls of despair, of repression, of self-hatred, and of silence begin to crack and, stone by stone, are dismantled. We have seen how these protagonists express value, obligations, and qualities of character in response to their ancestors' and their own suffering and vision; how they learn to make decisions in dialogue with conflicting claims on their energies and loyalties; and how they construct identities that embody with integrity their own and their communities' futures.

CHAPTER SIX

TOWARDS A FEMINIST ETHIC OF SOLIDARITY IN THE CANADIAN RADICAL CHRISTIAN TRADITION

Summary of the Study

We are made invisible in the mainstream. And there is talk about "coming from the woman's perspective, coming from the woman's standpoint." It seems to me very empty, this standpoint, because I do not know who this woman is that they are talking about.[1]

The need to engage elided women's voices as crucial and critical resources for theological ethics has shaped and fueled this study. I have particularly attended to the suffering of such women to grasp the radical existence of sin and the consequent need for grace. It is particularly necessary that we identify and celebrate the sources of experienced hope in their lives. In the process, I have systematically explored amplification of the methods and sources that can move a Canadian feminist theological ethic to this deeper accountability. My hope is that this study will contribute to the creation of alternative ways of living out Christian faith in local, global, and ecological solidarity.

My theological method has employed the complementary analyses of political economics and cultural-literary theory as diverse means of naming, feeling, assessing, and confronting everyday realities of in-

---

[1] Himani Bannerji, "We Appear Silent to People Who are Deaf to What We Say," in *Fireweed: Issue 16, Women of Colour* (May 1983), 9.

justice and forms of resistance in women's lives. If we are not to render particular women invisible by making false generalizations about "women's experience," then women's experience in feminist theology and ethics must be specified in ever more subtle and concrete ways. I have tried to keep before me Adrienne Rich's poetic expression of the pain and power of women's lives, as a reminder to remain faithful to both the potency of women's agency and their particular experiences of victimization.

> It's an oldfashioned, an outrageous thing
> to believe one has a "destiny"
>
> --a thought often peculiar to those
> who possess privilege--
>
> but there is something else: the faith
> of those despised and endangered
>
> that they are not merely the sum
> of the damages done to them:
>
> have kept beyond violence the knowledge
> arranged in patterns like kente-cloth
>
> unexpected as in batik
> recurrent as bitter herbs and unleavened bread
>
> of being a connective link
> in a long, continuous way
>
> of ordering hunger, weather, death, desire
> and the nearness of chaos.[1]

This project has sought to address the following question: how do the needs central to my liberation--work, safe space, friendships, housing, spirituality--take form in and come to expression in the lives of those who are doubly or triply oppressed? Accountability to race and class and the texture of specific cultures enables this dialogue. We do not possess familiarity with contexts different than ours, but we must find new ways of listening and learning.

---

[1]Adrienne Rich, "Sources, XV," in *Your Native Land, Your Life* (New York: W. W. Norton and Co., 1986), 17.

As we have seen, some of the contours of a contextual theological method in Canada contribute to this agenda because we can only begin where we are.[1] As Robert McAfee Brown argues, contextualization is essential to theological formation:

> the presupposition we must accept is that our own position, whatever it is, is *not* normative, but is itself the product of many factors that may heretofore have escaped our notice: our race, class, sex, economic status, geographical location, or whatever. It is this *awareness of our own context* that . . . can liberate us from seeking to exercise over others a kind of theological imperialism. . . .[2]

This contextualization must be amplified if our ethic is to be consistent with justice-making and committed to a destiny inclusive of all women's visions. Locating this project in continuity with the indigenous Canadian religious movement, Radical Christianity, gives us a new way to initiate this contextualization and appropriate our heritage.   I have reviewed the roots of a Radical Christian contextual theological ethic, and suggested how these roots will be enhanced by an appropriation of feminist political economy.

Since this tradition claims human experience and relatedness as the loci of revelation, it has given us a theological perspective that is sensitive to the limitations of theologies that stress human dependence on divine control and fear of self-direction. Recognizing that such theologies are likely to reproduce social relations of domination and subordination, Radical Christianity's norm of mutuality is based on its reading of Jesus' ethic of loving our neighbour as ourselves. Radical Christianity's theological tenet, that love is most present in relations of justice, correlates well with feminist liberation norms. Therefore, its characterization of Christian love as mutuality, reciprocity, communion, and solidarity, and its application of love to both personal and social life, must be retained.

Radical Christianity's recognition that sin is social, that anything which opposes or thwarts the norm of mutuality is evil, also remains a

---

[1] This presupposition is basic to feminist theological practice; see for example, Letty Russell, *Household of Freedom: Authority in Feminist Theology*, 65.

[2] Brown, "What is Contextual Theology?" in *Changing Contexts of our Faith*, ed. Letty Russell (Philadelphia: Fortress, 1985), 59; emphasis added.

vital legacy. The movement recognized that capitalism is especially dangerous because its premises are individualism and the exploitation of human persons. Radical Christianity's rejection of capitalism, on the grounds of its contradiction of basic theological tenets which affirm that we are social creatures who become fully human only in communities directed towards love and justice, must also be retained.

Another basepoint of Radical Christianity, that moral agency and solidarity are the key to divine-human relationship, also needs to be re-affirmed. Active struggle against social sin and participation in creating communities based on mutuality enable an encounter with grace. Its oft-repeated emphasis on the integrity of personal and social well-being continues to serve us well.

Finally, for Radical Christianity utopias, or imaginative yearnings and visions, play an essential role in encouraging a critical conversion to the reality and possibility of the realm of God, even though no possible social order is equivalent to that realm. Liturgies and the shared struggle for justice are of central importance to this task of nourishing utopian visions of shalom.[1]

While embracing this Radical Christian legacy, I have identified some definite weaknesses in the tradition. My critical feminist reading in terms of socio-economic and cultural theory has informed this critique. One result is an extension of the concept of mutuality, since Radical Christianity's reading of this norm neglected the *interpersonal specifics of power relationships*, thus mystifying the range of racial/ethnic, class, and gender privilege operative within the Radical Christians' social locations. I have argued that a norm of mutual relationship must be grounded in terms of embodiment which requires awareness of the specific cultural-historical contexts that mediate our actions, perceptions, and beliefs.

Like the norm of mutuality, the Radical Christian conception of social sin as fueled chiefly by capitalism took account only of social sin in the public arena. From a feminist viewpoint, structural sin is often named as *patriarchy*, but patriarchy must be understood to include in-

---

[1] As I was preparing this summary of the continuities between my project and the Canadian Radical Christianity, I welcomed Gregory Baum's reflections on, among other books, the reprinted edition of *Towards the Christian Revolution* (Kingston, Ont.: Ronald Frye and Co., 1989); see his "United Church Theology Offers Food," *Catholic New Times*, Fall Book Supplement (8 October 1989).

terlocking structures of sexism, heterosexism, racism, classism, cultur-al imperialism, and ecological destruction.[1] I have argued that our understanding of what creating just relationships involves must be radi-cally deepened to include our understanding of the particularities of women's moral agency. Acknowledging and enabling women to be-come moral agents is essential and inseparable from the theological and ethical task of building rightly-ordered communities.

Significant developments in the Canadian faith-and-justice tradi-tion for clarifying economic justice have received special attention here. These statements on economic justice must be appropriated criti-cally from the standpoints of women's experience. This economic ethic extends our legacy by embracing theological norms of creation and human participation, and affirms work as essential to full humanity. It affirms an advocacy stance that consistently expresses the viewpoint of victims of the global capitalist economic system. Finally, people are placed at the centre of its vision of moral value: the goal of economic ethics is to develop shalom communities of whole persons.

Nevertheless, these Radical Christian approaches to economic justice do not illumine women's work as a key to an adequate ethics. As I demonstrated, the everyday lives of women were invisible in early work, and continue to be marginal to recent ecclesial analyses. Assum-ing that economic reality is the same for women as for men and that a changed economic system would bring justice equally for women and men is an error. Without awareness of women's work, the types, causes, and pervasiveness of human alienation and oppression can neither be named or challenged. When unemployment is presumed to be the fundamental problem (or evil) in the economic crisis, the chief victims of that crisis are waged workers. I have argued that the dehu-manization of labour that women's lives reveal deepens our understand-ing of economic ethics. Such an approach also strengthens links with those who are differently exploited and oppressed. Nor would full

---

[1]Patriarchy is not always understood so complexly in feminist theory. Delores Williams, in "The Color of Feminism," argues that white women often define patriarchy in ways that do not include black women's experience of white oppression in which white women participate and reap benefits. Williams proposes that the more adequate term for women of colour is demonarchy. On patriarchy complexly defined, see for example Caroline Ramazanoglu, *Feminism and the Con-tradictions of Oppression*, and Sheila Collins, *A Different Heaven and Earth*.

employment strategies proposed by Radical Christianity affect women's lives as positively as men's lives, since the domestic sphere is left untouched, as are the patriarchal and racist dynamics within systems of capitalist exploitation.

To redress this major lacuna of Radical Christianity, I focused on a social analysis of Canadian women's situations through the lens of political-economy. Like Radical Christianity, feminist political economic analysis insists that social power is largely predicated on economic power, and that concrete social justice is necessary for full personal well-being. To make women's labour visible, however, I investigated the distinctiveness of women's economic suffering and agency. The general picture of women's labour included evaluating the role of the public-private split enshrined in white-supremacist, capitalist-patriarchy as the root cause of women's oppression and exploitation; the nature of women's alienated and shadow work; and the inadequacy of wage labour as a potential solution to women's problems.

Out of this research I affirmed criteria for a feminist liberative theological ethic that defines the work of women's everyday lives as an issue of moral value in a misogynist, sexist, and homophobic culture. How, then, can women's everyday work experience be conveyed more adequately? Women's work is structured by the *productive* and *reproductive/cultural* systems. The latter is as basic as the former for human survival because the transmission of material life, human values, meaning, and purpose all depend upon it. From the vantage point of women's experience cross-culturally, our notions of work must be transformed to include creative involvement in building relationships, and enhancing the dignity of persons and communities in love and justice. Such transformation requires a broader conception of social responsibility, in which "people share responsibility for each other, both directly and through the socialization of many forms of labour that must now be performed or paid for by private individuals and families."[1] Lastly, and most importantly, I concluded that the norm for economic justice, as for all other areas of women's lives, is empowerment.

After arguing for the methodological priority of investigating political economic dynamics specifically in women's lives, the second step of this inquiry was to strengthen another methodological basepoint

---

[1] Sarvasy and Allen, "Fighting the Feminization of Poverty," 100.

to enable a liberative ethics to incorporate the elided voices of women. How can we gain access to the cultural specifics of women's lives and further develop a critical cultural analysis in Canadian theological ethics? I explored a framework for cultural analysis consistent with feminist aims and norms by drawing on contextual and liberation theological insights and on critical cultural conceptions of culture in terms of hegemony, ideology, and power. Because women's experience, like the word of God, is socially constructed and lived out within the boundaries of a given culture and society, the embodied uniqueness of those struggling to practice justice must not be reduced to the sum of their social statistics. Therefore, cultural analysis must be used in relation to the insights gained from the analyses of political economy.

The cultural resources of empowering cultural practices, insights, meanings, and codes provide "a surplus of experience"[1] which is dependent on, and inseparable from, lived-world experience, but not entirely contained within the limits of the social givens. This cultural surplus of experience enables us to seek *common* goals but in ways which confront differences of oppression experienced by women, and respect differences of insight, skill and liberating culture. To appropriate critically women's experience in cultural terms, we must clarify the terms of female responsibility as the ground for authentic moral freedom. Therefore, we must ask *whose* culture and *whose* experience are shaping theological ethics. Without including the widest possible range of experiences, especially the experiences of those who suffer most from dominant social arrangements, our theological ethics will remain truncated, and lacking the vitality and accountability conducive to human liberation. To this end, I have aligned my work with a critically appropriated transformational understanding of the cultural context in doing theological ethics. My central thesis has been that critical attention must be given to the cultural practices of everyday life if women's voices are to have their due authority in the theological task of shaping justice in relationships with God, self, and others.

Within the construct of hegemony, this method of cultural analysis acknowledges that culture can be both oppressive and emancipatory, either open to the creation of authentic identities within configurations

---

[1]This term is from Briggs, "Sexual Justice and the 'Righteousness of God,'" in *Sex and God*, ed. Hurcombe, 274.

of restraint or an arena of subjugation. The import of this approach to culture is that it enables us to engage cultural resources in a way that discloses the problematic of women's everyday social contexts and to approach culture as a generative context of concrete transformation. A critical hermeneutics of women's experience will attend to the dynamic connections between social-cultural orders, and the subjective forms by which we live and create meaning, such as consciousness, emotions, memories, and the sense of oneself, others, and God. This approach to culture equips us to identify and interpret those cultural factors which restrict, crush, or encourage women in their varied struggles to become moral agents. A feminist liberationist ethic of culture seeks to study the fabric of women's struggles for justice that provides the context for theological expressions. In particular, we examine critically the ways in which power is abused or shared. In order to make women's experience central *without* perpetuating further distortions of women's suffering and hope, the realities of conflict, multiplicity, contradiction, and commonality in women's lives must be disclosed respectfully, not objectified. To this end, feminist liberation theology focuses on women's own stories of their struggles to embrace life authentically.

Narrative is a valuable cultural resource for including women's elided voices which open up "the surplus of experience." If women are to become moral subjects and if we are to author our own lives, the importance of naming our own experience cannot be overestimated. An exploration of narrative can both tell the truth about the differences and commonalities of women's experience under varying power dynamics and keep our theological ethics accountable to women's lived-world experience. To enable a focus on the *specificity* of women's experience, we must hear women's stories from *varied positions of outsiderhood*. We must also count as moral activity that which has long been considered outside the domain of public morality: the so-called private social relations for which women have long been accorded responsibility and which are necessary for the functioning of all social relations. The importance of women's narratives for feminist ethics lies in their portrayal of women learning how to live, of women's "lifeline politics"[1] which have been muted or submerged by hegemonic cul-

---

[1] This term is from Delores Williams, "Women's Oppression and Lifeline Politics in Black Women's Religious Narratives," 58-71.

tural schemes. In order to resist horizontal violence, narratives by and about women whose experience is different from, as well as similar to, one's own can enable us to hear one another across barriers that divide.

To demonstrate how such a theory of culture might work I investigated selected narratives to discover imaginative insights which would enable us to learn of the complex power dynamics which shape personal, cultural, sexual, and social matrices. I elaborated a feminist cultural hermeneutic to guide my reading of three narratives about the process of female self-invention. Narrative can function as a privileged resource for a self-critical politics of diversity. Most importantly, perhaps, we can read fiction as narratives that help us in our common task of constructing communities in which our hearts and minds, bodies and souls, will be integrated in right relationship.

I selected three Canadian novels for a close analysis, choosing these narratives: because they were set in recent cross-cultural situations on the prairies, because they developed female protagonists who were struggling for their own lives against great odds, and because the characters struggled to live into their own power despite severe wounds, ostracism, and rejection. We saw how each author explores the context of the prairie and the particular horizon and destiny her characters inherited. The stories evolve out of the painful contradictions which each protagonist discovers and needs to confront in order to embrace the liberative possibilities in her context.

Theological Implications of Elided Voices in Canadian Women's Fiction

For those of us who are still rooted in Christian discourse and tradition, what are some theological implications of these voices? While I want to be sensitive to a possible misuse of these narratives, I will now briefly develop some theological themes. In reading these narratives, I have observed significant parallels with some threads of white feminist theology, namely how we define sin, spiritual conversion, sacred power, and salvation.

A major contribution of these narratives to the continuing work of feminist theological ethics is their correlation of personal and social histories. The novels said a great deal about power as a living, historical phenomenon, mostly about its abuses, and also about its effects on the characters' everyday lives. This literature encourages us to clarify our commitments and loyalties in terms of the explicit starting point of a liberative ethic: a praxis for justice which never violates the human person in her social context. We must start from where we are, but these narratives enlarge the horizon with particular journeys, sufferings, and resources for empowerment. They invite us to deepen our own naming of the marginalized histories and shared moral wisdom available for the collective task of making love through justice.

These narratives depict the spiritual struggles of their protagonists to move into their own creative power. That is the meaning given to grace: the gift of claiming responsibility for one's life, of love of self and neighbour, of the assumption of healthy power over one's life and circumstances.

Sin in feminist theology is anything which contradicts the gospel: the good news of freedom and dignity for all. It has many manifestations.[1] For example, it can be the acceptance of dehumanization, or it can mean denying others the room to live and breathe. In the characterization of April Raintree, Morag Gunn, and Naomi Nakane, sin is aptly portrayed as muteness, that is, the absence of the power to interpret rightly. Personal sin is sometimes acceptance of isolation, self-denial, and the failure to take responsibility for oneself. Each protagonist has different constraints on her agency, yet each discovers that she has the capacity either to perpetuate her own "otherness" or to commit herself to breaking apart the stereotypes and lies in order to emerge as a co-creator. For example, when each character takes courage and searches for appropriate knowledge and images of herself, she discovers rich blessing in coming to accept the identity of her people. Sin is also depicted as a corporate power that does evil against whole groups of people. Corporate sin as exposed and described in the novels denies to Native, Japanese, rural, artist, and working Canadians the possibility of communal self-creation. In other words, the personal, interpersonal, and social exclusion and coercion of racism, sexism, and class and cultural elitism are denounced as sinful throughout the narratives.

---

[1] See Judith Plaskow's conclusions on white western women's experiences of sin and grace, in *Sex, Sin and Grace: Women's Experience and the Theologies of Reinhold Niebuhr and Paul Tillich* (Washington, D.C.: University Press of America, 1980), 149-76; and Aruna Gnanadason, "Women's Oppression: A Sinful Situation," in *With Passion and Compassion*, eds. Fabella and Oduyoye, 69-75.

The characters' failure to realize their own freedom, however, was not simply their own fault. The authors stand in judgment on any blaming of victims. Sin is that which brings about death in relationships among people; it is therefore quite specific to particular contexts and histories. The narratives portray their protagonists as those who are sinned-against. In other words, while their particular hopes for full life were at times thwarted by their passivity, the characters' inner resolve developed due to a deepening understanding of their own histories and to their attempts to exorcise internalized self-hate for which, they come to realize, they are not responsible.

In all three novels, we are shown that suffering has no meaning unless it has been freely chosen for a greater good. The only meaning that can be ascribed to the brutal pain experienced by the destruction of April and Cheryl's and Naomi's peoples is in their choice to *resist* oppression and confront abuse.[1] Different oppressions lead them to search for different expressions of freedoms and spiritual life. In Kogawa's metaphor, the search is for the freeing word, the living word from the stone of silence. Finally, near the close of her novel, she names that word as Love. In the persecution of the Japanese Canadian people and through the character of Naomi, we learn about a horrific reality of Canada that has been silenced. It is a country peopled by "an unlikely planting," where its cruelty and hope are mingled in "the wise, fearful, compassionate and corrupt."[2] In Culleton, the search for belonging and respect, for spiritual power and a future for the children of mixed ancestry, the symbol of transformation of suffering is in April's sister Cheryl: "[She] was that stalk in the field of grain which never bent to the mighty winds of authority. At the same time, that stalk could bend to the gentle breezes of compassion."[3] Again, resistance and self-determination are the keys to shedding false consciousness about the value of "being white." And for Laurence, the symbol for Morag's learning to live by her own approval and creativity in com-

---

[1]For an excellent treatment of the issue of suffering in the context of sexual and domestic violence, see Marie Fortune, "The Transformation of Suffering: A Biblical and Theological Perspective," in *Christianity, Patriarchy and Abuse*, eds. Joanne Carlson Brown and Carole Bohn (New York: Pilgrim Press, 1989).

[2]Kogawa, *Obasan*, 226.

[3]Culleton, *In Search of April Raintree*, 121.

munity is the art of divining. Her search for submerged histories and transforming, life-giving values to pass along as inheritance to the next generation is nourished by her commitment to take her own life seriously and take responsibility for her gifts of divining. The rare Blue Heron is Laurence's symbol of transcendence whose soaring and measured flight is as certain as the promise of rightness in relationships when people learn to live the means of grace: life is both a gift and a task.

For resurrection to happen, for this promise of right-relationship to be fulfilled, all three novelists identified particular stones which their protagonists must help to roll away: economic dependence, broken family bonds and lifeless marriages, ignorance, and stultifying self-images, to name a few. For example, we can notice that grace appears in these narratives as power arising from a sharing of burdens and a commitment to embodied spiritual wholeness. We learn that grief can be the place of deepened relationship because in grief we recognize the value of that which is loved. We read of the wisdom of compassion, portrayed as coming close enough to be touched, risking relation at the cost of great pain, and letting grief be a bridge to self-respect and healing. We recognize the forgiving acknowledgment of the dignity and value of unexpendable persons: as April Raintree does for her sister Cheryl, as Naomi Nakane does for her mother, and as Morag Gunn does for her lifelong lover, Jules Tonnerre. In these acts of compassion we recognize choices which incarnate God and we are reminded that it is we ourselves who are accountable for the incarnation of love and dignity among us.[1]

Salvation must be specifically named, then, in relation to characters who struggle for survival on the edges of society. We are shown their response to adversity. Often they face choices between relative deprivations--as April, Naomi, and Morag did in choosing to stay in lifeless marriages or jobs--and the insecurity of uncharted paths. These characters are women who come into their co-creative power by struggling to embrace life through confrontations with otherness, and their own nothingness. In them we encounter creative power, the power to

---

[1]On human responsibility for incarnating divine love, Carter Heyward, *The Redemption of God*, 159, observes: "There may be nothing more difficult than for us to realize and claim our power to effect good, our capacity to make a positive difference in the world, our co-creative ability to sustain relational power."

save from apathy and denial, as "the power to renew the world for someone or for a community. Through it [they] attempt to rebuild the house of life out of the ruins in which [they] now live."[1] In other words, to understand the protagonists' stories theologically, we need to hear their deepest yearnings for the courage to act as co-creators and participate in the goodness of creation by resisting evil.

Each protagonist learns that evil is only undone by joining with others to undo it. Each moves onto sacred ground in those moments when she organizes her life with what we who practice a Christian faith would name the power of the divine Spirit. These women's deepest and active joy is depicted in epiphanies of thanksgiving and love--April with her nephew or with Cheryl at the Pow Wow; Naomi on the prairie communing with her mother; or Morag by the river, happy to be alive.

All three characters discover their passion for life. It is no accident that Culleton, Kogawa, and Laurence portray salvation as a process of transformation involving the total well-being of creation. They offer us images of the faith necessary to claim life as a gift meant for all people. For those whose lives have been slashed and scarred by subjugation and exploitation, salvation *is* liberation, social and spiritual, personal and physical. In these narratives we find fictional portrayals of women empowered into agency, even at times empowered to shape the conditions for freedom. If we read these stories as spiritual odysseys, faith is that fulfilling dimension of learning to "breathe out loud," learning to live deeply into their own rightly claimed lives.

Theologically, these narratives contribute to an understanding of Sacred and Holy Power specifically in the integration of the many dimensions that compose personhood. The protagonists develop a common conviction that we know transcendence in the immediacy of human love, in relationships which give them affirmation and space to grow. We can recall the relationships of Jules and Morag, April and Cheryl, Naomi and her aunts. Never do these women meet Sacred Power by denying someone else's personhood. They are portrayed as possessing an amazing integrity; their spirituality is profoundly body, earth, and life affirming.

We are not, however, spared seeing and hearing the fears and agonizing doubts, the nightmares and abuse which characterize the sto-

---

[1] Sölle, *To Work and To Love*, 37.

ries of these women. Without endorsing pain and suffering as salvific in itself, these authors nonetheless have dwelt on how the struggle towards authentic human power goes through, not around, the deepest sorrow and suffering. Above all, these protagonists teach us that God is known when we are most fully present to ourselves through self-acceptance and love. We are thereby related to one another, belly-wise, as Naomi was to her mother. Such belly wisdom opens up the different yet integrated ways in which we are able to journey into the Power of Relation who is God: by weaving together private and public, facts and truth, politics and spirituality, bodies and souls. The power of abundant life is portrayed as present in the inseparability and interconnectedness of the characters in these narratives with their ancestors, their futures, and the land. Images of Sacred Power which emerge from these narratives as resources for visions of alternative futures include the God who is in all the Space in Between, the God who is in the dead of Winter, and the God who Relates Us to our Cultures.

In short, the novelists portray a profound sense of the spiritual journeys involved in their characters' coming to terms with their ancestors and their own sense of place as independent, and interdependent, "bloody-minded" women. All three protagonists suffer deeply, often through inherited injustice. They search for the wisdom specific to their communities. In this search they learn that in the power of remembrance lies hope for the future. In the process of surviving and creating themselves, they discover spiritual empowerment and a knowledge of rightness and belonging in themselves and among their people. In this struggle, they come to know a power beyond themselves, but known only through their own everyday struggles.

These stories teach us of the possibilities of taking courage, of believing that through one another's presence and energy we will realize the power to act our way into personhood and peoplehood. These narratives open our eyes to the incredible determination and grace possible when we take our own lives seriously. They also present diverse purposive senses of vocation[1] which urge us towards a sobered, yet deeper understanding of the differing concerns and priorities women embrace in their specific struggles for liberation. A theological reading of these narratives, then, must carefully examine the different obsta-

---

[1]This term is from Emmet, *The Moral Prism*, 5-6.

cles, such as racism, poverty, illiteracy, ethnocentrism, and heterosexism, to name a few, as well as sources of empowerment.

While I am very cautious in moving towards constructing a
common vision, we must now consider further learnings from this study for naming and honouring difference in women's experience.

Power and Particularity

Power, as understood in terms of women's work and narratives,
has been named as spiritual and physical energy, empowerment, endurance, creative work, connection with nature, making meaningful
lives out of chaos, enjoying sensual/sexual experience. Power shared
enables women to become persons in their own right and create a space
where they can breathe freely. One of these sources of power for
women is their work as culture-bearers. Bell Hooks identifies the significance of speech as the phenomenon of formerly silenced women
"talking back."

> Moving from silence into speech is for the oppressed, the colonized, the ex-
> ploited, and those who stand and struggle side by side, a gesture of defiance
> that heals, that makes new life and new growth possible. It is that act of
> speech, of "talking back," that is no mere gesture of empty words, that is the
> expression of our movement from object to subject--the liberated voice.[1]

This learned skill of "talking back" is crucial to forming right relation
with ourselves, our communities, and our God/dess. In examining
some aspects of difference in Canadian traditions of culture and theology, I have discovered the active, liberating Spirit at work in "the talking back" of the lives and movements dedicated to their own and each
others' well-being. In a movement among women which believes that
there is no liberation without genuine community, we understand that
for power to be authentic and life-giving, it must be shared.

This ethic of shared power has been described as the main theme
of a Canadian liberative theological tradition. The stories of women's
spiritual struggles for freedom have concretely reminded us that women
learn to live by needing and nurturing one another, by shaping communities in which self-creation and total human liberation are inseparable.

---

[1]Hooks, *Talking Back*, 9.

The central theological claim of an incarnational ethic of mutuality is that we must always attempt the difficult task of integrating the struggle for social transformation with our personal spiritual liberation.[1] It is a basic conclusion of this thesis that many women, because we are culture-bearers cross-culturally, can learn what Audre Lorde speaks:

> Without community there is no liberation and genuine community involves learning how to take our differences and make them strengths especially among those who stand outside the circle of this society's definition of acceptable women--poor, lesbian, colored, older women.[2]

Resources of power among persons and groups differ markedly: power cannot be treated isomorphically.[3] For example, power invested in kings or the state is not the same as power invested in prophets or artists. The concreteness of a cultural resource such as narrative can help us break down the mind-body split upon which such isomorphic treatments of experience and power are based. The integration of women's elided narratives has the potential not only to honour the particularity of specific experience, but also to minimize and correct the domination of moral theology by abstraction and false universalism. The theological commitment to change the systemic powers which structure relations of domination can be nourished if we remain in touch with the life-forces,

---

[1]Gregory Baum, long-time advocate of global justice and of solidarity with the victims of Canadian society, made the following comments about going gently into the struggle to integrate the personal and the political: "We can never get it all together. While we make statements . . . to reach out for some sort of interconnection between these various forms of oppression, in one's personal life . . . you cannot fight equally on all fronts. In other words, in a broken world we can't be totally reconciled in our private lives. . . . This is impossible because the contradictions are in the objective order and therefore we have to involve ourselves in slightly one-sided movements. If we don't do that, then we relativize everything. . . . We are just against oppression in general and then we don't really engage ourselves [or] experience brokenness. . . . Not having things all together means also having to take risks and get involved in onesidedness. Yes, it's a pain to be onesided but it is necessary if we are not to relativize great oppression." Lecture notes from Baum's course on "The Interstructuring of Oppressions and Christian Witness," Address to Conference on Hope for Human Liberation, Queen's Theological College, Kingston, Ontario, 1979.

[2]Lorde, "The Master's Tools Will Never Dismantle the Master's House," *Sister Outsider*, 112.

[3]I am indebted to a discussion with Michael Poellet for the following analysis of power.

both near and far, at work in our world. If we cannot *feel* our world there is no hope for moral values![1]

The "surplus of experience" reflected in narrative is one way of keeping in touch with our own and others' pain and contradictions. The sum of personal narratives does not, for example, necessarily constitute a feminist understanding of social life nor are all experiences of oppression the same. Our commitment to ourselves, the discarded, the poor, the suffering, and the oppressed is ultimately rooted in the passion of our faith in the God who works in and with us for full life. As Eleanor Humes Haney states: "Claiming to speak about human nature and revelation and God, when that speech is not informed by realities of life for *all*, is immoral."[2] Thus, we must recognize that our narratives about the world, like our theologies, are always partial and incomplete. They are limited to speaking the truth about what we know and to attempting to encourage solidarity with all those seeking to "mobilize against the exploitation, victimization, marginality, expendability, powerlessness, suppressed rage, and degradation that characterize . . . the experience of being oppressed."[3]

The problem of particularity in the theological appropriation of experience is not the limited specificity of experience *per se*. The issue is, rather, one of false universalizing from the particular. Hence, particularity is not the problem: theology cannot deal with so-called universal experience, because we are unable to compute such infinite variety of human contexts. The historical concreteness of the representations of sin and grace in the scriptural texts gives us additional warrant to value the relation between the particular and the universal as one which merits our constant vigilance. If we are to take particularity seriously as a resource for personal and social transformation, then we need to explicate some of the responsibilities attending this task. I concur with Robert McAfee Brown's important insight:

---

[1]See for example Toinette M. Eugene, "While Love is Unfashionable: An Exploration of Black Feminist Spirituality and Sexuality," in *Women's Consciousness, Women's Conscience*, eds. Andolsen et al., 121-42; and Harrison, "The Power of Anger in the Work of Love," in *Making the Connections*, 3-20.

[2]Haney, "What is Feminist Ethics?," 127.

[3]Tania Modeleski, "Feminism and the Power of Interpretation," *Feminist Studies/Critical Studies*, ed. De Lauretis, 158.

> In order to overcome the blind spots, the flawed perspectives, the failures of understanding, *we need firsthand exposure to other contexts than our own,* so that we can not only understand them but also have our understanding transformed by them. The sheer human responsibility of understanding another's position is a prerequisite here, but the other part of the task is even more important, namely, allowing our own perspectives to be opened up, challenged, transformed by immediate contact with the perspective of the other.[1]

For such transformation to occur, as crucial as social and discursive analysis are for a liberative feminist ethic, this work alone is not adequate to the long struggle of forging new communities of love and justice. Without the presence of different voices, we also cannot improve our understanding of our own sufferings, complicities, and shape a common vision. Without stories, metaphors, and images, we run the risk of objectifying and reducing ourselves, *and* those whose lives are different from our own to an I-It relationship. The challenge is well put, in another context, in a poem by Marzieh Ahmadi Ooskwi:

> I am a woman
> A woman for whom
> In your shameful vocabulary
> There is no word
> Corresponding to my significance.[2]

If we are to heed this cry in a Canadian context we must become practiced in the art of *bricolage* within a normative stance of seeking justice.[3] As ethical *bricoleurs* we must persist in articulating the roots of suffering and the sources of empowerment specific to Canadian

---

[1]Brown, "What is Contextual Theology," in *Changing Contexts of Our Faith,* ed. Russell, 92.

[2]"Honor," 12, in Churches in Solidarity with Women, *Prayers and Poems, Songs and Stories: Ecumenical Decade, 1988-1998* (Geneva: World Council of Churches Publications, 1988). The following introduces the poem: "Marzieh Ahmadi Ooskwi (Iran) identifies with the poor and working women of Iran. Her poem, like her life, is a cry of outrage at the invisibility of her sisters. She knows who she is, and her despair is overlaid with indignation and anger. Her outrage and combativeness cost her life: in 1974 she was assassinated on orders of the Shah."

[3]While I am aware of Jeffrey Stout's recent use of this metaphor, in *Ethics After Babel: The Languages of Morals and Their Discontents* (Boston: Beacon Press, 1988), 74-78 and passim, I derive it from my own experiences with artists and use it independently here.

women's cultural contexts. For the Christian faith to take root on these rocks and in these soils, we need to express our lived experiences of the Co-creating Power. Hence, the significance of suffering and of God's redemptive purposes and promises of abundant life for all will be registered in language and metaphors arising out of women's struggles for full and meaningful life. Only on this cultural basis does theological reflection become possible. Thus, as Judith Plaskow has asserted: "Human particularity represents not just limit but also possibility."[1] For example, in an attempt to expose our class, cultural and race blindness, we learn most about the distortions of power from those who, like the characters April and Cheryl Raintree, Morag Gunn, and Naomi Nakane and her aunts, have had to wrest creative power from traditions and cultural relations which would keep them mute and indifferent.

In attending to the diversity of women's experience of oppression, however, we must learn, as Audre Lorde insists, to make difference a non-threatening, creative source of strength. "Only within that interdependency of different strengths, acknowledged and equal, can the power to seek new ways of being in the world generate, as well as the courage and sustenance to act where there are no charters."[2] The importance of making common cause across the barriers that divide must continually be stressed, since difference can often be experienced as an oppressive power over another, rather than as solidarity in which difference is a source not of alienation, but of strength. Genuine community, Lorde advises, involves learning how to take our differences and make them strengths. The difficulties of accomplishing this are massive, but not insurmountable.

The Grace of Difference and Solidarity

This study has discovered that the politics of identity and struggle experienced by women differ widely. There is no "essential woman" but rather different kinds of women and gender identities shaped by the varying manifestations and consequences of different forms of oppres-

---

[1]Judith Plaskow, *Sex, Sin and Grace*, 174.

[2]Lorde, "The Master's Tools Will Never Dismantle the Master's House," in *Sister Outsider*, 111.

sion.[1] Thus the recognition of difference is essential to the work of feminist moral theologies. Feminist transformation, then, requires a revolution of cultural consciousness and conceptions of which groups to which we belong. If we are going to make common cause across barriers that divide women, then it is incumbent upon those of us with some power to listen to and learn about the cultures of women's lives, and their struggles for identity and, often, for a very different liberation than we might imagine. We have seen that feminism always requires contextualization. All difference is not equal difference--we still must distinguish between varying kinds of oppression because relationships of domination and subordination are historically constituted and there-fore capable of shifting, such that the oppressed can become the op-pressor by using their class, race, education, and other privilege to oppress others in new configurations of power and control.

Given this possibility, we must reflect further on the use of the metaphor of "margin and centre."[2] The term "marginalized" must be employed with care, especially in a theological method that uses con-versation as a key.[3] There are various margins, each dependent upon particular configurations of power. For example, in cultural relations premised on misogyny and dualism, societal fear and hatred of women disguise and suppress female power. Here women are subordinated to men by the structures of sexism and heterosexism. Another specific form of marginalization is illustrated by Harry Braverman's under-standing of exploitation: "the working class is the animate part of capi-tal which will set in motion the process that yields to the total capital its increment of surplus value. As such the working class is first of all raw material for exploitation."[4] In comparison to the term exploita-

---

[1] See Elizabeth Spelman, *Inessential Woman*.

[2] I am indebted to Raymond Whitehead's reflections on this topic, "Middle Kingdom Ethics: The Centre and the Margin as Moral Metaphors," Presidential Address to the Canadian Theological Society, June 1, 1988.

[3] See, for example, David Tracy, *Plurality and Ambiguity: Hermeneutics, Religion and Hope* (New York: Harper & Row, 1987). Tracy's model of conver-sation lacks the recognition of concrete difference in power among conversation partners, treating them as isomorphic interlocutors and thus, in practice, excluding many he says that he intends to include in the conversation.

[4] Braverman, *Labor and Monopoly Capital*, 377.

tion, the term "oppressed" in feminist theory refers to women and minorities within patriarchal, racist, and capitalist relations; it is inclusive of the notion of exploitation, and reflects a more complex, multi-faceted reality.[1] Perhaps a more useful term for exploring the power relations undergirding various oppressions is objectification.

> Objectification implies a continuous attempt by some human beings to dominate and control others. . . . But this in no way means that those who are at the receiving end of this process merely sit passively on the sidelines of history and allow others to oppress them.[2]

The "margin and centre" metaphor can, however, perpetuate the very dynamics it seeks to overthrow by creating a sense that those "in the margins" are passive and less significant than those "in the centre." And, as Raymond Whitehead points out, "to claim the centre in theology or society is always to marginalize someone else."[3] The spatial metaphor of margin-centre may be useful for an oppressed person or group to use when they come to consciousness of themselves as subjugated, and when they realise that they must develop their own culture and live from a different set of values from that of the dominant ideology. It may also be helpful for describing some economic relations of power. The margin-centre metaphor, however, can also function to reinforce dualistic, objectifying relations. On the one hand, everything at the so-called centre is not wrong or bad. On the other hand, the oppressed or marginalized can easily become objectified by this kind of theological discourse and so further excluded. Finally, would anyone want to identify themselves as marginal when, in fact, they were trying to gain a different kind of power from that which exists in the centre?[4]

The problem in using margin-centre metaphors is a result of an ahistorical understanding of power relations which posits power as a

---

[1]See Brittan and Maynard's helpful discussion in *Sexism, Racism and Oppression*, 21 ff.

[2]Ibid., 285.

[3]Whitehead, "Middle Kingdom Ethics," 19.

[4]Canadian theorist Smaro Kamboureli prefers to call the way power is reshaped between competing claims a process of dialogics; see "Dialogue with the Other: The Use of Myth in Canadian Women's Poetry," in *In the Feminine: Women and Words*, eds. Dybikowski, et al., 107-08.

static given, instead of exploring the varied, uneven, dynamic nature of all social relations. The ambiguity of margin-centre metaphors, then, reflects the dominant logic of patriarchal cultures, and can actually de-privilege the oppressed and marginalized. Katie Cannon has pointed to the difficulty of using margin-centre language in liberative discourse:

> To marginalize is to disempower, to push to the outer edge of the hub of the life-decision-making-center. . . . Marginality also means that one is removed from the nurturing and sustaining sources of life's energy. It can render one docile, ignorant of self and therefore willingly susceptible to whatever comes down the pike. Marginality places women's communities and racial ethnic interest in throwaway, expendable positions, diluting our potency.[1]

In attempts to specify women's experience, problems with "marginality" can be addressed by using "difference" to engage the particularities of women's lives. Elizabeth Ellsworth discusses the meaning of difference, as a result of teaching a course on "Media and Anti-Racist Pedagogies" as part of a protracted struggle against racist infractions on her university campus.

> By the end of the semester, many of us began to understand ourselves as inhabiting intersections of multiple, contradictory, overlapping social positions not reducible to either race, or class, or gender. . . . Depending upon the moment and the context, the degree to which any one of us "differs" from the mythical norm . . . varies along multiple axes, and so do the consequences. I began using the terms "students of difference," "professor of difference," to refer to social positionings in relation to the mythical norm (based on ability, size, color, sexual preference, gender, ethnicity, and so on).[2]

I concur with Ellsworth's insight into the importance of recognizing the very real differences that women face daily in their struggles for full life. For example, "[w]ords spoken for survival come already validated in a radically different arena of proof and carry no option or luxury of choice."[3] That is, it is inappropriate to respond to marginalized

---

[1]Mudflower Collective, *God's Fierce Whimsy*, 45.

[2]Elizabeth Ellsworth, "Why Doesn't This Feel Empowering? Working Through the Repressive Myths of Critical Pedagogy," *Harvard Educational Review* 59, no. 3 (August 1989), 302. I am indebted to Elizabeth Bounds for calling this essay to my attention, and to her and Pamela Brubaker for many conversations on the subject of difference.

[3]Ibid.

voices written about survival with rationalist debates about their validity. Thus we can recognize that all voices are *not* equal in a multi-dimensional paradigm where justice is the norm and that the concept of *difference* enables us to keep in dynamic relationship varied and multivocal positions among different people.[1]

This problematic of the language used to describe women's experiences raises the question of our precise understanding of solidarity: Is solidarity with the most vulnerable an act of paternalistic charity, or is it a recognition of shared interests in the transformation of a society which, at present, denies the great majority of us creative and meaningful work, recognition, and value? To conceptualize the principle of difference in relation to the work of solidarity is to recognize the ambiguity of both terms.

Given that the category of woman is fragmented and multiple, how can women hope to work across differences that concretely divide us and look towards a shared liberation?[2] This study affirms learnings relevant for the work of solidarity. We need to bring our fears out into the open in order to dispel them. Emotional work is required for a liberative spirituality. Our theoretical work must also include reflection on the problems of reproducing our lives, on the drudgery, struggles and celebrations of everyday life. Feminist consciousness must come from the bag ladies as well as from farmers, from prostitutes as well as from academics. We can make alliances over common causes if we listen closely to the interpretations of those with different interests and learn to connect our struggles.

In theological terms, Dorothee Sölle describes solidarity as related to difference and the everyday work of resurrection and liberation.

> Where we break the neutrality of silence and abandon our complicity with injustice, the new life begins. People who earlier were invisible and forgot-

---

[1] I am inclined to agree with Raymond Whitehead's contention in his "Middle Kingdom Ethics" that while margin-centre rhetoric can be a heuristic device in some circumstances, "since it does expose certain truths," our emancipatory projects will be better served by metaphors such as feminists' "weaving," justice groups' "networking," Asian theologians' "option for the people," and images of "spiritually grounded and connected" persons, rather than centres and peripheries.

[2] For a helpful discussion, see Uma Narayan, "Working Together Across Difference: Some Considerations on Emotions and Political Practice," *Hypatia* 3, no. 2 (Summer 1988), 31-47.

ten become self-assured and find their own language. They stand up for their rights, and this revolt, this rebellion, is a sign of resurrection.[1]

Solidarity, according to Sölle, involves three elements: the creation of a common language, where "yours" and "mine" lose meaning; new life-styles based on communitarian, justice-seeking values; and, thus, new forms of community. Because solidarity is based on mutuality, those with power are called to relinquish or transform it. Mutuality demands concrete justice. For some women who hold power over other women, empowering women will mean some women losing their power over others. An incarnational method of doing feminist theological ethics will emphasize solidarity, then, as a process of working towards mutual responsibility, dignity, respect, and power. The criteria for emancipated life, then, are empowerment and the reduction of privileges and elimination of domination: "the value of a member of the group is assessed, not according to his/her natural gifts or his/her social position in the group, but according to the question how this member meets people's needs."[2]

What happens, then, if theological ethics attends to accounts of reality by those marginalized within dominant theology and culture? Lesbians, working class women, and women of colour have been challenging white, heterosexual middle-class women for years; if we share our "appraisal power,"[3] we will learn to correlate our language of sin and grace, suffering and hope, with women's diverse experiences. Without this correlation, we will also overlook places where the grace of God is enlivening and abounding.

This thesis concludes that feminist liberation ethics in Canada must be shaped by women who are doing their utmost to claim their own power, who are learning to recognize each other's problems and possibilities as the interconnecting basis for ongoing solidarity, and who are living into a future in which all persons can be whole. We

---

[1]Sölle, *Choosing Life*, trans. Margaret Kohl (Philadelphia: Fortress Press, 1981), 88-89.

[2]Ibid., 92-93.

[3]Esmerelda Thornhill, "Focus on Black Women!," in *Race, Class, Gender: Bonds and Barriers*, Socialist Studies, A Canadian Annual, No. 5, eds. Jesse Vorst et al. (Toronto: Between The Lines and The Society for Socialist Studies), 29.

glean the theological significance of women's experience when we are most like God: that is, when we struggle against conditions which crucify and perpetuate injustice. I believe that women thirst for knowledge and stories which encourage us to "believe ourselves to be called to resist evil, seek and live out justice and right relationships, to pray and laugh and weep, to know joy and suffering--to be women living as signs of God's gracious and compassionate love in a world in need of hope and healing."[1]

---

[1]Charlotte Caron, "The Significance of Women in Ministry," *Touchstone* 4, no. 1 (January 1986), 5.

SELECTED BIBLIOGRAPHY

Aitken, Johan Lyall. *Masques of Morality: Females in Fiction.* Toronto: Women's Press, 1987.

Allen, Richard, ed. *The Social Gospel in Canada.* Ottawa: National Museum of Man, 1975.

Allen, Richard. *The Social Passion: Religion and Social Reform in Canada: 1914-1928.* Toronto: University of Toronto Press, 1971.

Aman, Kenneth, ed. *Border Regions of Faith: An Anthology of Religion and Social Change.* Maryknoll, N.Y.: Orbis Books, 1987.

Amjad-Ali, Charles, and Pitcher, Alvin, eds. *Liberation and Ethics: Essays in Honor of Gibson Winter.* Chicago: Center for the Scientific Study of Religion, 1985.

Anderson, Elizabeth. "'Not by might, nor by power but by my spirit, saith the Lord of Hosts': Women Missionaries as Women of Faith, 1880-1935." Paper submitted at Emmanuel College, Toronto School of Theology (n.d.) (Photocopy.)

Anderson, Elizabeth. "Women in the Student Christian Movement: 1921-49." Paper submitted at Emmanuel College, Toronto School of Theology, n.d. (Photocopy.)

Anderson, Elizabeth. "Women Workers in the Methodist Church, 1889-1925." Paper submitted at Emmanuel College, Toronto School of Theology, 1985. (Photocopy.)

Anderson, G., and Stransky, T., eds. *Liberation Theologies: Mission Trends #4.* Grand Rapids, Michigan: William B. Eerdmans, 1979.

Andolsen, Barbara H.; Gudorf, Christine E.; and Pellauer, Mary D., eds. *Women's Consciousness, Women's Conscience: A Reader in Feminist Ethics.* Minneapolis: Winston Press, 1985.

Andrew, Caroline. "Women and the Welfare State." *Canadian Journal of Political Science* 17, no. 4 (December 1988): 671-73.

Armstrong, Jeanette. *Slash*. Penticton, British Columbia: Theytus Books, 1985.

Armstrong, Pat. *Labour Pains: Women's Work in Crisis*. Toronto: Women's Educational Press, 1984.

Armstrong, Pat, and Armstrong, Hugh. *The Double Ghetto: Canadian Women and their Segregated Work*. Toronto: McLelland and Stewart, 1978.

Armstrong, Pat, and Armstrong, Hugh. *A Working Majority: What Women Must Do for Pay*. Prepared for the Canadian Advisory Council on the Status of Women. Ottawa: Ministry of Supply and Services Canada, 1983.

Arnopolous, Sheila McLeod. *Problems of Immigrant Women in the Canadian Labour Force*. Ottawa: Advisory Council on the Status of Women. 1982.

Asian Women's Consultation. "Women's Oppression: A Sinful Situation, Composite Paper." *Proceedings, Asian Women's Consultation* Coordinator, Sun Ai Park. Manila, November 1985.

Atkinson, Clarissa W.; Buchanan, Constance H.; and Miles, Margaret R., eds. *Immaculate and Powerful: The Female in Sacred Image and Social Reality*. Boston: Beacon Press, 1985.

Bacchi, Carol Lee. *Liberation Deferred? The Ideas of the English Canadian Suffragists, 1877-1918*. Toronto: University of Toronto Press, 1985.

Bandarage, Asoka. "Women of Color: Towards a Celebration of Power." *Woman of Power* 4 (Fall 1986): 8-14.

Bannerji, Himani. "Introducing Racism: Notes Towards an Anti-Racist Feminism." *Resources for Feminist Research* 16, no. 1 (1987): 10-12.

Bannerji, Himani. "We Appear Silent to People Who are Deaf to What We Say." *Fireweed: Issue 16, Women of Colour* (May 1983): 8-17.

Barrett, Michele. "The Concept of Difference." *Feminist Review* 26 (1987): 29-41.

Barrett, Michele. *Women's Oppression Today*. London: Verso, 1980.

Barrett, Michele, and McIntosh, and Mary. *The Anti-Social Family*. London: Verso, 1982.

Barrett, Michele, and McIntosh, and Mary. "Ethnocentrism and Feminist Social Theory." *Feminist Review* 20 (1985): 23-46.

Barstow, Anne Llewelyn; Brown, Karen McCarthy; Gilkes, Cheryl Townsend; Hunt, Mary E.; and Fiorenza, Elisabeth Schüssler. "Roundtable Discussion: On Feminist Methodology." *Journal of Feminist Studies in Religion* 1, no. 2 (Fall 1985): 73-88.

Baum, Gregory. "Faith and Culture." *The Ecumenist* 24, no. 1 (November-December 1985): 9-13.

Baum, Gregory. "The Interstructuring of Oppressions and Christian Witness." Address to Conference on Hope for Human Liberation, Queen's Theological College, Kingston, Ontario, 1979.

Baum, Gregory. "Option for the Powerless." *The Ecumenist* 26, no. 1 (November-December 1987): 5-11.

Baum, Gregory. "Political Theologies in Conflict." *The Ecumenist* 22, no. 6 (September-October 1984): 84-85.

Baum, Gregory. *The Priority of Labor: A Commentary on "Laborem Exercens," Encyclical Letter of Pope John Paul II.* New York: Paulist Press, 1982.

Baum, Gregory. *Theology and Society.* Mahwah, New Jersey: Paulist Press, 1987.

Baum, Gregory. "Three Theses on Contextual Theology" *The Ecumenist* 24, no. 4 (May-June 1986): 49-59.

Baum, Gregory. "United Church Theology Offers Food." *Catholic New Times* (Toronto), Fall Book Supplement (October 1989).

Baum, Gregory, and Cameron, Duncan, eds. *Ethics and Economics: Canada's Catholic Bishops on the Economic Crisis.* Toronto: James Lorimer, 1984.

Bettenhausen, Elizabeth. "Blizzard: Pluralism and Ethics." Lecture delivered at St. Andrew's College, Saskatoon, February 12, 1990.

Birch, Bruce C., and Rasmussen, Larry R. *Bible and Ethics in Christian Life.* Revised Edition. Minneapolis: Augsburg Fortress, 1989.

Blodgett, E.D. *Configuration: Essays on the Canadian Literatures.* Downsview, Ontario: ECW Press, 1982.

Bolaria, B. Singh, and Li, Peter S., eds. *Racial Oppression in Canada.* Toronto: Garamond Press, 1985.

Bottomore, Tom, ed. *The Dictionary of Marxist Thought.* Cambridge, Mass.: Harvard University Press, 1983.

Bottomore, Tom. *Social Criticism in North America.* Toronto: Canadian Broadcasting Corporation, 1966.

Bounds, Elizabeth. "Narrative Lost, Narrative Regained? Some Postmodern Musings." Union Theological Seminary, 1988. (Photocopy.)

Brand, Dionne. "Black Women and Work: The Impact of Racially Constructed Gender Roles on the Sexual Division of Labor." *Fireweed* Issue 25 (Fall 1987): 28-37.

Braverman, Harry. *Labor and Monopoly Capital: The Degradation of Work in the Twentieth Century.* New York: Monthly Review Press, 1974.

Brewer, Rose. "Black Women in Poverty: Some Comments on Female-Headed Families." *Signs* 13, no. 2 (1988): 331-39.

Briggs, Sheila. "The Politics of Identity and of Interpretation." *Union Seminary Quarterly Review* 43, nos. 1-4 (1989): 163-80.

Brittan, Arthur, and Maynard, Mary. *Sexism, Racism and Oppression.* Oxford: Basil Blackwell, 1984; reprint, 1985.

Briskin, Linda. "Socialist Feminism: From the Standpoint of Practice." Toronto: York University, Social Sciences Division, 1988. (Photocopy.)

Briskin, Linda, and Yanz, Lynda. *Union Sisters: Women in the Labour Movement.* Toronto: The Women's Press, 1983.

Brown, Joanne Carlson, and Bohn, Carole, eds. *Christianity, Patriarchy and Abuse.* New York: Pilgrim Press, 1989.

Brown, Terry, and Lind, Christopher. *Justice as Mission: An Agenda for the Church.* Burlington, Ontario: Trinity Press, 1985.

Brubaker, Pamela. "Rendering the Invisible Visible: Women's Global Economic Reality and Christian Social Ethics." Ph. D. dissertation, Union Theological Seminary, New York, 1989.

Bruce, Phyllis. "*The Diviners.*" *The Canadian Forum* 54 (1974-75): 15-16.

Bulkin, Elly; Pratt, Minnie Bruce; and Smith, Barbara. *Yours in the Struggle: Three Feminist Perspectives on Anti-Semitism and Racism.* Brooklyn, New York: Long Haul Press, 1984.

Butcher, Dennis L.; Macdonald, Catherine; McPherson, Margaret E; Smith, Raymond R.; and Watts, A. McKibbin. *Prairie Spirit: Perspectives on the Heritage of the United Church of Canada in the West.* Winnipeg: University of Manitoba Press, 1985.

Cadorette, Curt. *From the Heart of the People: The Theology of Gustavo Gutiérrez*. Oak Park, Illinois: Meyer-Stone Books, 1988.

Cameron, A. Barry. *"The Diviners."* *Queen's Quarterly* 81 (1974): 639-40.

Campbell, Maria. *Halfbreed*. Toronto: McLelland and Stewart, 1973; reprint ed., Halifax: Goodread Biographies, 1983.

Cannon, Katie Geneva. *Black Womanist Ethics*. American Academy of Religion Series. Atlanta: Scholars Press, 1988.

Cardinal, Harold. *The Unjust Society: The Tragedy of Canada's Indians*. Edmonton: M. G. Hurtig, 1969.

Careless, J. M. *Colonists and Canadiens*. Toronto: Macmillan, 1971.

Caron, Charlotte. "Qualitative Methods: An Experiment in Feminist Theological Method." Paper submitted at Carleton University, Ottawa, 1988. (Photocopy.)

Caron, Charlotte. "The Significance of Women in Ministry." *Touchstone* 4, no. 1 (January 1986): 3-5.

Casalis, George. *Correct Ideas Don't Fall from the Skies: Elements for an Inductive Theology*. Maryknoll, New York: Orbis Books, 1984.

Centre for Contemporary Cultural Studies. *On Ideology*. London: Hutchinson and Co., 1978.

Chopp, Rebecca. "Feminism's Theological Pragmatics." *Journal of Religion* 67 (1987): 239-256.

Chopp, Rebecca. *The Praxis of Suffering: An Interpretation of Liberation and Political Theologies*. Maryknoll, New York: Orbis Books, 1986.

Christ, Carol P. *Diving Deep and Surfacing: Women Writers on Spiritual Quest*. Boston: Beacon Press, 1980.

Christ, Carol P., and Plaskow, Judith. *Womanspirit Rising: A Feminist Reader in Religion*. New York: Harper & Row, 1979.

Chu, Theresa, and Lind, Christopher, eds. *A New Beginning*. Toronto: Canada China Programme of the Canadian Council of Churches, 1983.

Churches in Solidarity with Women. *Prayers and Poems, Songs and Stories: Ecumenical Decade, 1988-1998*. Geneva: World Council of Churches Publications, 1988.

Clark, L., and Lange, L. *The Sexism of Political and Economic Theory.* Toronto: University of Toronto Press, 1979.

Clarke, Margaret. "Revisioning April Raintree." *Prairie Fire* 7 (Autumn 1986): 136-42.

Cocks, Joan. *The Oppositional Imagination: Feminism, Critique and Political Theory.* London and New York: Routledge and Kegan Paul, 1989.

Collins, Sheila. *A Different Heaven and Earth.* Valley Forge: Judson Press, 1974.

Collins, Sheila. "Reclaiming the Bible through Storytelling." In *Must We Choose Sides: Christian Commitment for the 1980's*, pp. 98-100. Inter-Religious Task Force for Social Analysis. Oakland, California: Inter-Religious Task Force for Social Analysis, 1979.

Cone, James. *A Black Theology of Liberation.* Second Edition. Maryknoll, New York: Orbis Books, 1986.

Cooey, Paula M.; Farmer, Sharon A.; and Ross, Mary Ellen, eds. *Embodied Love: Sensuality and Relationship as Feminist Values.* San Francisco: Harper & Row, 1987.

Cook, Ramsey. *Canada: A Modern Study.* Toronto: Clarke Irwin and Co., 1963.

Cormie, Lee. "The Churches and the Economic Crisis." *The Ecumenist* 21, no. 3 (March-April 1983): 33-38.

Cormie, Lee. "The Epistemological Privilege of the Oppressed: Liberation Theologies, Biblical Faith, and Marxist Sociology of Knowledge." *Proceedings of the Catholic Theological Society of America* 33 (1978): 155-81.

Cross, Michael, ed. *The Consolidation of Capital: 1846-1924.* Toronto: McLelland and Stewart, 1978.

Cross, Michael, and Kealey, Gregory, eds. *Modern Canada: 1930-1980.* Toronto: McLelland and Stewart, 1983.

Culleton, Beatrice. *In Search of April Raintree.* Winnipeg: Pemmican Publications, 1983.

Culpepper, Emily Irwin. "New Tools for Theology: Writings by Women of Color." *Journal of Feminist Studies in Religion.* 4, no. 2 (Fall 1988).

Daniels, Douglas. "Louis Riel and Liberation Theology." *The Ecumenist* 25, no. 3 (March-April 1987): 33-36.

Davy, Shirley, project coordinator. *Women, Work & Worship in the United Church of Canada.* Toronto: United Church of Canada, 1983.

Daymond, Douglas, and Monkman, Leslie, eds. *Canadian Novelists and the Novel.* Ottawa: Borealis, 1981.

De Lauretis, Teresa, ed. *Feminist Studies/Critical Studies.* Bloomington: Indiana University Press, 1986.

Dixon, Sophia. "How Experiences of Women in Literature May Help Saskatchewan Women." *Adult Learning* 2, no. 3 (December 1937).

Drache, Daniel, and Clement, Wallace, eds. *The New Practical Guide to Canadian Political Economy.* Toronto: James Lorimer, 1985.

Driver, Tom F. *Christ in a Changing World.* New York: Crossroads, 1981.

Driver, Tom F. *Patterns of Grace: Human Experience as Word of God.* San Francisco: Harper & Row, 1977.

Driver, Tom F. "Theology of Culture." Paper written for the Study Commission on Theology, Education, and the Electronic Media, National Council of the Churches of Christ, New York, 1985.

Dubois, Ellen Carol; Kelly, Gail Paradise; Kennedy, Elizabeth Lapovsky; Korsmeyer, Carolyn W; and Robinson, Lillian S., eds. *Feminist Scholarship: Kindling in the Groves of Academe.* Urbana and Chicago: University of Illinois Press, 1987.

Dussel, Enrique. *Ethics and Community.* Maryknoll, New York: Orbis Books, 1988.

Dybikowski, Ann; Freeman, Victoria; Marlatt, Daphne; Pulling, Barbara; and Warland, Betsy, eds. *In the Feminine: Women and Words.* Edmonton: Longspoon Press, 1985.

Dyck, E. F., ed. *Essays on Saskatchewan Writing.* Regina: The Saskatchewan Writers Guild, 1986.

Eagleton, Mary. *Feminist Literary Theory: A Reader.* New York: Basil Blackwell, 1986.

Eagleton, Terry. *The Function of Criticism: From the Spectator to Post-Structuralism.* London: Verso, 1984.

Eagleton, Terry. *Marxism and Literary Criticism.* London: Methuen, 1976.

Elliot, Lorris, ed. *Other Voices: Writings by Blacks in Canada.* Toronto: Williams Wallace, 1985.

Ellsworth, Elizabeth. "Why Doesn't this Feel Empowering? Working Through the Repressive Myths of Critical Pedagogy." *Harvard Educational Review* 59, no. 3 (August 1989): 297-324.

Ellwood, Douglas J., ed. *Asian Christian Theology: Emerging Themes.* Philadelphia: Westminster Press, 1980.

Emmett, Dorothy. *The Moral Prism.* London: Macmillan Press, 1979.

Essed, Philomena. "Black Women in White Women's Organizations: Ethnic Differentiation and Problems of Racism in the Netherlands." *Resources for Feminist Research* 18, no. 4 (December 1989): 10-15.

Fabella, Virginia, and Oduyoye, Mercy Amba. *With Passion and Compassion: Third World Women Doing Theology.* Maryknoll, New York: Orbis Books, 1988.

Fabella, Virginia, and Torres, Sergio, eds. *Doing Theology in a Divided World.* Maryknoll, New York: Orbis Books, 1985.

Fairbanks, Carol. *Prairie Women: Images in American and Canadian Fiction.* New Haven and London: Yale University Press, 1986.

Fictive Collective, The. *Baker's Dozen: Stories by Women.* Toronto: The Women's Press, 1984.

Finn, Geraldine. "Feminism and Fiction: In Praise of *Praxis,* Beyond *Bodily Harm.*" *Socialist Studies: A Canadian Annual* (1983): 51-77.

Finn, Geraldine, and Miles, Angela, eds. *Feminism in Canada: From Pressure to Politics.* Montreal: Black Rose Books, 1982.

Fitzgerald, M.; Guberman, C.; and Wolfe, M. *Still Ain't Satisfied! Canadian Feminism Today.* Toronto: Women's Press, 1982.

Foucault, Michel. *Power/Knowledge: Selected Interviews and Other Writings, 1972-1977.* Edited by C. Gordon. New York: Pantheon, 1977.

Fourez, Gerard. *Liberation Ethics.* Translated and adapted by David Morris, Barbara Hogan, and Gerard Fourez. Foreword by John C. Raines. Philadelphia: Temple University Press, 1982.

Fox, Bonnie. *Hidden in the Household: Women's Domestic Labour Under Capitalism.* Toronto: The Women's Press, 1980.

Fox-Genovese, Elizabeth. "Placing Women's History in History." *New Left Review* 133 (May-June 1982): 5-29.

French, William. "Ecological Concern and the Anti-Foundationalist Debates: James Gustafson and Biospheric Constraints." *Annual of the Society of Christian Ethics* (1989): 113-30.

Frye, Joanne S. *Living Stories, Telling Lives: Women and the Novel in Contemporary Experience*. Ann Arbor: University of Michigan Press, 1986.

Glastonburg, Marion. "The Best Kept Secret--How Working-Class Women Live and What They Know." *Women's Studies International Quarterly* 2, no. 2 (1979): 171-81.

Godard, Barbara, ed. *Gynocrytics: Feminist Approaches to Writing by Canadian and Quebec Women*. Toronto: ECW Books, 1987.

Goldberg, Michael. *Theology and Narrative: A Critical Introduction*. Nashville: Abingdon Press, 1982.

Goldie, Terrie. "Folklore, Popular Culture, and Individuation in *Surfacing* and *The Diviners*." *Canadian Literature* 104 (Spring 1985): 95-108.

Gottlieb, Erika. "The Riddle of Concentric Worlds in *Obasan*." *Canadian Literature* 109 (Summer 1986): 34-53.

Graham, Scott. *More Than Survival: Viewpoints Toward a Theology of Nation*. Don Mills, Ontario: Canec, 1980.

Gramsci, Antonio. *Selections from the Prison Notebooks*. New York: International Publishers, 1971; reprint ed., 1983.

Grant, John Webster. *The Church in the Canadian Era: The First Century of Confederation*. Toronto: McGraw Hill Ryerson, 1972.

Greene, G., and Kahn, C. *Making a Difference: Feminist Literary Criticism*. London and New York: Methuen, 1986.

Grelle, Bruce. "Christian Political Ethics and Western Marxism." *Journal of Religious Ethics* 15, no. 2 (Fall 1987): 173-98.

Griffiths, Morwenna, and Whitford, Margaret, eds. *Feminist Perspectives in Philosophy*. Bloomington: Indiana University Press, 1988.

Gutiérrez, Gustavo. *The Power of the Poor in History: Selected Writings*. Translated by Robert Barr. Maryknoll, New York: Orbis Books, 1983.

Gutiérrez, Gustavo. *A Theology of Liberation: History, Politics and Salvation*. Translated and edited by Sister Caridad Inda and John Eagleson. Maryknoll, New York: Orbis Books, 1973.

Hall, Douglas John. *The Canada Crisis: A Christian Perspective*. Toronto: Anglican Book Centre, 1980.

Hall, Douglas John. "On Contextuality in Christian Theology." *Toronto Journal of Theology* 1, no. 1 (Spring 1985): 3-16.

Hall, Douglas John. "The Future of Religion in Canada." The Ebbutt Lecture. Sackville, New Brunswick: Mount Allison University, 1988.

Hamilton, Roberta, and Barrett, Michele, eds. *The Politics of Diversity* London: Verso, 1986.

Haney, Eleanor. "What is Feminist Ethics? A Proposal for Continuing Discussion." *Journal of Religious Ethics* 8, no. 1 (Spring 1980): 115-24.

Hannum, Nancy. "Gender Based Economic Activity." Paper prepared for the National Working Group on the Economy and Poverty of the United Church of Canada, March 9, 1989.

Harding, Sandra, and Hintikka, Merrill B. *Discovering Reality: Feminist Perspectives on Epistemology, Metaphysics, Methodology, and Philosophy of Science*. Boston: D. Reidel Publishing Co., 1983.

Harding, Sandra, and O'Barr, Jean F., eds. *Sex and Scientific Inquiry*. Chicago: University of Chicago Press, 1987.

Harrison, Beverly Wildung. "The Dream of a Common Language: Towards a Normative Theory of Justice in Christian Ethics." *Annual of the Society of Christian Ethics* (1983): 1-25.

Harrison, Beverly Wildung. *Making the Connections: Essays in Feminist Social Ethics*. Edited by Carol S. Robb. Boston: Beacon Press, 1983.

Harrison, Beverly Wildung. *Our Right to Choose*. Boston: Beacon Press, 1983.

Harrison, Beverly Wildung. "Restoring the Tapestry of Life: A Vocation of Feminist Theology." The Nelle Morton Lecture, March 8, 1984. In *The Drew Gateway*, 54, no. 1 (1984): 39-48.

Harrison, Deborah. *The Limits of Liberalism: The Making of Canadian Sociology*. Montreal: Black Rose Books, 1981.

Harrison, Dick. *Unnamed Country: The Struggle for a Canadian Prairie Fiction*. Edmonton: University of Alberta Press, 1977.

Hartsock, Nancy. *Money, Sex and Power: Toward a Feminist Historical Materialism*. Boston: Northeastern University Press, 1983.

Hartsock, Nancy. "Rethinking Modernism." *Cultural Critique* (Fall 1987): 187-206.

Hartsock, Nancy. "Staying Alive." *Quest* 3, no. 3 (1976-77): 3-14.

Hedenstrom, Joanne. "Puzzled Patriarchs and Free Women: Patterns of the Canadian Novel." *Atlantis* 4, no. 1 (Fall 1978): 2-9.

Heilbrun, Carolyn. *Writing a Woman's Life*. New York: W. W. Norton & Co., 1988.

Hessel, Dieter, ed. *Theological Education for Social Ministry*. New York: Pilgrim Press, 1988.

Heyward, Carter. "Heterosexist Theology: Being Above it All." *Journal of Feminist Studies in Religion* 3 (Spring 1987): 29-38.

Heyward, Carter. *Our Passion for Justice: Images of Power, Sexuality, and Liberation*. New York: Pilgrim Press, 1984.

Heyward, Carter. *The Redemption of God: A Theology of Mutual Relation*. Washington, D.C.: University Press of America, 1982.

Heyward, Carter. *Speaking of Christ: A Lesbian Feminist Voice*. New York: Pilgrim Press, 1989.

Heyward, Carter. *Touching Our Strength: The Erotic as Power and the Love of God*. San Francisco: Harper & Row, 1989.

Hinsdale, Mary Ann, and Leddy, Mary Jo, eds. *The Faith that Transforms: Essays in Honor of Gregory Baum*. Mahwah, New Jersey: Paulist Press, 1987.

Hoagland, Sarah. "Moral Agency Under Oppression." *Trivia* 9 (1986): 86-87.

Hooks, Bell. *Feminist Theory: From Margin to Center*. Boston: South End Press, 1984.

Hull, Gloria T.; Scott, Patricia Bell; and Smith, Barbara, eds. *All the Women are White, All the Blacks are Men, but Some of Us are Brave: Black Women's Studies*. Old Westbury, New York: The Feminist Press, 1982.

Humm, Maggie. *Feminist Criticism: Women as Contemporary Critics*. New York: St. Martin's Press, 1986.

Hunt, Mary. "Feminist Liberation Theology: The Development of Method in Construction." Ph. D. dissertation, Graduate Theological Union, Berkeley, 1980.

Hurcombe, Linda, ed. *Sex and God: Varieties of Women's Religious Experience.* New York: Routledge and Kegan Paul, 1987.

Hutchinson, Roger. "The Fellowship for a Christian Social Order: A Social Ethical Analysis of a Christian Socialist Movement." Th. D. dissertation, Emmanuel College, Toronto School of Theology, 1975.

Hyett, Catherine. "Theories of Dependency." *The Ecumenist* 25, no. 3 (March-April 1987): 37-44.

Irvine, Lorna. *Sub/version: Canadian Fiction by Women.* Toronto: ECW Press, 1986.

Irvine, Lorna. "Surfacing, Surviving, Surpassing: Canada's Women Writers." *The Journal of Popular Culture* 15, no. 3 (Winter 1981): 70-79.

Isasi-Díaz, Ada-María, and Tarango, Yolanda. *Hispanic Women: Prophetic Voice in the Church.* San Francisco: Harper & Row, 1988.

Jaggar, Alison. *Feminist Politics and Human Nature.* Totowa, New Jersey: Towman and Allanheld, 1983.

Johnson, Richard. "What is Cultural Studies Anyway?" *Social Text* 16 (Winter 1986-87): 38-80.

Johnston, Eleanor. "The Quest of *The Diviners.*" *Mosaic* 11, no. 3 (Spring 1978): 107-17.

Kalven, Janet, and Buckley, Mary I., eds. *Women's Spirit Bonding.* New York: Pilgrim Press, 1984.

Kaplan, Cora. *Sea Changes: Culture and Feminism.* New York: Schocken Books, 1986.

Kelly, Joan. *Women, History and Theory: The Essays of Joan Kelly.* Chicago: University of Chicago Press, 1984.

Keohane, Nannerl O., and Gelpi, Barbara C. *Feminist Theory: A Critique of Ideology.* Sussex: Harvester Press, 1982.

King, Thomas, and Hay, Helen, eds. *The Native in Canadian Literature.* Toronto: ECW Press, 1987.

Kogawa, Joy. *Obasan.* Toronto: Lester and Orpen Denys. 1981; reprint ed., Markham, Ontario: Penguin Books, 1982.

Kristjana, Gunners, ed. *Crossing the River: Essays in Honor of Margaret Laurence.* Winnipeg: Turnstone Press, 1988.

Kwok Pui Lan. "Discovering the Bible in the Non-Biblical World." *Semeia* 47 (1989): 24-42.

Lambertson, Michiko. "*Obasan.*" *Canadian Woman Studies* 4, no. 2 (1982): 94-95.

Larrain, Jorge. *The Concept of Ideology.* London: Hutchinson and Co., 1979.

Laurence, Margaret. *The Diviners.* Toronto: McLelland and Stewart, 1974; reprint ed., New York: Bantam Windstone, 1982.

Lauret, Maria. "Seizing Time and Making New: Feminist Criticism, Politics and Contemporary Feminist Fiction." *Feminist Review* 31 (Spring 1989): 94-106.

Lebacqz, Karen. *Justice in an Unjust World: Foundations for a Christian Approach to Injustice.* Minneapolis: Augsburg Press, 1987.

Lefkowitz, Rochelle, and Withorn, Ann, eds. *For Crying Out Loud: Women and Poverty in the United States.* New York: Pilgrim Press, 1986.

Le Sueur, Meridel. *Ripening: Selected Works, 1927-1980.* Edited and with Introduction by Elaine Hedges. Old Westbury, New York: The Feminist Press, 1982.

Lind Christopher. "An Invitation to Canadian Theology." *Toronto Journal of Theology* 1, no. 1 (Spring 1985): 17-26.

Lind, Christopher. "Ethics, Economics and Canada's Catholic Bishops." *Canadian Journal of Political and Social Theory* 7, no. 3 (Fall 1983): 150-66.

Livingstone, David, ed. *Critical Pedagogy and Cultural Power.* Toronto: Bergin and Garvey, 1985.

Lorde, Audre. *Sister Outsider: Essays and Speeches.* Trumansburg, New York: The Crossing Press, 1984.

Lugones, Maria, and Spelman, E. V. "Have We Got a Theory for You! Feminist Theory, Cultural Imperialism and the Demand for 'the Women's Voice.'" *Women's Studies International Forum* 6, no. 6 (1983): 573-82.

Luxton, Meg. *More than a Labour of Love: Three Generations of Women's Work.* Toronto: The Women's Press, 1980.

Luxton, Meg, and Rosenburg, Harriet. *Through the Kitchen Window: The Politics of Home and Family.* Toronto: Garamond Press, 1986.

McKale, Michael. "Culture and Human Liberation." *Radical Religion* 5 (1980): 5-15.

McLessan, David. *Ideology*. Minneapolis: University of Minnesota Press, 1986.

Maguire, Daniel. *The Moral Choice*. Minneapolis: Winston Press, 1978.

Mahan, Brian, and Richesin, L. Dale, eds. *The Challenge of Liberation Theology: A First World Response*. Maryknoll, New York: Orbis Books, 1981.

Martens, Debra. "The Problem of Difference: Sexual Difference and Feminist Literary Criticism." Manuscript. Montreal, 1983.

Martindale, Kathleen. "On the Ethics of 'Voice' in Feminist Literary Criticism." *Resources for Feminist Research* 16, no. 3 (September 1987): 6-19.

Manuel, George, and Poslins, Michael. *The Fourth World: An Indian Reality*. New York: Macmillan, 1974.

Marchak, Patricia. "Canadian Political Economy." *Canadian Review of Sociology and Anthropology* 22, no. 5 (1985): 673-709.

Marchak, Patricia, ed. *The Working Sexes*. Vancouver: University of British Columbia, Institute of Industrial Relations, 1977.

Maroney, Heather Jon, and Luxton, Meg. *Feminism and Political Economy: Women's Work, Women's Struggle* Toronto: Methuen, 1987.

Mies, Maria. *Patriarchy and Accumulation on a World Scale: Women in the International Division of Labour*. London: Zed Books, 1986.

Mitchell, Juliet, and Oakley, Ann, eds. *What is Feminism?* New York: Pantheon Books, 1986.

Mitter, Swasti. *Common Fate, Common Bond: Women and the Global Economy*. London: Pluto Press, 1986.

Moi, Toril. *Sexual/Textual Politics*. London and New York: Methuen, 1985.

Mollenkott, Virginia Ramey. *The Divine Feminine: The Biblical Imagery of God as Female*. New York: Crossroad, 1983.

Monkman, Leslie. *A Native Heritage: Images of the Indian in English-Canadian Literature*. Toronto: University of Toronto Press, 1981.

Moraga, Cherie. *Loving in the War Years*. Boston: South End Press, 1983.

Moraga, Cherie, and Anzaldua, Gloria, eds. *This Bridge Called My Back: Writings by Radical Women of Color*. Watertown, Massachusetts: Persephone Press, 1981.

Morgan, Kathryn Pauly. "Women and Moral Madness." *Canadian Journal of Philosophy* Supplementary Volume 13 (n.d.): 210-26.

Morton, Nelle. *The Journey is Home*. Boston: Beacon Press, 1985.

Mudflower Collective, The. *God's Fierce Whimsy: Christian Feminism and Theological Education*. New York: Pilgrim Press, 1985.

Murray, Pauli. "Black, Feminist Theologies: Links, Parallels and Tensions." *Christianity and Crisis* 40, no. 6 (April 14, 1980): 86-95.

Narayan, Uma. "Working Together Across Difference: Some Considerations on Emotions and Political Practice." *Hypatia* 3, no. 2 (Summer 1988): 31-47.

Nelson, Cary, and Grossberg, L., eds. *Marxism and the Interpretation of Culture*. Urbana and Chicago: University of Illinois Press, 1988.

Nemiroff, Greta Hoffman, ed. *Women and Men: Interdisciplinary Reading on Gender*. Toronto: Fitzhenry and Whiteside, 1987.

Neuman, Shirley, and Kamboureli, Smaro, eds. *Amazing Space: Writing Canadian Women Writing*. Edmonton: Longspoon/ NeWest, 1986.

Newton, Judith, and Rosenfelt, Deborah. *Feminist Criticism and Social Change: Sex, Class and Race in Literature and Culture*. New York: Methuen, 1985.

O'Brien, Mary. "Fiction and Fact." *Resources for Feminist Research* 16, no. 2 (June 1987): 57-59.

O'Brien, Mary. *The Politics of Reproduction*. London: Routledge and Kegan Paul, 1981.

O'Donovan, Theresa. "On Human Work: A Feminist Critique of LABOREM EXERCENS." M. A. thesis, St. Michael's College, Toronto School of Theology, 1988.

Oduyoye, Mercy Amba. *Hearing and Knowing: Theological Reflections on Christianity in Africa*. Maryknoll, New York: Orbis Books, 1986.

Olsen, Tillie. *Silences*. New York: Delacorte Press, 1978.

Overall, Christine, "Review of Elizabeth V. Spelman's *Inessential Woman: Problems of Exclusion in Feminist Thought*." *Resources for Feminist Research* 18, no. 4 (December 1989): 40-41.

Panitch, Leo, ed. *The Canadian State: Political Economy and Political Power*. Toronto: University of Toronto Press, 1977; reprint, 1983.

Penney, Jennifer. *Hard Earned Wages*. Toronto: Women's Educational Press, 1983.

Phillips, Paul. *Regional Disparities*. Canadian Issues Series. Updated Version. Toronto: James Lorimer and Co., 1982.

Phillips, Paul, and Phillips, Erin. *Women and Work: Inequality in the Labour Market*. Toronto: James Lorimer and Co., 1983.

Plaskow, Judith. *Sex, Sin and Grace: Women's Experience and the Theologies of Reinhold Niebuhr and Paul Tillich*. Washington, D.C.: University Press of America, 1980.

Plaskow, Judith, and Christ, Carol P. *Weaving the Visions: New Patterns in Feminist Spirituality*. San Francisco: Harper & Row, 1989.

Pobee, John S., and von Wartenberg-Potter, Barbel, eds. *New Eyes for Reading: Biblical and Theological Reflections by Women from the Third World*. Geneva: World Council of Churches, 1986.

Poelzer, Dolores, and Poelzer, Irene. *In Our Own Words: Northern Saskatchewan Metis Women Speak Out*. Saskatoon, Saskatchewan: Lindenblatt and Hamonic Publishing, Inc., 1986.

Pratt, Annie. *Archetypal Patterns in Women's Fiction*. Brighton: Harvester, 1982.

Ramazanoglu, Caroline. *Feminism and the Contradictions of Oppression*. New York: Routledge and Kegan Paul, 1989.

Rasmussen, Larry R. "New Dynamics in Theology: Politically Active and Culturally Significant." *Christianity and Crisis* 28, no. 8 (May 16, 1988): 178-83.

Rasmussen, Linda; Rasmussen, Lorna; Savage, Candace; and Wheeler, Anne. *A Harvest Yet to Reap: A History of Prairie Women*. Toronto: The Women's Press, 1976.

Reeve, Ted. "The Church and the Economic Crisis: A Study of the United Church's Continuing Concern for Social Justice." M. Th. thesis, Emmanuel College, Toronto School of Theology, 1986.

Rich, Adrienne. *The Dream of a Common Language: Poems, 1974-1977*. New York: W. W. Norton and Co., 1978.

Rich, Adrienne. *On Lies, Secrets and Silences: Selected Prose, 1966-1978*. New York: W. W. Norton and Co., 1979.

Rich, Adrienne. *Your Native Land, Your Life*. New York: W. W. Norton and Co., 1986.

Robinson, Lillian. *Sex, Class and Culture*. Bloomington: Indiana University Press, 1978.

Ronan, Marian. "A Liturgy of Women's Lives: A Call to Celebration." *Cross Currents* (Spring 1988): 19-31.

Rosaldo, Michele Zimbalist, and Lamphere, Louise, eds. *Woman, Culture and Society*. Stanford, California: Stanford University Press, 1974.

Ross, Malcolm. "The Imaginative Sense and the Canadian Question." *Mosaic* 9, no. 1 (Fall 1987): 1-13.

Ruether, Rosemary. *Sexism and God-Talk: Toward a Feminist Theology*. Boston: Beacon Press, 1983.

Russell, Letty M., ed. *Changing Contexts of Our Faith*. Philadelphia: Fortress Press, 1985.

Russell, Letty M., ed. *Feminist Interpretation of the Bible*. Philadelphia: Westminster Press, 1985.

Russell, Letty M. *Household of Freedom: Authority in Feminist Theology*. Philadelphia: Westminster Press, 1987.

Russell, Letty M. "Universality and Contextualism." *The Ecumenical Review* 30 (1979): 23-26.

Russell, Letty M.; Kwok Pui-Lan; Isasi-Diaz, Ada-Maria; and Cannon, Katie Geneva. *Inheriting Our Mothers' Gardens: Feminist Theology in Third World Perspective*. Philadelphia: Westminster Press, 1988.

St. Andrews, B. A. "Reclaiming a Canadian Heritage: Kogawa's *Obasan*." *The International Fiction Review* 13, no. 1 (1986): 29-31.

Sandwell, B. K. "Social Function of Fiction." *Queen's Quarterly* 49, no. 4 (1942): 322-22.

Sarvasy, Wendy, and Van Allen, Judith. "Fighting the Feminization of Poverty: Socialist Feminist Analysis and Strategy." *Review of Radical Political Economics* 16, no. 4 (1984): 98-110.

Schechter, Patricia; Harrison, Beverly Wildung; Kwok Pui Lan; Miles, Margaret R.; Weems, Renita J.; and Suchocki, Marjorie. "Roundtable Discussion: A Vision of Feminist Religious Scholarship." *Journal of Feminist Studies in Religion* 3, no. 1 (Spring 1987): 91-111.

Schüssler Fiorenza, Elisabeth. *Bread Not Stone: The Challenge of Feminist Biblical Interpretation*. Boston: Beacon Press, 1984.

Schüssler Fiorenza, Elisabeth. "The Ethics of Biblical Interpretation: Decentering Biblical Scholarship." *Journal of Biblical Literature* 107, no. 1 (Winter 1988): 3-17.

Schüssler Fiorenza, Elisabeth. "Feminist Theology as a Critical Theology of Liberation." *Theological Studies* 36 (1975): 605-26.

Schüssler Fiorenza, Elisabeth. *In Memory of Her: A Feminist Theological Reconstruction of Christian Origins*. New York: Crossroads, 1983.

Scott, Hilda. *Does Socialism Liberate Women?* Boston: Beacon Press, 1974.

Scott, Hilda. *Working Your Way to the Bottom: The Feminization of Poverty*. London: Pandora Press, 1984.

Scott, R. B. Y., and Vlastos, Gregory, eds. *Towards the Christian Revolution*. Chicago: Willett Clark and Company, 1936; reprint ed., Kingston, Ontario: Ronald Frye and Co., 1989.

Segundo, Juan Luis. *The Liberation of Theology*. Translated by John Drury. Maryknoll, New York: Orbis Books, 1982.

Sen, Gita, and Gown, Caren. *Development, Crises, and Alternative Visions: Third World Women's Perspectives*. New York: Monthly Review Press, 1987.

Showalter, Elaine, ed. *The New Feminist Criticism: Essays on Women, Literature and Theory*. New York: Pantheon, 1985.

Sidel, Ruth. *Women and Children Last: The Plight of Poor Women in Affluent America*. New York: Viking Press, 1986.

Silvera, Makeda. *Silenced*. Toronto: Williams-Wallace, 1983.

Sivard, Ruth Leger. *Women . . . A World Survey*. Washington, D.C.: World Priorities, 1985.

Slater, Peter, ed. *Religion and Culture in Canada*. Waterloo, Ontario: Canadian Group for Studies in Religion, 1977.

Smillie, Benjamin, ed. *Political Theology in the Canadian Context*. Waterloo, Ontario: Wilfred Laurier University Press, 1982.

Smith, Dorothy. *The Everyday World as Problematic: A Feminist Sociology*. Toronto: University of Toronto Press, 1987.

Smith, Ruth, and Valenze, Deborah. "Mutuality and Marginality: Liberal Moral Theory and Working Class Women in Nineteenth-Century England." *Signs: Journal of Women in Culture and Society* 13, no. 2 (Winter 1988): 277-98.

Sobrino, Jon. *Christology at the Crossroads*. Maryknoll, New York: Orbis Books, 1978.

Sölle, Dorothee. *Choosing Life*. Translated by Margaret Kohl. Philadelphia: Fortress Press, 1981.

Sölle, Dorothee. *Revolutionary Patience*. Translated by Rita and Robert Kimber. Maryknoll, New York: Orbis Books, 1977.

Sölle, Dorothee, with Cloyes, Shirley. *To Work and to Love: A Theology of Creation*. Philadelphia: Fortress Press, 1984.

Spelman, Elizabeth. *Inessential Woman: Problems of Exclusion in Feminist Thought*. Boston: Beacon Press, 1988.

Spetnak, C., ed. *The Politics of Women's Spirituality*. Garden City, New York: Anchor/Doubleday, 1982.

Sproxton, Birk, ed. *Trace: Prairie Writers on Writing*. Winnipeg: Turnstone Press, 1986.

Staines, David, ed. *The Canadian Imagination*. Cambridge, Massachusetts: Harvard University Press, 1977.

Stallard, Karin; and Ehrenreich, Barbara; and Sklar, Holly. *Poverty in the American Dream*. Boston: South End Press, 1983.

Stasiulis, Daria K. "Rainbow Feminism: Perspectives on Minority Women in Canada." *Resources for Feminist Research*. 16, no. 1 (March 1987): 5-9.

The State of the World's Women, 1985. Oxford: New Internationalist Publications, 1985.

Stephenson, Marylee, ed. *Women in Canada*. Revised Edition. Don Mills, Ontario: General Publishing, 1977.

Stout, Jeffrey. *Ethics After Babel: The Languages of Morals and Their Discontents*. Boston: Beacon Press, 1988.

Strong-Boag, Veronica. "Working Women and the State: The Case of Canada, 1889-1945." *Atlantis* 6, no. 2 (Spring 1981): 1-9.

Strong-Boag, Veronica, and Fellman, Anita Clair, eds. *Rethinking Canada: The Promise of Women' History*. Toronto: Copp Clark Pitman, 1986.

Student Christian Movement of Canada. *The Student Christian Movement: A Brief History, 1921-1974.* Toronto: SCM, 1975.

Sullivan, Rosemary, ed. *Stories by Canadian Women.* Toronto: Oxford University Press, 1984.

Swingewood, Alan. "Hegemony, Praxis and the Novel Form." *Praxis* 1 (Spring 1975): 98-110.

Tabb, William K., ed. *Churches in Struggle: Liberation Theologies and Social Change in North America.* New York: Monthly Review Press, 1986.

Tamez, Elsa. *Bible of the Oppressed.* Maryknoll, New York: Orbis Books, 1982.

Thistlethwaite, Susan B. "Narrative and Connection." *Christianity and Crisis* (March 2, 1987): 71-75.

Thompson, Kenneth. *Beliefs and Ideology.* Sussex and London: Tavistock and Ellis Harwood, 1986.

Tobique Women's Group with Silman, Janet. *Enough is Enough: Aboriginal Women Speak Out.* Toronto: Women's Press, 1987.

Toye, William, ed. *The Oxford Companion to Canadian Literature.* Toronto: Oxford University Press, 1983.

Tracy, David. *Plurality and Ambiguity: Hermeneutics, Religion and Hope.* New York: Harper & Row, 1987.

Trofimenkoff, Susan Mann. *The Dream of Nation: A Social and Intellectual History of Quebec.* Toronto: Gage, 1983.

United Church of Canada. "The Church and the Economic Crisis." Toronto: United Church of Canada, 1984.

United Church of Canada. "Women and the Economy: Grounding Assumptions." Reprinted from Women's Research Centre, "Women and the Economy Kit." *Women's Concerns Newsletter.* (Spring 1987): 3-4.

Verduyn, Christl, ed. *Margaret Laurence: An Appreciation.* Peterborough, Ontario: Broadview Press, 1988.

Vlastos, Gregory. "Justice and Love." *The Canadian Student* 50, no. 2 (1937).

Vlastos, Gregory. "Reclaim the Gospel of Solidarity." *Christian Century.* 59 (February 25, 1942): 245-47.

Vorst, Jesse, et al. *Race, Class, Gender: Bonds and Barriers*. Socialist Studies: A Canadian Annual, No. 5. Toronto: Between The Lines and The Society for Socialist Studies, 1989.

Wagner, Linda W. "Margaret Laurence's *The Diviners*." *University of Windsor Review* 16, no. 2 (Spring-Summer 1982): 5-17.

Walker, Alice. *The Color Purple*. New York: Simon and Schuster, 1982.

Walker, Alice. *In Search of Our Mothers' Gardens*. New York: Harcourt Brace Jovanovich, 1983.

Wallace, Carole. "Women and the Deficit." *Status of Women News* 10, no. 1 (November 1984): 18-25.

Watson, Barbara Bellow. "On Power and the Literary Text." *Signs* 1, no. 1 (Autumn 1975): 111-18.

Wells, Harold, and Hutchinson, Roger, eds. *A Long and Faithful March: "Towards the Christian Revolution," 1930s/1980s*. Toronto: The United Church Publishing House, 1989.

Wendell, Susan. "Oppression, Victimization, Choice and Responsibility." Department of Philosophy, Simon Fraser University, Burnaby, British Columbia. (Photocopy.)

West, Charles. "Culture, Power and Ideology in Third World Theologies." *Missiology: An International Review* 12, no. 4 (October 1984): 405-20.

West, Cornel. *Prophesy Deliverance! An Afro-American Revolutionary Christianity*. Philadelphia: Westminster Press, 1982.

West, Cornel. *Prophetic Fragments*. Grand Rapids, Michigan and Trenton, New Jersey: William B. Eerdmans and Africa World Press, 1988.

West, Cornel; Guidote, Caridad; and Coakley, Margaret, eds. *Theology in the Americas: Detroit II*. Maryknoll, New York: Orbis Books, 1982.

Whitehead, Raymond. "Middle Kingdom Ethics: The Centre and the Margin as Moral Metaphors." Presidential Address to the Canadian Theological Society, June 1, 1988.

Williams, Delores S. "The Color of Feminism." *Journal of Religious Thought* 43, no. 1 (Spring-Summer 1986): 42-58.

Williams, Delores S. "What are Women Theologians Saying?" Paper presented at Auburn Theological Seminary Conference, New York, 1988.

Williams, Delores S. "Women's Oppression and Lifeline Politics in Black Women's Religious Narratives." *Journal of Feminist Studies in Religion* 1 & 2 (Fall 1985): 59-71.

Williams, Raymond. *Marxism and Literature*. Oxford: Oxford University Press, 1977.

Williams, Raymond. *Politics and Letters: Interviews with New Left Review*. London: New Left Books, 1979.

Wilson, Paul. "First Novels." *Books in Canada* (February 1984): 30.

Woodcock, George, ed. *A Place to Stand On: Essays by and About Margaret Laurence*. Edmonton: NeWest Press, 1983.

Wuthnow, Robert. *Meaning and Moral Order: Explorations in Cultural Analysis* Berkeley and Los Angeles: University of California Press, 1987.

Wuthnow, Robert; Hunter, James Davidson; Bergesen, Albert; and Kurzweil, Edith. *Cultural Analysis: The Work of Peter L. Berger, Mary Douglas, Michel Foucault and Juergen Habermas*. Boston: Routledge and Kegan Paul, 1984.

Zaretsky, Eli. *Capitalism, the Family and Personal Life*. New York: Harper & Row, 1976.

Zimmerman, Bonnie. "What Has Never Been: An Overview of Lesbian Literary Criticism." *Feminist Studies* 7, no. 3 (Fall 1981): 463-64.